LIBRARY OF NEW TESTAMENT STUDIES

277

formerly the Journal for the Study of the New Testament Supplement Series

Editor
Mark Goodacre

To the biblical studies faculty of the Lutheran School of Theology at Chicago,
κράτιστοι διδάσκαλοι

To Karen,
ἀγαπητάτη γυνή

To Chris,
ἀγαπήτατος υἱός

To Raymond Kauppi (1925–2005),
ἀγαπήτατος πατὴρ καὶ τεχνίτης

FOREIGN BUT FAMILIAR GODS

Greco-Romans Read Religion in Acts

LYNN ALLAN KAUPPI

t&t clark

Published by T&T Clark International
A Continuum imprint
The Tower Building, 11 York Road, London SE1 7NX
80 Maiden Lane, Suite 704, New York, NY 10038

www.tandtclark.com

British Library Cataloguing-in-Publication Data
A catalogue record for this book is available from the British Library

ISBN 0-567-08097-8 (hardback)

Typeset by ISB Typesetting, Sheffield
Printed on acid-free paper in Great Britain by Biddles Ltd, Kings Lynn, Norfolk

CONTENTS

LIST OF TABLES

ABBREVIATIONS

AB	Anchor Bible
ABD	D.N. Freedman (ed.), *Anchor Bible Dictionary* (New York, 1992)
AJA	*American Journal of Archaeology*
ALGRM	W.H. Roscher (ed.), *Ausführliches Lexikon der griechischen und römischen Mythologie* (Leipzig, B.G. Teubner, 1884–1937)
ANRW	H. Temporini and W. Haase (eds), *Aufstieg und Niedergang der römischen Welt: Geschichte und Kultur Roms im Spiegel der neueren Forschung* (Berlin, 1972)
ASNU	Acta seminarii neotestamentici upsaliensis
ARW	*Archiv für Reformationsgeschichte*
ATLA	American Theological Library Association
BARev	*Biblical Archaeology Review*
BCH	*Bulletin de correspondence hellénique*
BETL	Bibliotheca ephemeridum theologicarum lovaniensium
BibInt	*Biblical Interpretation*
BMCR	*Bryn Mawr Classical Review*
BTB	*Biblical Theology Bulletin*
BZ	*Biblische Zeitschrift*
BZNW	Beihefte zur Zeitschrift für die neutestamentliche Wissenschaft
CAGN	B.P. Reardon (ed.), *Collected Ancient Greek Novels* (Berkeley, 1989)
CahRB	Cahiers de la Revue Biblique
CAM	*Civilizations of the Ancient Mediterranean*
CBET	Contributions to Biblical Exegesis and Theology
CBQ	*Catholic Biblical Quarterly*
CIG	*Corpus inscriptionum graecarum*
CIL	*Corpus inscriptionum latinarum*
ClQ	*Classical Quarterly*
ConBNT	Coniectanea biblica: New Testament Series
CP	*Classical Philology*
DACL	F. Cabrol (ed.), *Dictionnaire d'archéologie chrétienne et de liturgie* (Paris, 1907–53)
DDD	K. van der Toorn, B. Becking and P.W. van der Horst (eds), *Dictionary of Deities and Demons in the Bible* (Leiden, 1995)
Ebib	*Etudes bibliques*
EncJud	*Encyclopaedia Judaica* (Jerusalem, 1972)
EKKNT	Evangelisch-katholischer Kommentar zum Neuen Testament
EPRO	Etudes préliminaires aux religions orientales dans l'empire romain
ER	*Encyclopedia of Religion.* M. Eliade (ed.); New York, 1987
FGH	*Die Fragmente der griechischen Historiker.* F. Jacoby (ed.); Leiden, 1954–64
FHG	Fragmenta Historica Graecorum (Paris, 1841–70)

FRLANT	Forschungen zur Religion und Literatur des Alten und Neuen Testaments
GRBS	*Greek, Roman and Byzantine Studies*
HB	Hebrew Bible
HDR	Harvard Dissertations in Religion
HTKNT	Herders theologischer Kommentar zum Neuen Testament
HTR	*Harvard Theological Review*
I.Eph.	H. Wankel *et al.* (eds), *Die Inschriften von Ephesos* (7 vols and index; Bonn: Habelt, 1974–84)
IG	*Inscriptiones Graecae* (Berlin, 1924–)
IGR	*Inscriptiones Graecae ad res Romanas pertinentes*
ILS	*Inscriptiones Latinae Selectae*
JAAR	*Jounal of the American Academy of Religion*
JAC	*Jahrbuch für Antike und Christentum*
JBL	*Journal of Biblical Literature*
JewEnc	*The Jewish Encyclopedia*
JHS	*Journal of Hellenic Studies*
JR	*Journal of Religion*
JRH	*Journal of Religious History*
JRS	*Journal of Roman Studies*
JSNT	*Journal for the Study of the New Testament*
JSNTSup	Journal for the Study of the New Testament: Supplement Series
JSPSup	Journal for the Study of the Pseudepigrapha: Supplement Series
JTS	*Journal of Theological Studies*
KBS	*Kölner Beitrage zur Sportswissenschaft*
LIMC	H.C. Ackerman and J.-R. Gisler (eds), *Lexicon iconographicum mythologiae classicae* (Zurich, 1981–97)
LEC	*Library of Early Christianity*
LXX	Septuagint
MAMA	*Monumenta Asiae Minoris Antiqua* (Manchester and London, 1928–93)
MDAI	*Mitteilungen des Deutschen Archäologischen Institutes*
Neot	*Neotestamentica*
NewDocs	G.H.R. Horsley and S. Llewelyn (eds), *New Documents Illustrating Early Christianity.* (North Ryde, NSW, 1981–)
NICNT	New International Commentary on the New Testament
NovT	*Novum Testamentum*
NovTSup	Novum Testamentum Supplements
NTD	Das Neue Testament Deutsch
NTS	*New Testament Studies*
OCD	S. Hornblower and A. Spawforth (eds), *Oxford Classical Dictionary* (Oxford)
OCT	Oxford Classical Texts
OGIS	W. Dittenberger (ed.), *Orientis graeci inscriptiones selectae* (Leipzig, 1903–1905)
OHCW	Oxford History of the Classical World
PGM	K. Preisendanz (ed.), *Papyri graecae magicae: Die griechischen Zauberpapyri* (Berlin, 1928)
PRSt	Perspectives in Religious Studies
PTMS	Pittsburgh Theological Monograph Series
PW	G.Wissowa (ed.), *Paulys Realencyclopädie der classischen Altertumswissenschaft* (Munich, 1980)
PWSup	Supplement to PW

RAC	T. Kluser *et al.* (eds), *Reallexikon für Antike und Christentum* (Stuttgart, 1950–)
Rarch	*Revue archéologique*
RGRW	Religions in the Greco-Roman World
RVV	*Religionsgeschichtliche Versuche und Vorarbeiten*
SANT	Studien zum Alten und Neuen Testaments
SBLDS	Society of Biblical Literature Dissertation Series
SBLSBS	Society of Biblical Literature Sources for Biblical Study
SBLSP	*Society of Biblical Literature Seminar Papers*
SEG	Supplementum epigraphicum graecum
SGRR	Studies in Greek and Roman Religion
SJLA	Studies in Judaism in Late Antiquity
SNTSMS	Society for New Testament Studies Monograph Series
SO	Symbolae osloenses
SP	Sacra pagina
TAPA	*Transactions of the American Philological Association*
TDNT	G. Kittel and G. Friedrich (eds), *Theological Dictionary of the New Testament* (trans. G.W. Bromiley; Grand Rapids, 1974–)
TynBul	*Tyndale Bulletin*
TZ	*Theologische Zeitschrift*
WUNT	Wissenschaftliche Untersuchungen zum Neuen Testament
ZNW	*Zeitschrift für die neutestamentliche Wissenschaft*
ZST	*Zeitschrift für systematische Theologie*
ZThK	*Zeitschrift für Theologie und Kirche*
b. Ber.	Babylonian Talmud, tractate *Berakot*
Mek. R. Ishmael	*Mekilta de Rabbi Ishmael*
Ag.	Aeschylus, *Agamemnon*
Aen.	Virgil, *Aeneid*
Aeth.	Heliodorus, *Aethiopika*
Aj.	Sophocles, *Ajax*
Alex.	Lucian, *Alexander the False Prophet*
Ann.	Tacitus, *Annales*
Ant.	Josephus, *Jewish Antiquities*
Ant. Rom.	Dionysius of Halicarnassus, *Roman Antiquities*
Anth. Pal.	*Anthologia Palatina*
Apol.	Apuleius, *Apology*
Argon.	Apollonius Rhodius, *Argonautica*
Att.	Cicero, *Epistulae ad Atticum*
Bell. Civ.	Appian, *Civil Wars*
Bibl.	Apollodorus, *Bibliotheca*
Bis acc.	Lucian, *Bis accusatus*
Carm.	Claudian, *Carmina*
Charid.	Dio Chrysostom, *De dei cognitionae*
Daphn.	Longus, *Daphnis and Chloe*
De Div.	Cicero, *De divinatione*
Def. Orac.	Plutarch, *De defectu oraculorum*
Dei cogn.	Dio Chrysostom,
Deipn.	Athenaeus, *Deipnosophistae*
De Rer. Nat.	Lucretius, *De rerum natura*

Dem.	Plutarch, *Demosthenes*
Ecl.	Virgil, *Eclogae*
Ep.	Seneca, *Epistulae moracles*
Epid.	Hippocrates, *Epidemiae*
Epit.	Livy, *Epitome*
Eum.	Aeschylus, *Eumenides*
Euthyphr.	Plato, *Euthyphro*
Fast.	Ovid, *Fasti*
Flam.	Plutarch, *Titus Flamininus*
Frat. amor.	Plutarch, *De fraterno amore*
h. Ap.	*Homeric Hymn to Apollo*
Hann.	Appian, *Hannibal*
Heracl.	Euripides, *Heraclidae*
Hist.	Tacitus, *Historiae*
Hist.	Diodorus Siculus, *Historia*
Hist. Rom. Ep.	Cassio Dio, *Historika Romaika* Epitome
Il.	Homer, *Iliad*
Iph. taur.	Euripides, *Iphigeneia at Tauris*
Jul.	Suetonius, *Divus Julius*
Leg.	Cicero, *De legibus*
Leu. Clit.	Achilles Tatius, *Leucippe et Clitophon*
Lex.	Lucian, *Lexiphanes*
Mem.	Xenophon, *Memorabilia*
Metam.	Ovid, *Metamorphoses*
Mim.	Herodas, *Mimiambi*
Mith.	Appian, *Mithridates*
Mor.	Plutarch, *Moralia*
Nat.	Pliny the Elder, *Naturalis historia*
Nat. an.	Aelian, *De natura animalium*
Nat. d.	Cicero, *De natura deorum*
Nem. Ode	Pindar, *Nemean Odes*
Od.	Homer, *Odyssey*
Oed. Col.	Sophocles, *Oedipus coloneus*
Omn. Prob. Lib.	Philo, *Quod omnis probus liber sit*
Onir.	Artemidorus, *Onirocritica*
Or.	Aelius Aristides,
Orest.	Euripides, *Orestes*
Pan.	Pliny the Younger, *Panegyricus*
Peri Eus.	Theophrastus,
Phaed.	Plato, *Phaedrus*
Phaen.	Aratus, *Phaenomena*
Ps.-Cl. Hom.	*Pseudo-Clementine Homilies*
Ps.-Cl. Rec.	*Pseudo-Clementine Recognitions*
Pyth. Orac.	Plutarch, *De Pythiae oraculis*
Sacr.	Lucian, *De sacrificiis*
Satyr.	Petronius, *Satryicon*
Silv.	Statius, *Silvae*
Soph.	Plato, *Sophista*
Somn.	Philo, *De somniis*
Spect.	Martial, *Spectacula*
Spir.	Hero, *Spiritalia*

Stoic Rep.	Plutarch, *De Stoicorum repugnantiis*
Strat.	Polyaenus, *Strategems of War*
Strom.	Clement of Alexandria, *Stromata*
Syr.	Lucian, *De syria dea*
Theb.	Statius, *Thebaid*
Tim.	Lucian, *Timon*
Tr. Pont.	Ovid, *Tristia ex Ponto*
Tusc.	Cicero, *Tusculanae disputationes*
Vesp.	Aristophanes, *Vespae*
Vit. Apoll.	Philostratus, *Vita Apollonii*
Vit auct.	Lucian, *Vitarum auctio*
War	Josephus, *Jewish War*

PREFACE

This monograph is the substantial revision of my 1999 doctoral dissertation, 'ΞΕΝΩΝ ΔΑΙΜΟΝΙΩΝ: Greco-Romans Read Religion in the Book of Acts', written under the direction of David Rhoads at the Lutheran School of Theology at Chicago.

My text critical base for biblical texts includes the NA[27] Greek text, the 1979 edition of the Rahlfs *Septuaginta*, and the *BHS* Hebrew text. Acts is notoriously rife with text critical issues. I accept the NA[27] text of Acts for the purposes of my analysis and discuss pertinent variants and relevant translation as needed.[1] For non-biblical Greek texts I have usually cited the standard Teubner or Oxford Classical Text editions.[2] Because of the paucity and brevity of the quoted Latin texts, I have relied upon the texts in the Loeb Classical Library for my Latin sources. For the sake of consistency, when citing critical Greek texts I have converted all iota adscripts found in modern critical texts into iota subscripts.

Unless otherwise indicated, all English translations are my own. I have lightly edited quoted translations to remove and update Elizabethan English ('thee' or 'thou') and archaic expressions such as the use of 'baneful' to mean 'poisonous'. Unless otherwise indicated, translations of Latin texts are from the Loeb Classical Library. All English translations from the Greek reflect the degree of gender inclusivity or exclusivity in the original text. For purposes of inclusive language, I have avoided the cumbersome 'he/she', 'his/her', 'he or she', and 'his or her', but instead use the generic third person plural pronouns 'they' and 'their' in both my translations and discussion.

I have transliterated Greek names following the contemporary practices of classical scholarship: names are transliterated and not Latinized excepting those established by long and customary usage. For example, I transliterate 'Sokrates' but retain Plato.

Throughout this study, I assume the time of writing for Luke-Acts to be between 80–100 CE. Whether or not Luke was a companion of Paul does not materially affect my discussion. If Luke was Paul's companion in the We-sections,

---

1. Jenny Read-Heimerdinger has recently argued that D, Codex Bezae, represents the original text of Acts (*The Bezan Text of Acts: A Contribution of Discourse Analysis to Textual Criticism* [JSNTSup, 236; Sheffield: Sheffield Academic Press, 2003]). Klaus Wachtel has argued that her position is vitiated because she methodologically ignores other textual traditions beyond that of B and D and her *petitio principi*; see his review of her monograph, *RBL* (online), http://www.bookreviews. org/pdf/3197_3576.pdf (2004). Full engagement with her text critical and linguistic arguments is beyond the scope of this monograph.

2. The relevant text critical details are discussed in Kauppi, 'ΞΕΝΩΝ ΔΑΙΜΟΝΙΩΝ', throughout.

he adapted his recollection of historical events to his authorial purposes. If he was not Paul's companion, he similarly adapted his sources. I make no assumptions about the place of composition.

I consistently translate ἐκ τοῦ οὐρανοῦ and ἐξ οὐρανοῦ as 'from the realm of the gods' when dealing with both non-Christian and non-Judean Greco-Roman texts. This avoids the implicit Judeo-Christianizing assumptions of the translation 'from heaven' and the secularizing assumptions translating as 'the sky'.

John H. Elliott has demonstrated the inappropriateness of applying the words 'Jew', 'Jews', or 'Jewish' to the first century.[3] Therefore, I translate Ἰουδαῖοι as 'Judeans'. The term 'Judean' can have four different meanings: (1) those who lived in the region of Judea in southern Palestine, (2) those who lived in the province of Judea, (3) those who lived outside of Judea but who had origins there, and (4) those who embraced the religion of Judea. Context will make clear the appropriate meaning of the word.[4]

Unfortunately, there is no adequate non-anachronistic term to indicate 'Christians' or 'Christianity'. As used in this study, 'Christians' indicates *both* Luke's understanding of a group whose theological allegiance was to Jesus *and* the historical community that lies behind the text. 'Christianity' and the adjective 'Christian' denote both Luke's theology and the historical early followers of Jesus.

Except in direct quotations, I have resolutely refrained from using the word 'pagan'. In a number of contexts this word pejoratively connotes an individual who adheres to superstitious and irrational polytheistic beliefs.[5] Using this term does not take the ancient adherents of Greco-Roman religion and their religious devotion with sufficient seriousness. Thus, though I do not believe in or have allegiance to Isis, I must certainly respect Apuleius' profound awe of, reverence toward, respect for, and belief in his goddess (*Metam.* 11). I have tried to grant Greco-Roman religion as much respect 'as I am capable of demonstrating to any system of belief which does not number me among its adherents'.[6]

All mistakes are my own.

---

3. John H. Elliott, 'Jesus Wasn't a Christian. Historical, Social, and Theological Implications of the Disparaging Label Christianos and Other Nomenclature' (unpublished paper presented to the annual meeting of the Context Group; Portland, OR, 13–16 March 1997); esp. p. 19 n. 76.

4. David Rhoads, *The Challenge of Diversity: The Witness of Paul and the Gospels* (Minneapolis: Fortress Press, 1996), pp. 35–36, also pp. 82–83.

5. I thank Frederick Danker and Edgar Krentz for this insight about the word 'pagan'.

6. Robert Garland, *Introducing New Gods: The Politics of Athenian Religion* (Baltimore, MD: The Johns Hopkins University Press, 1992), p. 173.

ACKNOWLEDGMENTS

Special thanks to John H. Elliot and Dennis MacDonald for allowing a total stranger to read and cite unpublished manuscripts; to Adriana Destro and Mauro Pesce for providing English translations of their Italian manuscript; to Christopher A. Faraone, N. Clayton Croy, and Geoffrey S. Sumi, for bibliographic suggestions and various advice; to Chris Forbes, Rick Strelan, and F. Stanley Jones for discussion; William H. Race for help with Pindar, to the members of the Acts-L electronic discussion group for ideas and bibliography; and to Martin Breen of the Jesuit-Krause-McCormick Library and the inter-library loan staff at the Nashville Public Library.

Deepest thanks to my dissertation committee: Ralph Klein, Edgar Krentz, David Aune, and David Rhoads, my advisor. Their input has sharpened the focus of my work and helped me to avoid errors of substance and style. I especially thank David Aune for agreeing (by email no less!) to read a total stranger's dissertation and for his critique that has saved me from egregious errors and clarified my logic. I also specially thank David Rhoads for his detailed efforts on my behalf, unflagging enthusiasm, deft editorial pen, and determination to drag a traditionalist historical-critical student exegete into the new – to me – frontiers of using reader response theory in New Testament exegesis.

Special thanks to the Continuum staff for their patience, support and hard work: Rebecca Vaughan-Williams, Rebecca Mulhearn (now with SPCK), Haaris Naqvi and Joanna Taylor. Also, my thanks to Dr Mark M. Newby for his copy-editing, which saved me from a serious gaffe.

My greatest and most profound thanks are to my wife Karen and our son Chris for their love, endurance, and support during my doctoral study and during the preparation of this monograph; and to my late father, Raymond Kauppi, for teaching me the value of both theological inquiry and craftsmanship in the entirety of one's life.

I dedicate this book to David Rhoads, Edgar Krentz, David Aune, Ralph Klein, my family and, most especially, Dad.

Κλείετε δ' ἀθανάτων ἱερὸν γένος αἰὲν ἐόντων,
οἵ Γῆς ἐξεγένοντο καὶ Οὐρανοῦ ἀστερόεντος,
Νυκτός τε δνοφερῆς, οὕς θ' ἁλμυρὸς ἔτρεφε Πόντος.

Sing the praises of the deathless holy ones, the always existing race,
the ones born of Earth and starry Heaven,
the ones born of dark Night, whom salt Sea fathered.

Hesiod, *Theog.* 105-7

εὐαγγελιζόμενοι ὑμᾶς ἀπὸ τούτων τῶν ματαίων ἐπιστρέφειν ἐπὶ θεὸν ζῶντα, ὃς
ἐποίησεν τὸν οὐρανὸν καὶ τὴν γῆν καὶ τὴν θάλασσαν καὶ πάντα τὰ ἐν θῦτοῖς·

[We are] proclaiming good news to you so that you may turn from these empty things to
the living God, who made heaven and earth and the sea and everything in them.

Acts 14.15

Chapter 1

INTRODUCTION

In Acts 17.18, Greek philosophers understand Paul to be speaking about ξένια δαιμονία, 'foreign gods'. For an ancient Greco-Roman reader, there is a note of heavy irony here. For the Greek philosophers, Jesus and 'Resurrection' are 'foreign gods', because the city did not formally recognize them to receive public worship. For Luke and the early Christian members of his audience, the 'foreign gods' are the diverse gods of the Greco-Roman world. Thus for an early Greco-Roman Christian encountering this text, Jesus, Resurrection, and the various gods mentioned in Acts (Zeus and Hermes in 14.8–20, Artemis in 19.21–41, and the two Dioskuroi, Castor and Pollux, in 28.11 are simultaneously both familiar and foreign. In contrast to other New Testament writings, Luke specifically mentions these gods and the following aspects of Greco-Roman religion: sacrificial cult (14.8–19), ἄγνωστος θεός, the 'unknown god' (17.22), and the personified abstraction Δική, 'Justice' (28.1–6). He seems to allude to Greco-Roman oracles and divination (1.17–26 and 16.16–18), the imperial cult (12.20–23), and to Aeschylus' *Eumenides* by referring to ἀνάστασις, 'resurrection' (17.18, 33).

We can address key questions to these texts:

1. In overt references to Greco-Roman religious phenomena in Acts, are there previously unexplored issues?
2. Did a Greco-Roman audience perceive references and allusions to Greco-Roman religions or religious phenomena in Acts that are overlooked by modern readers?
3. What cultural knowledge did Luke's ancient Greco-Roman readers bring to these references and allusions to Greco-Roman religion that informed their reading of Acts?
4. When reading Acts, would Greco-Romans have seen an implicit contrast between Greco-Roman religion and early Christianity?
5. Does understanding the perceptions of a Greco-Roman audience help us to better understand Lukan theology?
6. When reading Acts, would Greco-Romans have seen an implicit contrast between Greco-Roman religion and early Christianity?

My thesis is simple: various passages in Acts reflect either Luke's mention of Greco-Roman religion for his own theological purposes or may have been interpreted by Luke's Greco-Roman audience in light of their personal knowledge of and participation in Greco-Roman religions. A premise of this thesis is that we cannot obtain a thorough understanding of Luke's theology and purpose and his original audience's comprehension of his work unless we have a full understanding of these references to Greco-Roman religions. The purpose of this study, therefore, is to explore a Greco-Roman reader's perception of Luke's references to Greco-Roman religion with a view to showing how relevant they might be for understanding Luke's theology and purpose. I will do this by asking how Luke's Greco-Roman audience might have understood these references in light of the popular knowledge and experience of Greco-Roman religions that might be assumed of such an audience. Modern readers must engage in the scholarly reconstruction of that ancient religious world in order to understand either Luke's technique and purpose or the cultural knowledge of his audience. According to literary critic Hans R. Jauss the modern interpreter's task in relation to a work whose author is unknown is to consider the text in light of the literary, artistic works, historical events, and religious practices that 'the author could expect the contemporary public to know either explicitly or implicitly'.[1]

My study seeks to contribute to such a reconstruction by investigating overlooked references to Greco-Roman religion in Acts within their first-century Greco-Roman religious context and by tentatively suggesting Acts texts that a Greco-Roman reader could possibly have understood as allusions to various aspects of Greco-Roman religion. I make no claims for having elucidated every reference or allusion to Greco-Roman religion in Acts. Nor do I claim to have created a comprehensive synthesis regarding Luke's 'theology of Greco-Roman religion'.

Review of Research

Surveying Acts scholarship shows that scholars generally study Greco-Roman religion in Acts by either analyzing specific texts or by attempting synthetic treatments.[2] To my knowledge, only six scholars have attempted to study Luke's use of Greco-Roman religions as a whole: Bernard Tremel, Bruno Wildhaber, Robert M. Grant, Graham Soffe, H.J. Klauck, and David W.J. Gill.[3] Tremel

---

1. Hans R. Jauss, 'Literary History as a Challenge to Literary Theory', *New Literary History* 2 (1970), pp. 7–38, citing p. 19. See also Jauss' theoretical expansion of this essay in his *Toward an Aesthetic of Reception* (trans. Timothy Bahti; Theory and History of Literature 2; Minneapolis: University of Minnesota Press, 1982), pp. 3–45.

2. See the succeeding chapters for citation and discussion of the various scholarly analyses of specific texts in Acts.

3. Bernard Tremel, 'Voie du salut et religion populaire. Paul et Luc face au resque de paganisation', *Lumière et Vie* 30 (1981), pp. 87–108; Bruno Wildhaber, *Paganisme populaire et prédication apostolique, d'après l'exégèse de quelques séquences des Actes* (Le Monde de la Bible; Geneva: Labor et Fides, 1987); Robert M. Grant, *Gods and the One God* (LEC, 1; Philadelphia: Westminster Press, 1986), pp. 19–28; Graham Soffe, 'Christians, Jews and Pagans in the Acts of the Apostles', in Martin Henig and Anthony King (eds), *Pagan Gods and Shrines of the Roman Empire* (Oxford University Committee for Archaeology Monograph, 8; Oxford: Oxford University Committee for Archaeology, 1986), pp. 239–56; H.J. Klauck, 'With Paul in Paphos and Lystra: Magic and Paganism in the Acts of the Apostles', *Neot* 28 (1994), pp. 93–107; *idem, Magie und Heidentum in der*

examines Acts 13.4–12 (Paul in conflict with the magician Bar Jesus), 14.8–20 (Paul and Barnabas are hailed as Hermes and Zeus), 16.16–40 (the Philippian Pythia), 19.11–20 (the seven sons of Sceva), 19.21–40 (Artemis of Ephesus) and 28.1–10 (Paul's miracles on Malta) in light of 'popular religion' and the risk of 'paganization'. Tremel's article is intended for a lay audience and therefore cites almost no primary or secondary literature and does not analyze the historical and cultural backgrounds of the religious phenomena he discusses.

Bruno Wildhaber, Tremel's student, attempts a broadly-based general synthesis of 'popular paganism' and the risks of syncretism for the early Christian community in Acts through exegesis of the following Acts texts. Simon Magus (8.4–25), the death of Agrippa I (12.20–23), the magician Bar Jesus (13.4–12), Paul and Barnabas proclaimed Hermes and Zeus (14.8–20), the oracular slave (16.16–24), the seven sons of Sceva (Acts 19.8–20), Artemis of Ephesus and the silversmiths (19.23–41) and the miracles on Malta (28.1–6, 7–10). He presents a number of useful insights, attempts to synthesize Luke's 'theology of paganism', and provides relevant primary sources in his notes. Because of his emphasis on the perils of syncretism, paganism, and magic for the early Christian community, Wildhaber does not fully integrate the primary sources as cultural backgrounds for the original audience of Acts into his analysis.

Grant is interested in placing the development of early Christian monotheism in its polytheistic and syncretistic Hellenistic religious environment and continues with observations about Luke's silence about Athena in Athens, Aphrodite on Cyprus, and Zeus on the Areopagus. He devotes a short chapter to the Greco-Roman divinities mentioned in Acts and concludes that Luke made no 'direct denunciation of paganism though magic and divination were self-evidently wrong... This is not to say that Luke accepted paganism any more than his heroes did... A violent attack on pagan religion...could not have produced a favorable response. Luke is setting forth an ideal pattern for pagan and Christian relations'.[4] Grant does not support these conclusions nor does he define 'an ideal pattern for pagan and Christian relations'.

Soffe intends to examine 'the relationships between earliest Christianity, Judaism, and paganism' as seen in Acts.[5] His essay is very general with unremarkable conclusions: Judaism was more important 'in creating a ceremonial form for early Christianity within a Graeco-Roman environment', individual *ekklesia*

Apostelgeschichte des Lukas (SBS, 167; Stuttgart: Katholisches Bibelwerk, 1996), rev. in English trans. as *Magic and Paganism in Early Christianity: The World of the Acts of the Apostles* (Edinburgh: T&T Clark, 2000 [all references to this edition]); and David W.J. Gill, 'Acts and Roman Religion, A. Religion in a Local Setting', in David W.J. Gill and Conrad Gempf (eds), *The Book of Acts in Its Graeco-Roman Setting*, vol. 2 in the five-volume set *The Book of Acts in Its First Century Setting* (ed. Bruce W. Winter; Grand Rapids: Eerdmans, 1994), pp. 79–102.

Additional brief discussion about Greco-Roman religion in Acts in Heikki Räisänen, 'Coexistence and Conflict: Early Christian Attitudes to Adherents of Traditional Cults', *Temenos: Studies in Comparative Religion* 31 (1995), pp. 163–80; and Peter Stockmeier, 'Christlicher Glaube und antike Religiosität', *ANRW* II/23, part 2 (1980), pp. 871–909.

4. Grant, *Gods and the One God*, pp. 20 and 22.
5. Soffe, 'Christians, Jews, and Pagans', p. 239.

borrowed secular habits (especially in the language of dogma and exhortation) from Greco-Roman society, the larger society initially greeted early Christians and their message with interest but rejected and persecuted them when Christian religion conflicted with the material components of Greco-Roman society, and because of their exclusive religious outlook, the Christians wished to displace Greco-Roman religion.[6] Soffe's discussion is frequently irrelevant to Acts. For example, he discusses Greco-Roman mystery religions without connecting them to any text in Acts.[7]

Klauck attempts to trace the narrative 'red threads' of early Christianity's encounter with Greco-Roman religion and magic through the entire book of Acts by studying two texts: Acts 13.4–12 and 14.8–20.[8] He concludes that Luke whole-heartedly, but in a nuanced manner, condemned Greco-Roman idolatry, even showing 'sympathy for individual pagans and gentiles'. In contrast to 'paganism', where there is a permeable border 'between the divine and the human', Luke stresses the 'necessary distinction between God, the creator, and all his creatures' thus putting Christian missionary miracle-working in the proper perspective and emphasizing Jesus Christ's unique position as the only Son of God. But Greco-Roman religion is in Luke's view also open for the Christian message because they contain some 'ideas about the divine which might prove useful'. Luke is thereby 'venturing into the ambitious program of acculturation and evangeliza-tion' in which he adapts 'as far as necessary and possible to different cultural situations' and transforming these cultures through 'the power of the gospel'.[9] His lack of in-depth analysis does not sufficiently support these conclusions. For example, his sweeping and never defined use of the term 'magic' causes him to equate the oracular slave girl of 16.16–18 and Greco-Roman 'popular' divination with 'magic', thus implying that the ancient marginality of what we now call 'magic' extended to divination when in reality, divination was an established and accepted social practice.

Klauck's monograph *Magic and Paganism in the Acts of the Apostles* expands the discussion in his earlier article by studying Greco-Roman religion and Lukan theology in thirteen passages: Acts 1.1–14 (introduction and missionary program), 2.1–47 (Pentecost), 8.4–25 (Philip and Simon Magus), 8.26–40 (Philip and the Ethiopian eunuch), 10.1–11, 18 (the God-fearing centurion Cornelius), 12.20–23 (Herod Agrippa I), 13.4–12 (Paul and Barjesus), 14.8–20 (Paul and Barnabas acclaimed as Hermes and Zeus), 16.16–24 (the oracular slave woman), 17.16–21, 32–34 (Paul's speech in Athens), 17.22–31 (the unknown God), 19.11–20 (Paul and magicians), 19.23–40 (Artemis of Ephesus), 27.1–44 (sea voyage and ship-wreck), 28.1–11 (Paul and the snake, the Dioskuroi) and 28.16–31 (preaching in Rome). Klauck's emphasis in this book is pastoral and theological in that he relates

6.   Soffe, 'Christians, Jews, and Pagans', p. 253.
7.   Soffe, 'Christians, Jews, and Pagans', p. 247.
8.   Klauck also discusses 'paganism' in Acts 3.12; 10.25–26; 12.21–23; 16.29–30; 17.16–41; and 28.1–10 but devotes less than two pages to their interpretation. His treatment of the texts dealing with magic is similarly brief.
9.   Klauck, 'With Paul in Paphos and Lystra', p. 105.

each passage to modern theological concerns, especially that of acculturation or the cultural accommodation of the Christian faith. One cannot fault Klauck the believing Christian for attempting to apply the Acts texts that mention Greco-Roman religion to contemporary concerns. However, he does not exegete any of these texts in detail, cites primary sources minimally, and often either reaches conclusions that are untenable or simply accepts the results of earlier research without in depth investigation. He also makes Christianizing errors of fact by making assertions such as: '[The decline of the Delphic Oracle] was not least due to the cheap offers [i.e., other oracles] available everywhere' with the questions posed of such oracles being 'sometimes very *banal*'.[10] Many of the inquiries to Delphi, whether real or legendary, typically dealt with 'banal' matters: whether to establish a cult to honor a hero, whether to establish a new temple, etc. Additionally, what sort of questions should an ancient enquirer of an oracle have asked so as not be considered 'banal' by a twenty-first century exegete? Therefore, Klauck's book is insufficient for detailed understanding of the Greco-Roman religious background of Acts.

David W.J. Gill treat Acts as a chronologically accurate history of the early church.[11] Luke mentions Greco-Roman divinities only because they were the divinities and religious practices that Luke and Paul encountered on the four missionary journeys of Paul recounted in Acts. Gill treats Luke's use of Greco-Roman religion atomistically by briefly discussing each Greco-Roman cult that Paul encounters, or which Luke implies that Paul encountered, in the Acts narrative. He concludes:

> Pagan cults play a noticeably low profile within the narrative of Acts… Within Acts, the expanding Christian community is brought face to face with the range of religious cults found within the Roman Empire. *Some of these contacts are made explicit within the text, such as the incident at Lystra or Paul's reaction to Athens. Other contacts with this range of cults are implied by the places visited on the journeys.* Clearly as Gentiles joined the Christian community, the Jewish group had to come to terms with pagan cult. Thus the Jerusalem council required Gentiles 'who turn to God…to abstain from the pollutions of idols' (Acts 15.19–20).[12]

By so emphasizing Luke's historical accuracy in the book of Acts, Gill does not utilize his rich mine of primary and secondary sources to study the function of Greco-Roman religions in Acts for both Luke and his audience.

The Approach of This Investigation

My review of the literature shows that scholars who have studied the Greco-Roman religions mentioned in Acts usually do so within the context of a particular passage. A few have attempted synthetic studies that are frequently generalizing and cursory surveys of Greco-Roman religion in their ancient contexts and lack in-depth analysis.

---

10. Klauck, *Magic and Paganism in Early Christianity*, pp. 66–67, my emphasis.
11. Gill, 'Acts and Roman Religion', pp. 79–92.
12. Gill, 'Acts and Roman Religion', pp. 80 and 92, my emphasis.

The social world or social location of Luke and his audience was quadricultural encompassing various local, Judean, Greco-Roman, and early Christian
literary, cultural, and religious traditions. In this study, I will specifically focus
on a detailed contextual analysis of one portion, Greco-Roman religion, of this
quadricultural social location. In the same way that identifying allusions and
references to the LXX or early Christian worship helps us understand Luke's text,
my analysis should help indicate: (1) how his Greco-Roman auditors/readers may
have construed such materials in light of their own cultural knowledge, (2) how
Luke uses these religions in his narrative and (3) enable modern readers to better
comprehend Acts.

Methods and Assumptions

Core Samples and Soundings. To use geological and hydrological metaphors, I
will perform two types of investigation: (1) I will make 'core samples' or detailed
analyses of those texts that overtly mention Greco-Roman gods or religious practices to see what cultural knowledge lies beneath or behind Luke's text for both
the ancient and modern reader. (2) I will make 'soundings' or tentative explora-
tions of various Acts texts that contain the presence of Lukan allusions to Greco-
Roman oracles, the imperial cult, and mythology. In my conclusions, I will
synthesize these 'core samples' and 'soundings' to ask what they contribute to
our understanding of a Greco-Roman audience's understanding of these allusions
and references and the implications of the ancient understanding of Greco-
Roman religion in Acts for our contemporary understanding of Acts.[13]

In terms of probability, I draw a distinction between core samples and soundings in my analysis. In geology, core samples provide data about a known substrate
such as the ocean floor or a surface rock formation. In this study, core samples
provide relatively assured results because they analyze Lukan texts that everyone
agrees mention Greco-Roman religion. For example, analyzing the cultural, literary, and archaeological backgrounds of Ephesian Artemis and her temple in Acts
19.23–41 (see Chapter 6) is a core sample because the text explicitly mentions
Ephesian Artemis and her temple (vv. 24, 27, 28, 34, 35).

---

13. Two influential scholars have recently used similar methodological metaphors: Gian Biagio
Conte describes the philologist's study of an ancient text (for Conte, the study of Latin poetry) as a
vertical dissection or 'the plumbing of the space beneath the tough compact surface' to see the text as
a 'profoundly contextualized network of association, echoes, imitations, allusions – a rich root system
reaching down and entwined with the fibers of the culture in its historical dimension' (*The Rhetoric of
Imitation: Genre and Poetic Memory in Virgil and Other Poets* [Cornell Studies in Classical Philology,
44; Ithaca, NY: Cornell University Press, 1986] p. 49). Eldon Jay Epp, in his 2003 Society of Biblical
Literature Presidential Address, uses several 'core samples' of the sociocultural soil of ancient
Oxyrhynchus to probe the local context of New Testament papyri in their local context by analyzing
other Oxyrhynchus papyri (including letters, hymns, prayers, treatises, and petitions) to provide
insights to the use and interpretation of New Testament texts within the context of ancient Oxyrhynchus; later published as 'The Oxyrhynchus New Testament Papyri: "Not Without Honor Except
in Their Hometown?" ', *JBL* 123 (2004), pp. 5–55, esp. pp. 20–55.

In hydrology, oceanography, navigation and cartography, one uses soundings when the depth of a channel is unknown. In this study, soundings are tentative and exploratory because I test the 'textual depths' to determine if allusions to Greco-Roman religion can be hypothesized. In making 'textual soundings', I either develop the brief suggestions of other exegetes or note possible cultural and literary parallels between passages in Acts and Greco-Roman literature and religious practices unmentioned in earlier scholarly literature. My very hypothetical suggestion, based on a slender parallel, that there is a possible allusion to Aeschylus' *Eum.* 647 in Acts 17.18, 32 is a sounding because I am exploring the tentative undeveloped suggestion made by F.F. Bruce and others that such an allusion exists (see chapter 5).[14] In chapter 2, I tentatively suggest, without any support from previous scholarship, that there may be an allusion to Greco-Roman divination in Acts 1.15–26. Again, this is a 'sounding' because of my suggestion's highly hypothetical nature.

Methodologies Used. The combined use of several methods will govern this study. First, I will accumulate the data for these analyses by using the social-description approach of John E. Stambaugh and David L. Balch.[15] This involves cataloging and describing the various aspects of the deity, myth, or religious practice in question using textual, artistic, archaeological, epigraphic and numismatic evidence.

Secondly, following the example of Charles H. Talbert, I rely upon the concept of 'authorial audience' as developed by Hans Robert Jauss and Peter J. Rabinowitz.[16] Rabinowitz distinguishes four reading audiences for any text: the 'actual audience' (the flesh and blood audience who is physically reading or listening to a text), the 'authorial audience' (the author's intended audience who shares the author's background knowledge that is presumed within the text), the 'narrative audience' (the audience that the narrator communicates with, whose understanding of reality does not necessarily cohere with the actual or authorial audience), and the 'ideal narrative audience'(the audience that accepts the narrator's perspective even if the narrative or authorial audience does not). This is not the 'implied reader' as postulated by Wolfgang Iser, which is constructed from the autonomous

14. F.F. Bruce, *Book of the Acts* (rev. edn; *NICNT*; Grand Rapids: Eerdmans, 1988), p. 343; Bruce W. Winter, 'In Public and in Private: Early Christian Interactions with Religious Pluralism', in Andrew D. Clarke and Bruce W. Winter (eds), *One God One Lord in a World of Religious Pluralism* (Cambridge: Tyndale House, 1991), pp. 112–34 (129); Charles H. Talbert, *Reading Acts: A Literary and Theological Commentary on The Acts of the Apostles* (Reading the New Testament Series; New York: Crossroad, 1997), p. 165; and Ben Witherington III, *The Acts of the Apostles: A Socio-Rhetorical Commentary* (Grand Rapids: Eerdmanns, 1997), p. 532.

15. John E. Stambaugh and David L. Balch, *The New Testament in Its Social Environment* (LEC, 2; Philadelphia: Westminster Press, 1986). Also, Edgar Krentz, *The Historical-Critical Method* (Guides to Biblical Scholarship, Old Testament Series; Philadelphia: Fortress Press, 1975), pp. 39–41.

16. Jauss, 'Literary History'; Peter J. Rabinowitz, 'Truth in Fiction: A Reexamination of Audiences', *Critical Inquiry* 4 (1977), pp. 121–141; *idem, Before Reading: Narrative Conventions and the Politics of Interpretation* (Ithaca, NY: Cornell University Press, 1987) esp. pp. 15–46; *idem*, 'Whirl Without End: Audience Oriented Criticism', in G. Douglas Atkins (ed.), *Contemporary Literary Criticism* (Amherst, MA: University of Massachusetts Press, 1989), pp. 81–100; Charles H. Talbert, *Reading Luke-Acts in Its Mediterranean Milieu* (NovTSup, 107; Leiden: Brill, 2003) esp. pp. 14–18.

text and is thus disconnected from the context of reading: 'A theory of response [i.e., reading] has its roots in the text'.[17] By focusing on the authorial audience, the first-century audience Luke addressed, I avoid searching for Luke's psyche and personal musings. Rather, I am studying the 'communicative and interpretive community' of Luke's first-century world. Authors and readers relinquish total freedom of expression and interpretation when communicating through the author's text; they rely upon common cultural assumptions and unconscious social agreements to communicate. Luke's audience accepted his 'invitation to read in a particular socially constituted way...shared by [Luke] and his... expected readers'.[18]

Luke and his first-century audience shared common knowledge about the beliefs, myths and rituals of Greco-Roman religions. By mentioning these aspects of the first-century religious world, Luke endeavored to communicate part of his theological message. What would his first-century audience, the authorial audience, have understood when reading or hearing about lotteries, a mere mortal man accepting divine honors, a sacrificial ritual, the Ephesian Artemis, and so forth? In attempting to understand a first-century audience's appropriation of references and allusions to Greco-Roman religion in Acts, I minimize the split between the cultural knowledge bases of the actual (twenty-first-century) and authorial (first-century) audiences. As noted above, contemporary scholarship has sometimes misinterpreted Greco-Roman religion in Acts or, more frequently, all but ignored it. By reconstructing the assumptions and understandings of Luke's world regarding Greco-Roman religions, we can better understand Luke's message and his first-century audience's understanding of his message.

Thirdly, I, at least implicitly, approach Greco-Roman religion with a critically and historically serious validation of Greco-Roman religion as a religion (or more appropriately 'religions') fundamentally constituted by ritual. Biblical scholarship has generally relegated ritual in religion to the ephemeral aspects of critical study rather than as an essential component. This is in large part due to modern biblical scholarship's roots in both the Reformation, which reacted against the perceived liturgical excesses of the medieval Roman Catholic Church, and the rationalistic assumtions of the Enlightenment. By emphasizing theological (what the biblical authors believed stated propositionally) and historical (what happened, or in the nineteenth century German historian von Ranke famous words: '*wie es eigentlich gewesen*') concerns, biblical exegetes have overlooked the fundamental importance of ritual in the ancient Mediterranean.[19]

Both the Greeks and the Romans point to ritual as the foundational basis for their modes of religious thought and expression. Isocrates commented: '[The

---

17. Wolfgang Iser, *The Act of Reading: A Theory of Aesthetic Response* (Baltimore: The Johns Hopkins University Press, 1978), p. x; also, *idem, The Implied Reader: Patterns in Communication in Prose Fiction from Bunyan to Beckett* (Baltimore: The Johns Hopkins University Press, 1974). Cf. Rabinowitz, 'Whirl', p. 84; and Talbert, *Reading Luke-Acts,* p. 44.

18. Rabinowitz, *Before Reading,* p. 22.

19. Frank H. Gorman Jr., 'Ritual Studies and Biblical Studies: Assessment of the Past; Prospects for the Future', *Semeia* 67 (1994), pp. 13–36, esp. 14–20.

Athenians] recognized that *piety* consists...in preserving unchanged the rites their ancestors handed down to them' (*Areiopagitikos* 30).[20] Herodotus records that the Athenians in part defined their self-identity as Greeks as sharing 'the same cults, sacrifices, and religious outlook' (8.144.2).[21] In his *Euthyphro*, Plato has Euthyphro define religion to Socrates as: 'If someone knows how to say and to do what is agreeable to the gods by both praying and *sacrificing*, this is holiness, and these things save both private families and city-states. The opposite of what is gratifying to the gods is impious, which, quite obviously, overturns and destroys everything' (14). The Roman poet-philosopher Lucretius argued against the traditional ritual-based Roman understanding of religion when he wrote:

> Nor is it any piety frequently to be seen, head covered, turning to a [sacred] stone and advancing towards every altar; or to fall face to the ground and stretch out one's hands before the gods' shrines; or to shower the altars with the copious blood of oxen; or to heap vow upon vow (*De Rer. Nat.* 5.1197–1201).[22]

My ritual-studies methodology follows the ethnographic approaches of Ronald L. Grimes and Catherine Bell.[23] Their method requires an analysis of the ritual itself (participants, costumes, space, props, music, sound, language) and the ritual's own cultural and historical context.[24] Obviously ethnographic study of ancient texts is impossible. But by close reading of the ritual elements within the text (ritual language, indications of space and gesture, mentions of costume, etc.) one can tentatively form a sketch of the ritual itself and its larger ritual and socio-cultural context.

Implicit throughout my study is a fourth approach (closely related to the second and third approaches) that relies upon the notion of intertextuality in terms of *allusions* and *cultural competencies*. For several texts (Acts 1.17–26; 12.20–23; 14.23–41; 16.16–18; and 17.16–31) I argue that a Greco-Roman reader may have seen a Lukan *allusion* to various expressions of Greco-Roman religion or mythology. For my purposes, I use 'allusion' and 'allude' as defined by Chris Baldick:

20. Trans. Robert Garland, *Introducing New Gods: The Politics of Athenian Religion* (Baltimore: The Johns Hopkins University Press), p. 23.

21. Trans. Garland, *Introducing New Gods*, p. 113.

22. Trans. Ken Dowden, *Religion and the Romans* (Classical World Series; Bristol: Bristol Classical Press, 1992), p. 1.

23. Ronald L. Grimes, *Beginnings in Ritual Studies* (Studies in Comparative Religion; Columbia, SC: University of South Carolina Press, 1995), pp. 24–39; and Catherine Bell, *Ritual: Perspectives and Dimensions* (New York and Oxford: Oxford University Press, 1997), pp. 171–72. For detailed theoretical discussion, see Bell's *Ritual Theory, Ritual Practice* (New York and Oxford: Oxford University Press, 1992). A modern example of this approach is Grimes' ethnographic study of an annual festival in Santa Fe, New Mexico (*Symbol and Conquest: Public Ritual and Drama in Santa Fe* [Ithaca, NY: Cornell University Press, 1976]).

24. Ronald L. Grimes, *Research in Ritual Studies: A Programmatic Essay and Bibliography* (ATLA Bibliography Series, 14; Metuchen, NJ: American Theological Library Association and Scarecrow, 1985), p. 1; *idem, Ritual Criticism: Case Studies in Its Practice, Essays on Its Theory* (Studies in Comparative Religion; Columbia, SC: University of South Carolina Press, 1990), pp. 90, 219; and Bell, *Ritual: Perspectives and Dimensions*, p. 171.

> An indirect or passing reference to some event, person, place, or artistic work, the nature and relevance of which is not explained by the writer but relies on the reader's familiarity with what is thus mentioned... Allusion is an economical means of calling upon the history or the literary tradition that author and reader are assumed to share.[25]

According to J.A. Cuddon, allusions may be of four types: a reference to events and people, a reference to facts about the author, metaphorical references, and allusions that imitate the style or structure of another author.[26]

Richard B. Hays has demonstrated Paul's allusive intertextual relationship to the Hebrew Scriptures.[27] My arguments are analogous to Hays' investigation in that my analysis builds upon a general understanding of allusion and a general sensitivity to its occurrence rather than a detailed theory or taxonomy of allusion.[28]

Intertextuality also extends beyond texts to cultural phenomena. Building upon modern literary criticism and cultural analysis, Vernon K. Robbins has broadened the scope of allusions by developing 'socio-rhetorical interpretation', which includes 'cultural intertexture'.[29] Cultural intertexture is the interrelationship of a text to cultural knowledge and values. For Robbins, an allusion: 'is a statement that presupposes a tradition that exists in textual form, but the text being interpreted is not attempting to 'recite' the text...the text interacts with phrases, concepts, and traditions that are 'cultural' possessions that anyone who knows a particular culture may use'.[30] For my purposes, then, an allusion may be a reference to 'cultural possessions' that are not necessarily textual. The personification of Δίκη in Acts 28.4 is an allusion to a long standing cultural tradition in both the Greek and Roman worlds that is noted not only in texts such as Hesiod's *Theogeny* but also on coins and in vase paintings, and formed the basis of various cults and their associated temples, e.g. a temple to *Pax* or deified Peace. It is precisely Luke's veiled references to ancient 'religious cultural possessions', or more precisely, his Greco-Roman reader's perception of such references, that I seek to identify and comprehend in this study.

Both Hays and Robbins treat allusions from the viewpoint of the author. Implicit in my 'intertextual' approach is that the ancient readers or auditors of Acts shared cultural and literary 'competencies', which Luke expected of them.[31]

---

25. Chris Baldick, *The Concise Oxford Dictionary of Literary Terms* (Oxford : Oxford University Press, 1990), p. 6.

26. J.A. Cuddon, *A Dictionary of Literary Terms* (Oxford: Blackwell, 3rd rev. edn., 1991), p. 29.

27. Richard B. Hays, *Echoes of Scripture in the Letters of Paul* (New Haven : Yale University Press, 1989), esp. pp. 14–21. Hays, in turn, builds his argument upon John Hollander (*The Figure of Echo: A Mode of Allusion in Milton and After* [Berkeley: University of California Press, 1981]).

28. Hays, *Echoes of Scripture*, pp. 20–21.

29. Vernon K. Robbins, *Exploring the Texture of Texts: A Guide to Socio-Rhetorical Interpretation* (Valley Forge, PA: Trinity, 1996), pp. 58–60.

30. Robbins, *Exploring the Texture*, p. 59. Also note Jonathan Culler's remarks, 'Intertextuality thus becomes less a name for a work's relation to prior texts than a designation of its participation in the discursive space of a culture' (*The Pursuit of Signs: Semiotics, Literature, Deconstruction* [Ithaca, NY: Cornell University Press, 1981], p. 103).

31. S. John Roth, *The Lame, The Blind, and the Poor: Character Types in Luke-Acts* (JSNTSup, 144; Sheffield: Sheffield Academic Press, 1997), pp. 22–23. Also, Jonathan Culler, *Structuralist*

From the reader's perspective, these competencies form the basis of allusions. These competencies help the reader to construe meaning in a text, especially in those instances where there are 'gaps', silences, or inconsistencies in the narrative.[32] Such gaps require the reader to apply their cultural knowledge, either consciously or unconsciously, to understand the text. There are four overlapping competencies: (1) commonly known historical events and personalities, (2) the audience's literary canon, (3) standard literary conventions and (4) social norms and structures.[33] My analysis relies largely upon categories 1, 2, and 4 in relationship to Greco-Roman religion as found in the book of Acts. What are the well-known, i.e., well-known to ancient Greco-Roman auditors or readers, historical events or personalities that lie behind the mention of a particular Greco-Roman divinity or religious practice? What are the ancient literary texts with which Luke and his audience would have been familiar and that form a cultural backdrop for the passage in question? What first-century social norms and relationships are implicit in Luke's narratives involving Greco-Roman religion?[34]

By emphasizing the Greco-Roman reader of Acts, I avoid attempting to determine Luke's authorial intention. A Greco-Roman reader would apply their religious cultural competencies to Luke's text and would either understand overt references to Greco-Roman religion in light of these competencies or interpret

Poetics: Structuralism, Linguistics, and the Study of Literature (Ithaca, NY: Cornell University Press, 1975), pp. 137–48.

32. On the notion of textual gaps and the construal of textual meaning, see Roth, *The Lame, The Blind, and the Poor*, pp. 62–68. Roth's understanding of textual gaps is dependent upon Iser, *The Act of Reading*, esp. pp. 53–85.

I am not using 'gaps' and inconsistencies quite in the same way as Joel Marcus, 'Blanks and Gaps in the Markan Parable of the Sower', *BibInt* 5 (1997), pp. 247–67, relying on Meir Sternberg, *The Poetics of Biblical Narrative: Ideological Literature and the Drama of Reading* (Indiana Studies in Biblical Literature; Bloomington, IN: Indiana University Press, 1985), pp. 191–92. Marcus, following Steinberg, posits 'blanks' where there is 'an inadvertent failure to supply necessary information or an accidental transmission of confusing narrative signals' (p. 247) and 'gaps' where there is a 'deliberate ambiguity in the narrative' that is sometimes intentional so as to permit 'various interpretations within the overarching structure of narrative or ideological coherence…[and was] clear to the original readers' (pp. 247–48). My focus is not on whether or not a given interpretive lacuna in a text is deliberate (a literary analysis) or lost in textual transmission (text criticism). Instead my focus is on how Luke's authorial audience could have interpreted any such lacuna in light of their cultural knowledge.

33. John Darr, 'Glorified in the Presence of Kings: A Literary Critical Study of Herod the Tetrarch in Luke-Acts' (PhD dissertation, Vanderbilt University, 1987), pp. 62–68, 79–83, 125–39; see also his updated and partially modified discussion in *idem, Herod the Fox: Audience Criticism and Lukan Characterization* (JSNTSup, 163; Sheffield: Sheffield Academic Press, 1998), pp. 53, 62, 76, 92–100.

34. My methodological emphasis is upon the cultural competencies of a Greco-Roman audience who noticed elements of Greco-Roman religion in Acts. In this limited sense, my methodology is that of 'reader-response criticism'. In contrast to reader-response criticism, I *am not* studying the 'implied author', the 'implied reader', or other subtle modern theoretical constructs based purely upon an autonomous text irrespective of that text's original cultural, social, and historical setting. I am investigating Acts from the perspective of the explicit and implicit cultural religious knowledge of *real* Greco-Roman readers in the first century CE.

portions of the text as allusions to Greco-Roman religion in light of these cultural competencies. However, a consistent pattern of perceived allusions *may* suggestive one aspect of Luke's authorial intention. I do not 'banish the author' nor require an absolute understanding of Luke's authorial intention. I adopt a middle road in which 'authorial intention cannot be invoked to validate intertextual and allusive resonances, but audience-oriented readings must acknowledge that most readers do in fact try to reconstruct an author's intentions; they may perhaps fail, but a reader's meaning is very much bound up with the idea of an author'.[35]

Since I investigate the *cultural competencies* and *not the historicity* of Luke's narrative, I have bracketed out the entire question of the historicity of Acts. Does Luke write an absolutely chronologically accurate early Christian history? Or does he write an early Christian novel? These questions are irrelevant for this inquiry because, as G.W. Bowersock convincingly argues, one can derive cultural data with equal ease from ancient novels, poetry, myth, or historical narrative.[36]

At what point do I leave off pursuing allusions to Greco-Roman religion? Hays cautions:

> As we move farther away from [the] overt citation [of an ancient cultural phenomenon] …the demand placed on the reader's listening powers grows greater. As we near the vanishing point of the [allusion], it inevitably becomes difficult to decide whether we are really hearing an [allusion] at all, or whether we are only conjuring things out of the murmurings of our own imaginations.[37]

My use of 'thickly described' social description identifies the availability of an allusion to Luke and his audience and determines the historical plausibility of such an allusion. Detailed examination of the ancient history and cultural nature of a Greco-Roman religious phenomenon assures the historical plausibility of my reconstructions of possible allusions to Greco-Roman religion in Acts.

Passages and Religions Studied

In this study, I will investigate the mention of or allusion to the following traditional, established Greco-Roman deities, religious practices, or myths: oracles and divination, the imperial cult, the Greco-Roman sacrificial system, Athenian civic-foundation mythology as seen in Aeschylus' *Eumenides*, the Artemis cult, votive offerings, διοπετής objects, snakes in Greek religion, Δίκη, personified abstractions, and the Διόσκουροι. Because of this focus, I have excluded two

---

35. Christopher Nappa, review of Stephen Hinds, *Allusion and Intertext: Dynamics of Appropriation in Roman Poetry* (Cambridge: Cambridge University Press, 1998), in *Bryn Mawr Classical Review* (online), http.//ccat.sas.upenn.edu/bmcr/1998/1998–09–08.html. Nappa continues that a completely authorless reading distorts the interpretative process as much as a reading that grants authorial omnipotence over the text.

36. G.W. Bowersock, *Fiction as History: Nero to Julian* (Sather Classical Lectures, 58; Berkeley: University of California Press, 1994). Fergus Millar has written a stellar example of discovering cultural data from ancient fiction, 'The World of *The Golden Ass*', *JRS* 71 (1981), pp. 63–75. For Greek mythology, see, Paul Veyne, *Did the Greeks Believe Their Myths? A Study in the Constitutive Imagination* (Chicago: University of Chicago Press, 1988).

37. Hays, *Echoes of Scripture*, p. 23.

broad categories of ancient religious phenomena that appear in Acts: 'magic' (Acts 8.4–25; 13.4–12; 14.8–20; 16.16–18; and 19.11–20) and philosophical religion (Acts 17.16–33). I *do* investigate Acts 14.8–20 and 16.18–20 but not in terms of the demonic or magical, but in terms of those elements of traditional Greco-Roman religion referenced in the two passages.[38] Similarly I investigate Acts 17.16–33 but only insofar as it reflects the Athenian civic-foundation myth reflected in Aeschylus' *Eumenides*.[39]

I focus on several aspects of Greco-Roman religion in Acts that are not adequately investigated elsewhere and are in need of further explanation. Though my investigation is quite detailed, I neither make any pretense that it is exhaustive nor am I attempting to write an overall synthesis of Lukan theology in regard to Greco-Roman religion. Instead, I am trying to show how the exploration of these aspects of Greco-Roman religion in Acts may contribute to our understanding of the first-century network of coded cultural communication between Luke and his audience.

In Chapter 2, I make soundings into the parallels between Greco-Roman kleromantic divination and oracles, the choice of Matthias by lottery (Acts 1.25–26), Judas' death (1.17–18), and Paul's encounter with the oracular slave girl in Philippi (16.16–18). In Chapter 3, I investigate the possibility of allusions to Greco-Roman ruler cult in the narrative about Herod Agrippa's death (12. 20–23). In Chapter 4, I investigate the nature of Greco-Roman sacrificial processions and rituals to show that Luke parodies Greco-Roman sacrifice by ironic reversal (14.8–18). In Chapter 5, I follow up on suggestions made by several scholars that there is a possible allusion or parallel between Aeschylus' *Eumenides* and Acts 17.16–31. In Chapter 6, I make a sounding into the presence of votive offerings and the διοπετής an 'object descended from the realm of the gods', to suggest that there may be parallels between Lk. 18.9–14, 10.18 and Acts 19.21–41. In Chapter 7, I take core samples of Greco-Roman views of snakes as agents of divine justice, the personified abstraction Δίκη (28.1–6) to show how Luke reinforces his superlative evaluation of Paul and the authenticity of Paul's message. I also take soundings to follow up the suggestion of several exegetes that Luke mocks images of the Greco-Roman gods by referring to the Διόσκουροι (Castor and Pollux; 28.11). In the concluding chapter, I summarize my findings with reference to their contributions to Lukan theology in terms of an understanding of Luke's symbolic universe, the Lukan view of prophecy, Luke and the imperial cult, Luke and Christian ritual, idolatry, the resurrection, the Lukan Paul, Luke's

38. For in-depth discussions of magic in Luke-Acts, see Susan R. Garrett (*The Demise of the Devil: Magic and the Demonic in Luke's Writings* [Minneapolis: Fortress Press, 1989]) and Klauck (*Magic and Paganism*, throughout).

39. On the Stoics and Epicureans mentioned in this passage, see David L. Balch, 'The Areopagus Speech: An Appeal to the Stoic Historian Posidonius against Later Stoics and the Epicureans' in David L. Balch (ed.), *Greeks, Romans, and Christians: Essays in Honor of Abraham L. Malherbe* (Minneapolis: Fortress Press, 1990), pp. 52–79; and Jerome H. Neyrey, 'Acts 17, Epicureans, and Theodicy', in Balch (ed.), *Greeks, Romans, and Christians*, pp. 118–34.

openness to practitioners of Greco-Roman religion, Luke's social location, and suggested avenues for further research.[40]

Assumptions and Definitions

Throughout my investigation, I assume Clifford Geertz' definition of a religion:

> (1) a system of symbols which acts to (2) establish powerful, pervasive, and long-lasting moods and motivations in men [*sic*], by (3) formulating conceptions of a general order of existence and (4) clothing these conceptions with such an aura of factuality that (5) the moods and motivations seem uniquely realistic.[41]

Geertz' definition permits a researcher to consider ancient Greco-Roman religious expressions as serious human symbolic endeavors that help to organize and comprehend reality.[42] This overcomes Christianizing assumptions about Greco-Roman 'paganism' that become all too easily dismissive, including such points of view as: ritual does not express true religiosity or is at best of secondary importance; the narrative of Acts is the narrative of Christianity's triumph over 'paganism'; the interpreter idealizes ancient Christian interpretations of Greco-Roman religious behavior; and the interpreter insists on analyzing Greco-Roman religion by contemporary Christian or post-Christian concepts.[43]

For Greco-Roman religion, I narrow the focus of Geertz' definition to the following components: the scrupulous sense of fulfilling obligations to the gods

40. I will not burden the reader with endless repetition of the words 'core samples', 'corings', or 'soundings'. I use these words less as jargon than as metaphors for the probability spectrum implicit in my exegeses.

41. Clifford Geertz, 'Religion as a Cultural System', in *idem, The Interpretation of Cultures* (San Francisco: Basic Books, a Division of HarperCollins, 1973), pp. 87–125, citing 90 in slightly modified form. Some scholars have raised serious theoretical objections to Geertz' approach: Talal Asad, *Genealogies of Religion: Discipline and Reasons of Power in Christianity and Islam* (Baltimore: Johns Hopkins University Press, 1993); Nancy Frankenberry and Hans Penner, 'Geertz's Long-Lasting Moods, Motivations, and Metaphysical Conceptions', *JR* 79 (1999): pp. 617–40. Kevin Shilbrak has cogently and convincingly answered these criticisms in his, 'Religion, Models of, and Reality: Are We Through with Geertz?', *JAAR* 73 (2005): pp. 429–52, esp. pp. 435–47.

42. See for example the studies of the Ephesian Artemis cult by Guy M. Rogers and Steven Friesen, both based on Geertz' concept of 'thick description': Guy M. Rogers, *The Sacred Identity of Ephesos: Foundation Myths of a Roman City* (New York: Routledge, 1991); Steven J. Friesen, *Twice Neokoros: Ephesus, Asia, and the Cult of the Flavian Imperial Family* (Leiden: Brill, 1993).

43. The following authors discuss and critique these Christianizing assumptions:
Denigration of ritual: S.R.F. Price, *Rituals and Power: The Roman Imperial Cult in Asia Minor* (Cambridge: Cambridge University Press, 1984), pp. 1–22; Mark McVann, introduction to *Transformations, Passages, and Processes: Ritual Approaches to Biblical Texts, Semeia* 67(1994), pp. 7–12; Gorman Jr, 'Ritual Studies and Biblical Studies', pp. 14–20; and Bobby C. Alexander, 'An Afterword on Ritual in Biblical Studies', *Semeia* 67 (1994), pp. 209–26.
Triumph over 'paganism': Richard E. Oster, 'The Ephesian Artemis as an Opponent of Early Christianity', *JAC* 19 (1976), pp. 24–44; Ramsay MacMullen, *Christianizing the Roman Empire: A.D. 100–400* (New Haven: Yale University Press, 1984), pp. 1–24; Rick Strelan, *Paul, Artemis, and the Jews in Ephesus* (BZNW, 80; Berlin: Walter de Gruyter, 1996), pp. 6–13, 79–94, 132–53, 163–65.
Idealization of Christian sources: MacMullen, *Christianizing the Roman Empire*, pp. 1–24.
Christianizing conceptual analysis: Price, *Rituals and Power*, pp. 1–24; Garland, *Introducing New Gods*, pp. 171–73.

in ritual, an emphasis upon public expressions of piety or fulfillment of the obliga-tions to the gods, and the structuring of corporate identity around shared cults and rituals.[44] Thus, not only do I analyze the cultural backgrounds of various deities, e.g. the Διόσκουροι (Chapter 7), but I also analyze ritual as important in and of itself (Chapters 3, 4 and 6). I also assume that Greco-Roman religion was a polymorphic system made evident in a variety of local forms. I *do not assume* that Greco-Roman religion expressed itself in a coherent belief system 'espoused by its adherents as a matter of conscious choice' to the exclusion of other belief systems.[45]

It may seem that I assume that Luke accurately depicts Greco-Roman religion instead of mocking it as idolatrous. My analyses focus on *specific details* in Luke's text. For example, in Acts 14.8–18, Luke mentions priest, bulls, garlands, and sacrifice. By cross-checking these narrative details against the ancient Greco-Roman religious context we can assess the cultural accuracy of Acts 14.4–18 and understand an original Greco-Roman audience's culturally conditioned appreci-ation and comprehension of these details. In Acts 14.8–18, Luke's details concur with the constituent components of ancient Greco-Roman public sacrifices, but the details of the narrative are ironic in light of an ancient audience's knowledge of Greco-Roman sacrificial ritual (Chapter 4).

'Greco-Romans' and 'Greco-Roman Religion' as Used in this Study
One may easily criticize an apparent weakness in my methodology: How can one possibly speak of 'Greco-Romans' and 'Greco-Roman religion' as unitary entities? As discussed below, I use these concepts very specifically and narrowly.

'Greco-Romans'. At Alexander the Great's death in 323 BCE, he had conquered the known eastern Mediterranean world and southwestern Asia to just east of the Indus River.[46] In doing so, he, and his successors after him, introduced Greek language (with Greek becoming the lingua franca of the eastern Mediterranean) and culture throughout the areas he had conquered.[47] In so doing, they erected a two-tiered society consisting of the indigenous population in a given area and the Hellenistic, i.e., essentially Greek, ruling classes. Internecine warfare among the successor kingdoms to Alexander resulted in Rome's intervention in the eastern

44. Following the discussions of Emily Kearns, 'Religion, Greek', *OCD* (3rd edn, 1996), pp. 1300–1301; Simon R.F. Price, 'Religion, Roman', *OCD* (3rd edn; 2003), pp. 1306–1307; John Scheid, 'Religion, Roman, terms relating to', *OCD* (3rd edn, 1996), p. 1307, and Mary Beard, John North, and Simon Price, *Religions of Rome*, vol. 1, *A History* (Cambridge: Cambridge University Press, 1998), pp. 42–54.
45. Kearns, 'Religion, Greek', p. 1300.
46. See map in Robert Morkot, *The Penguin Historical Atlas of Ancient Greece* (London: Penguin, 1996), pp. 120–21.
47. See discussion in Simon Price, 'The History of the Hellenistic Period', in John Boardman, Jasper Griffin and Oswyn Murray (eds), *Greece and the Hellenistic World* (OHCW; Oxford: Oxford University Press, 1988), pp. 309–31; Robin Lane Fox, 'Hellenistic Culture and Literature', in Board-man, Griffin and Murray (eds), *Greece and the Hellenistic World*, pp. 332–58, esp. pp. 332–42.

Mediterranean in 200 BCE. This resulted in Roman rule throughout most of the region by the first century CE. The Romans ruled various areas, either directly through governors or indirectly through client kings, and provided the military power to ensure the peace while the Greeks ruled their local cities.[48]

During the Hellenistic period, the Romans became increasingly philhellene. According to Horace, 'Greece the captive, took her savage victor captive, and introduced the arts to rustic Latium' (*Epistles* 2.1.156).[49] Greek art was avidly collected and widely dispersed through much of the Italian peninsula by the second and third centuries BCE.[50] Livius Andronicus translated Homer's *Odyssey* into Latin verse and adapted and translated Greek dramas for the Roman stage, the first being performed in 240 BCE in Rome. By 150, Romans had to be bilingual in Latin and Greek to be considered educated.

Therefore, for my purposes, a Greco-Roman was a first- or second-century resident of the eastern Mediterranean who could speak, read and write Greek and was familiar with the early imperial Greek and Roman culture as found in the eastern Mediterranean. This person would be able to comprehend references to and have knowledge of such cultural phenomena as the more 'popular' Greek and Roman literature, drama, the general organization of local civic governments, etc.

Greco-Roman Religion. Greco-Roman 'religion' was not a single, monolithic entity but instead a collection of Greek and Roman ritual practices, personnel (priests, temple attendants, oracles, etc.), individual behaviors ('magic' and so-called 'popular religion', schools of thought (philosophy and mystical metaphysics such as Orphism), and localized cults; thus more precisely, we are discussing Greco-Roman religion*s*. On the one hand, Roman religion, with one major exception, was limited to Rome and its immediate environs in the Italian peninsula, and those cities that Rome colonized, for example, Philippi and Corinth. Greek religion, on the other hand, was a collection of localized cults (perhaps as many as ten thousand in Athens alone[51]).

In common to both the religions of ancient Greece and Rome were an emphasis on ritual, especially sacrifice (on this, see Chapter 4), the Twelve Gods, priests

48. I am simplifying a complex situation in the extreme. For example, it appears that at least some native Egyptians of the original Egyptian elite classes maintained positions in the government during the Ptolemaic period (Alan B. Lloyd, 'The Egyptian Elite in the Early Ptolemaic Period. Some Hieroglyphic Evidence', in Daniel Ogden [ed.], *The Hellenistic World: New Perspectives* [Swansea, England: The Classical Press of Wales, 2002] pp. 117–36).

49. Trans. Susan E. Alcock, *Graecia Capta: The Landscapes of Roman Greece* (Cambridge: Cambridge University Press, 1993), p. 1.

50. For the following discussion, Erich S. Gruen, *The Hellenistic World and the Coming of Rome* (Berkeley: University of California Press, 1984), pp. 250–72; Elizabeth Rawson, 'The Expansion of Rome', in John Boardman, Jasper Griffin and Oswyn Murray (eds), *The Oxford Illustrated History of the Roman World* (Oxford: Oxford University Press, 1988), pp. 39–59, esp. pp. 55–58; Erich S. Gruen, *Studies in Greek Culture and Roman Policy* (Cincinnati Classical Studies, New Series, 7; Leiden: Brill, 1996); and Peter Sidney Derow, 'Philhellenism', *OCD* (3rd edn, 1996), pp.1159–60.

51. Robert Garland, *Religion and the Greeks* (Classical World Series; London: Bristol Classical Press, an imprint of Gerald Duckworth, 1995), p. 2.

(purely ritual supervisors rather than the Christian conception of pastoral counselors, theologians, and preachers), and during the imperial period, the imperial cult (see Chapter 3).[52] The Romans ritually and legally declared the equivalency of their most prominent gods and the most prominent Greek gods at a *lectisternium* (a formal banquet for the gods in which food was set before images of the gods set on dining couches) in 217 BCE (Livy 22.10.9): Jupiter = Zeus, Venus = Aphrodite, Mars = Ares, etc.[53] Additionally, the Romans had formally accepted such non-Roman deities as Asclepius in 239 BCE (Livy 10.47.7) and *Magna Mater* (or Cybele) in 205–204 BCE (Dionysius of Halicarnassus *Ant. Rom.* 2.19.3ff.) as worthy of worship.

The various Greek gods took on local characteristics: Artemis was the patron deity of Ephesus but also heavily influenced by Asiatic elements. Zeus was worshiped in Athens (and throughout the ancient world) under a variety of guises including Zeus Sōter (Zeus the Savior God) and Zeus Meilichios (Zeus who needs to be propitiated, often depicted in art as a huge snake).[54]

By the imperial era, a 'homogenous' Greco-Roman 'priestly system' had spread throughout the Mediterranean.[55] Whatever the original form of local 'religious authority'; local civic priesthoods increasingly modeled themselves after the Roman 'euergetic' model. Local aristocrats or Roman colonists performed the duties of the specific priesthood, which included supervising sacrifices and providing civic benefactions. For example Kleanax occupied the *prytaneis*, 'council chair', of Kyme in Asia Minor and provided for a pentennial celebration of local mysteries in which he entertained the city's citizens (of Greek descent), the local Anatolians, and the Romans.[56] He is thus an example of the religious multicultural complexity that existed by the first century.[57]

52. On the Twelve Gods, see Charlotte R. Long, *The Twelve Gods of Greece and Rome* (EPRO, 107; Leiden: Brill, 1987).

53. Robert Schillig and Jörg Rüpke, 'Roman Religion: The Early Period', *ER* (2nd edn),vol. 12. pp. 7997–8008, citing p. 7905.

54. On Artemis, see Paul Trebilco, 'Asia', in David W.J. Gill and Conrad Gempf (eds), *The Book of Acts in Its Graeco-Roman Setting*, vol. 2 of Bruce W. Winter (ed.),*The Book of Acts in Its First Century Setting* (Grand Rapids: Eerdmanns, 1994), pp. 316–57. For Zeus, see Fritz Graf, 'Zeus', *OCD* (3rd edn, 1996), p. 1637.

55. Following Richard Gordon, 'The Veil of Power', in Mary Beard and Jordan North (eds), *Pagan Priests: Religion and Power in the Ancient World* (Ithaca, NY: Cornell University Press, 1990), pp. 224–31; *idem*, 'Religion in the Roman Empire', in Beard and North (eds), *Pagan Priests*, esp. pp. 240–45. Gordon notes and explains the exceptional circumstances of Roman Egypt ('Religion in the Roman Empire', in Beard and North [eds], *Pagan Priests* pp. 241–42).

56. For further discussion of Kleanax, see Chapter 4.

57. See further P.M. Fraser, 'The Kings of Commagene and the Greek World', in Sencer Sahin, Elmar Schwertheim, and Jörg Wagner (eds), *Studien zur Religion und Kultur Kleinasiens: Festschrift für Friedrich Karl Dörner zum 65. Geburtstag am 28. Februar 1976* (EPRO, 66; Leiden: Brill, 1966) vol. 1 pp. 359–74; Richard D. Sullivan, 'Priesthoods of the Eastern Dynastic Aristocracy' in Sahin, Schwertheim, and Wagner (eds), *Studien zur Religion*, II, pp. 914–39; and Houwink ten Cate, *The Luwian Population Groups of Lycia and Cilicia Aspera During the Hellenistic Period* (Documenta et Monumenta Orientis Antiqui, 10; Leiden: Brill, 1961), esp. pp. 205, 201–203.

In light of the above, a Greek, a Roman, or a Hellenized native of the eastern Mediterranean, i.e. a 'Greco-Roman', could travel throughout the eastern Mediterranean and recognize a particular local god as a Roman god in Greek or local dress and perceive a general familiarity with localized religious practices. Thus for my purposes, 'Greco-Roman religion' is the sum total of religious practices encountered by a Greco-Roman in the daily course of civic life.

Chapter 2

ACTS 1.15–26; 16.16–18 AND GRECO-ROMAN ORACLES

Oracles and divination existed throughout the New Testament world in both Judean and Greco-Roman contexts.[1] Divination is 'the art or science of interpreting symbolic messages from the gods' that are often unpredictable or trivial.[2] An oracle is a message 'from the gods in human language', often given in response to an inquiry, or can also designate 'the place where such messages are requested or received'.[3] Acts 1.15–26 (esp. vv. 17, 23–26) and 16.16–18 use terminology or describe actions reminiscent of Greek divination and oracles. In this chapter, I suggest that Greco-Romans may have seen an allusion in these two texts to Greek inductive oracles and oracles of possession or inspiration because of this presence of technical kleromantic vocabulary and the mention of a πνεῦμα πύθωνα, a 'spirit of divination'.

Kleromancy in Acts 1.15–26

There are significant parallels between Acts 1.15–26 and certain aspects of Greco-Roman religion. In this section, I will briefly discuss the terms πληρόω,

---

1. W.R. Halliday, *Greek Divination: A Study of its Methods and Principles* (London: Macmillan, 1913; repr. Chicago: Argonaut, 1967); H.W. Parke and D.E. Wormell, *The Delphic Oracle* (2 vols; Oxford: Basil Blackwell, 1956); H.W. Parke, *The Oracles of Zeus: Dodona, Olympia, Ammon* (Oxford: Basil Blackwell, 1967); Robert Flacelière, *Greek Oracles* (2nd edn; London: Paul Elek, 1976); David E. Aune, *Prophecy in Early Christianity and the Ancient Mediterranean World* (Grand Rapids: Eerdmans, 1983), pp. 23–80; H.W. Parke, *The Oracles of Apollo in Asia Minor* (London: Croom Helm, 1985); Simon Price, 'Delphi and Divination', in P.E. Easterling and J.V. Muir (eds), *Greek Religion and Society* (Cambridge: Cambridge University Press, 1985), pp. 128–54; Joseph Fontenrose, *The Delphic Oracle: Its Responses and Operations with a Catalogue of Responses* (Berkeley: University of California Press, 1978); *idem, Didyma: Apollo's Oracle, Cult and Companions* (Berkeley: University of California Press, 1988); Saul Levin, 'The Old Greek Oracles in Decline', *ANRW* II/18, part 2 (1989), pp. 1598–1649; H.W. Parke, *Sibyls and Sibylline Prophecy in Classical Antiquity* (ed. B.C. McGing; London and New York: Routledge, 1988); Sarah Iles Johnston, introduction to 'Divination and Prophecy: Greece', in Sarah Iles Johnston (ed.), *Religions of the Ancient World: A Guide* (Harvard University Press Reference Library; Cambridge, MA: Belknap Press of Harvard University Press, 2004), pp. 370–71; Sarah Iles Johnston, 'Divination and Prophecy: Greece', in Johnston (ed.), *Religions of the Ancient World*, pp. 383–86; Richard L. Gordon, 'Divination and Prophecy: Rome', in Johnston (ed.), *Religions of the Ancient World*, pp. 387–89; and Sarah Iles Johnston and Peter T. Struck (eds), *Mantikê: Studies in Ancient Divination* (RGRW, 155; Leiden: Brill Academic, 2005).

2. Aune, *Prophecy in Early Christianity*, p. 23.

3. Aune, *Prophecy in Early Christianity*, p. 23.

προλέγω, and λαγχάνω as related to kleromancy, discuss kleromancy in the Greco-Roman world, and conclude by analyzing Acts 1.15–26 in light of the Greco-Roman context.

Kleromancy is divination performed by using lots, dice, or other items subject to forming random patterns.[4] Several Greek terms associated with kleromantic divination or Greco-Roman prophecy occur in Acts 1.15–26: κλῆρος, πληρόω, προλέγω, and λαγχάνω. Scholars have generally overlooked the verbal continuity between kleromantic terminology in 1.15–22 and 1.23–26 and their Greco-Roman parallels.[5] Bruce probably speaks for most exegetes when he discounts the importance of the lottery terminology in 1.17, 'Both λαγχεῖν and κλῆρος originally imply apportioning and receiving by lot, but this sense has disappeared; translate "he received his portion"'.[6] Understanding 1.17 purely in terms of 'ministerial service' or 'portion' overlooks the larger cultural context, the auditory connections between ἔλαχεν in 1.17 and ἐλακησεν in 1.18, and the connection of 1.15–22 to 1.23–26 by the repeated use of lottery terminology.[7]

πληρόω, προλέγω, and λαγχάνω

Luke's use of these three words in Acts 1.15–26 parallels their use in Greco-Roman oracles and prophecy. Luke uses πληρόω with the meaning 'to fulfill a prophetic oracle' in 1.16, ἔδει πληρωθῆναι τὴν γραφήν, 'it was necessary to fulfill the scriptures'. Polyaenus (second century CE) used πληρόω to indicate the fulfillment of an oracle, 'for were they not about to fulfill [πεπληρομένου] the prophecy?' (*Strat.* 1.18.).[8] Plutarch discussed the case of Cinna and Sulla

---

4.   Halliday, *Greek Divination*, pp. 205–35 esp. pp. 205–18; Fritz Graf, 'Rolling the Dice for an Answer', in Johnston and Struck (eds), *Mantikê*, pp. 51–98; and Cristiano Grottanelli, '*Sorte unica pro casibus pluribus enotata:* Literary Text and Lot Inscriptions as Sources for Ancient Kleromancy', in Johnston and Struck (eds), *Mantikê*, pp. 129–46.

5.   In studying Acts 1.15–26, most scholars have emphasized Luke's theology of completing the 'eschatological Israel' by bringing the inner apostolic circle back to twelve members, the historicity of the narrative, the Judas traditions, or the Judean backgrounds of the text; see the discussion of the *status quaestionis* in Arie W. Zwiep, *Judas and the Choice of Matthias: A Study on Context and Concern of Acts 1.15–26* (WUNT, 2/187; Tübingen: Mohr-Siebeck, 2004), pp. 1–32; and his bibliography, pp. 197–208.

6.   F.F. Bruce, *The Acts of the Apostles: the Greek Text with Introduction and Commentary* (3rd rev. and enlarged edn; Grand Rapids: Eerdmanns, 1990), p. 109. Luke Timothy Johnson, *The Acts of the Apostles* (Sacra Pagina 5; A Michael Glazier book; Collegeville, MN: Liturgical Press, 1992), p. 35, Ben Witherington (*The Acts of the Apostles: A Socio-Rhetorical Commentary* [Grand Rapids: Eerdmanns, 1997], p. 122), and Beverly Roberts Gaventa (*Acts* [Abingdon New Testament Commentaries; Nashville: Abingdon, 2003], p. 70) notice the κλῆρος motif in 1.15–26. Johnson sees a material-possessions symbolism in the passage related to Num. 18.21–26. Witherington also construes a relationship to Num. 18.21–26 but understands and translates κλῆρος as 'ministerial service'. Gaventa understands a reference to Judas' apostasy.

7.   John F. Brug has evaluated the evidence whether 1.26 refers to an election or a lottery and concludes that the evidence is inconclusive but slightly in favor of lot casting ('Acts 1.26 – Lottery or Election?', *Wisconsin Lutheran Quarterly* 95 [1998] pp. 212–114, esp. p. 214). He restricts his linguistic evidence strictly to the Hebrew Bible, LXX, and Greek New Testament.

8.   Trans. Peter Krentz, in Peter Krentz and Everett L. Wheeler (eds and trans.), *Polyaenus, Stratagems of War* (Chicago: Ares, 1994).

who, 'had fulfilled [their] destiny [πεπληρωκέναι] fated in a forged Sibylline oracle' (*Cicero* 17.4).

Luke uses προλέγω in the sense 'to foretell the future', ἣν προεῖπεν τὸ πνεῦμα τὸ ἅγιον, 'it was foretold by the Holy Spirit' (Acts 1.16). Plato also used προλέγω in this sense, 'when I say something in the assembly about the divine, foretelling [προλέγων] what is about to be to them, they laugh as if I am mad' (*Euthphr.* 3C).

λαγχάνω has the meanings 'to have one's place or destiny assigned' and 'to receive something by lot'. Luke uses the first meaning in Acts 1.17, ἔλαχεν τὸν κλῆρον τῆς διακονίας ταύτης, 'he received a share in this service'. Homer has the dead Patroclus say, 'but abhorrent fate has swallowed me up, which was assigned [λάχε] to me at birth' (*Il.* 23.78–80). Pindar comments, 'Let him know that he has had extraordinary joy allotted [λαχών] him by the gods' (*Nem. Ode* 9.45).[9]

Luke's use of λαγχάνω is part of his election and lottery vocabulary used in 1.15–26. He does not use λαγχάνω to mean 'to receive something by lottery' but instead uses the verb to describe Judas' fate as foreordained. However, Greco-Roman readers may have construed the semantic double association of the verb in this context of fate and lottery language.

Luke's use of πληρόω, προλέγω, and λαγχάνω in Acts 1.15–26 has interesting and remarkable parallels to the use of these terms in Greco-Roman texts about the fulfillment of oracles and prophecies, oracular predictions, and fate or destiny. This suggests that in Acts 1.15–26, either Luke alluded to Greco-Roman oracles and prophecies or that his Greco-Roman audience could have perceived references to Greco-Roman oracles and prophecies in the text.

Kleromancy in the Greco-Roman World

Kleromantic oracles, or oracles that involved lot casting, were a familiar part of Luke's Greek cultural context. Both individuals and larger institutions used kleromancy to fill cultic offices, to learn future events, and to determine future courses of action. A προφήτης or 'prophet' supervised the oracle at Didyma from at least 334 BCE through the Hadrianic era (117–38 CE). This official was chosen by lot from a list of up to five candidates (one for each deme in Milesia) from wealthy Milesian families. 'A man so chosen was obviously the god's choice'.[10]

Oracle consultations to determine future courses of action often used lotteries. The Athenian assembly was divided in 352 BCE over the propriety of leasing land

9.   Translation slightly adapted from John Sandys (trans.), *The Odes of Pindar: Including the Principal Fragments* (LCL; Cambridge, MA: Harvard University Press, 2nd rev. edn, 1919). For this passage, William Race translates λαχών as 'received' (*Pindar* [LCL; Cambridge: Harvard University Press, 1997]). The passage's context, a celebration of the Syracusan general Chromios' military victories and the favor that the gods have shown him, permits me to translate λαχών as 'allotted'. See also C.M. Bowra, who translates *Nem. Ode* 45.9 as 'Let him know that he has won/A wonderful fortune from the gods' (*The Odes of Pindar* [Penguin Classics; Harmondsworth, England: Penguin, 1969]).

10.   Fontenrose, *Didyma*, p. 46, citing a series of inscriptions in Albert Rehm and Richard Harder (eds), *Didyma II: Die Inschriften* (Berlin: Mann, 1958).

Foreign but Familiar Gods

dedicated to the Eleusinian goddesses, Demeter and Kore, and referred the question to Delphi. The Athenians believed that the Delphic oracle had all too frequently supported Spartan interests during the Peloponnesian war. Fearing that the Delphic priests would again intervene against Athenian interests, the Athenians inscribed answers to their question on two tin sheets. One answer permitted the leasing of the land; the other prohibited it. The Athenians concealed the inscriptions, placed them in separate vases, and had envoys carry them to Delphi. Presumably the Pythia, the Delphic seeress, had to answer the Athenians' question by choosing either of the two vases by lot or chance.[11]

> If [a citizen of Skiathos] appears for the consultation by two beans [φρυκτώ], the charge will be one Ae[ginetan] st[a]-
> te[r] for a public matter, [a smaller amount] for a private matter.
> [lacunae]
> [If he wants to consult the oracle, he will consecrate?]
> to the god [as a preliminary sacrifice on [the ta]ble a c[ho]ice goat an[d t]he other sacred offerings according to [c]ustom.[12]

Amandry interpreted φρυκτώ, the 'bean', as a lot used for the oracle. The remainder of the inscription stipulates the fees (for both private and public inquiries) and sacrifices necessary prior to consulting the oracle.[13]

Legend associated the Delphic oracle and the Pythia with the choice of the king of Thessaly by kleromancy:

> So Aleuas the Thessalian, who as an arrogant and insolent youth, was kept down and treated harshly by his father; but his uncle received him and attached him to himself, and when the Thessalians sent to the god at Delphi lots to determine who should be king, the uncle, without the father's knowledge, slipped in a lot [φρυκτούς] for Aleuas. When the Pythian priestess drew the lot [φρυκτόν] of Aleuas, his father denied that he had put in one for him, and to everyone it appeared that there had been some error in the recording of names. So they sent again and questioned the god a second time; and the prophetic priestess, as though to confirm fully her former declaration, answered: 'It is the red-haired man I mean, The child whom Archedice bore'. (*Frat. amor.* 21 [= *Mor.* 492B])[14]

11. Flacelière, *Greek Oracles,* pp. 69–71. P. Foucart first published the inscription recounting the Athenians' actions, 'Décret Athénien de L'Anée Trouvé a Éleusis', *BCH* 13 (1889), pp. 433–67.

12. Translation slightly adapted from Fontenrose, *Delphic Oracle,* p. 223. Text from Pierre Amandry, 'Convention religieuse conclue entre Delphes et Skiathos', *BCH* 63 (1939), pp. 183–219. esp. p. 184, ll. 15–24; and *idem, La mantique Apollinienne à Delphes: Essai sur le fonctionnement de l'Oracle* (Paris: Bocard, 1950), pp. 29–36, 84–85, 107–10, 232–33; cited in Fontenrose, *Delphic Oracle,* p. 222 n. 35 and p. 223 n. 36. Frank Egleston Robbins had previously suggested the existence of the lot oracle, 'The Lot Oracle at Delphi', *CP* 11 (1916), pp. 278–92. Recently, Massimo Di Salvator has confirmed the existence of lot oracles at Delphi, 'Il sorteggio fra politica e religion. Un caso tessalico', in Federica Cordano and Cristiano Grottanelli (eds), *Sorteggio pubblico e cleromanzia dall'antichità* (Milan: ET, 2001), pp. 119–30; cited in Grottanelli, '*Sorte unica*', p 130 n. 4.

13. Fontenrose dismisses the existence of Delphic kleromantic divination because this inscription is too fragmentary and open to other interpretations to suggest the use of a lottery oracle (*Delphic Oracle,* 219–23, following F. Solkolowski, 'Sur un passage de la convention Delphes-Skiathos', *RArch* 31/32 [1939] pp. 981–84).

14. Trans. W.C. Helmbold, *Plutarch's Moralia* (vol. 6; LCL; Cambridge: Harvard University Press, 1939).

Some Greek kleromantic oracles functioned without a human intermediary or supervisor. Pausanias mentions an oracle of Heracles in a cave near Bura:

> Here one can divine by means of a tablet and dice. He who inquires of the god offers up a prayer in front of the image [of Herakles in the cave], and after the prayer he takes four dice, a plentiful supply of which are placed by Herakles, and throws them upon the table. For every figure made by the dice there is an explanation expressly written on the tablet. (Pausanias, 7.25.10)[15]

The results of the dice throw yielded a series of numbers corresponding to a series of numbered oracular inscriptions on the tablet in the shrine.[16]

A similar type of kleromantic oracle operated at Phrygian Hierapolis. Twenty-four Greek sentences were inscribed on the temple walls of the oracle as a Greek alphabet acrostic. Georg Kaibel and Parke have suggested that an inquirer drew a lot marked with a letter of the Greek alphabet from a vessel. The inquirer then consulted the inscription beginning with the letter on the lot.[17]

One highly unusual votive offering suggests the gratitude of the favorable recipients of a lot oracle. Excavators uncovered an enormous cast bronze knuckle-bone (presumably one of a set of two) at Susa, the capital of ancient Persia.[18] Inscriptional evidence demonstrates that the knucklebone was originally dedicated as a gift to Apollo and later plundered by the Persians from Apollo's oracle sanctuary at Didyma in Asia Minor.

Zeus had his own kleromantic oracle at Dodona.[19] The exact procedure is unknown but the inquirers wrote the questions on strips of lead, which were then folded, given an identifying mark, and placed in a jar. Presumably the oracular priestess used lots such as colored beans to provide a yes or no response to the questions (Callisthenes, *FGH* 2B, 124 F 22). Cicero commented on a Spartan embassy to this oracle:

---

15. W.H.S. Jones (trans.), *Pausanias Description of Greece* (LCL; Cambridge: Harvard University Press, 1918).

16. Aune, *Prophecy in Early Christianity*, p. 25 and p. 350 nn. 25–26. Additional discussion and nineteenth century bibliography in James George Frazer, *Pausanias's Description of Greece* (London: Macmillan, 1897?; repr., New York: Biblo and Tannen, 1965), IV, pp.172–73.

17. See Parke, *Oracles of Apollo*, pp. 181, 224 n. 22 for discussion and references. For examples, see Georg Kaibel, *Epigrammata Graecae ex lapidibus conlecta* (Berlin: G. Reimer, 1878) no. 1038 (from Attalia in Pamphylia) and nos. 1039 and 1040 (from Hierapolis). The standard, but now dated, discussions of these oracular tablets are in F. Heinevetter, 'Würfel-und-Buchstaben Orakel in Griechenland und Kleinasien' (PhD dissertation, Breslau, 1912), cited in Aune, *Prophecy in Early Christianity*, p. 350 n. 25; and Gudmund Björck, 'Heidnische und Christlich Orakel mit Fertigen Antworten', *SO* 119 (1939), pp. 86–98.

18. Parke, *Oracles of Apollo in Asia Minor*, pp. 21–22, 30–32, 228 n. 26, and 229 n. 14. The excavation of the knucklebone was reported in J. de Morgan (ed.), *Délégation en Perse*, vol. 7 (Recherches Archélologiques, Deuxième série; Paris: Ministère de l'Instruction publique et des Beaux-Arts, 1905), p. 155, cited in Parke, *Oracles of Apollo* p. 228 n. 26.

19. My discussion follows Parke, *Oracles of Zeus*, pp. 108–12; and Aune, *Prophecy in Early Christianity*, p. 25. Examples of the inquiries in Parke, *Oracles of Zeus*, pp. 259–73 and *idem*, 'Three Enquiries from Dodona', *JHS* 87 (1969), pp. 132–33.

[The Spartans] sent to consult the oracle of Jupiter at Dodona as to the chances of victory. After their messengers had duly set up the vessel in which were the lots, an ape, kept by the king of Molossia for his amusement, disarranged the lots and everything else used in consulting the oracle and scattered them in all directions. (Cicero, *De Div.* 1.34)[20]

The Romans also used kleromancy: publicly for allotting provinces to members of the senatorial elite and privately for various individual questions (Livy 9.38.15, 10.24.16–17, 27.11.11, 37.51.1–6; Plautus *Casina* 345–46).[21] Cicero mentions the Italian oracle of *Fortuna* at Praeneste (*De Div.* 2.25, 41) in which oak tablets were inscribed with the oracular answers to various inquiries and drawn by children attached to the oracle center.[22] Various inscribed bronze lamellae, approximately dating from the early Republic to the early imperial era, have been unearthed in Italy and appear to be lots that provided the answer to an inquirer's question.[23]

An anonymous epigram from the early imperial period indicates how closely ancient Hellenistic literature linked kleromancy and fate (kleromantic technical terms in brackets):

One time three young girls played with lots [κλήρω],
to see who first would go to Hades.
And three times they threw [ἔβαλον] the die from their hands, but every time it fell
to one girl. She laughed at the lot [κλῆρον], her destiny.
For then, ill-fated, she unexpectedly slipped and fell from a roof,
she went to Hades, as fated [ἔλαχεν] by the lot.
The lot [ὁ κλῆρος] is not false when it is adverse, a better lot
neither mortal prayers nor mortal hands can achieve.
(*Anth. Pal.* 9.158)[24]

This epigram expresses the Greco-Roman belief that kleromantic divination accurately reveals either the will of the gods or, as in this case, the fate of the individual casting the lot or die.

20. Trans., William Armistead Falconer, *Cicero: De Senectute, De Amicitia, De Divinatione* (LCL; Cambridge: Harvard University Press, 1923).

21. Nathan Rosenstein, 'Sorting Out the Lot in Republican Rome', *AJP* 116 (1995), pp. 43–75; Roberta Office, *Public Office in Early Rome: Ritual Procedure and Political Practice* (Ann Arbor: University of Michigan Press, 1998); Sarah Iles Johnston, 'Lost in the Shuffle: Roman Sortition and Its Discontents', *Archiv für Religionsgeschichte* 5 (2003) 46–56; and the works cited in Fritz Graf, 'Rolling the Dice', p. 60 n. 38; and Grottanelli, 'Ancient Kleromancy', in Johnston and Struck (eds), *Mantikê*, throughout.

22. Discussion in Parke, *Oracles of Zeus*, pp. 111, 127 n. 28.

23. Grottanelli, 'Ancient Kleromancy', in Johnston and Struck (eds), *Mantikê*, pp. 138–41.

24. Translation adapted from D.L. Page, *Further Greek Epigrams* (rev. and prepared for publication by R.D. Dawe and J. Diggle; Cambridge: Cambridge University Press, 1981), p. 360. Dice are also associated with fate and death in four other epigrams from the *Greek Anthology*: 12.46 (Asklepiades, third century BCE), 7.422 (Leonidas of Tarentum, mid-third century BCE), 7.427 (Antiapter of Sidon, second century BCE), and 7.428 (Meleager, first century BCE); see also the discussion in Kathryn J. Gutzwiller, *Poetic Garlands: Hellenistic Epigrams in Context* (Hellenistic Culture and Society 28; Berkeley: University of California Press, 1998), pp. 143–44, 267–68, 269–71, and 273–76.

Acts 1.15–26 in Light of Greco-Roman Kleromantic Oracles

Acts 1.15–26 parallels Greco-Roman oracles in vocabulary. This text parallels Greco-Roman kleromantic oracles through the use of lots to fill a religious office and by using κλῆρος to refer to an individual's fate or destiny.

In Acts 1.15–26, Luke uses πληρόω, προεῖπον, and λαγχάνω parallel to use of these words in the surrounding Greco-Roman culture: πληρόω is 'to fulfill an oracle', προεῖπον is to foretell the future by means of oracles, and λαγχάνω is 'to receive knowledge of one's destiny, position, or office in life'. According to Luke, the Holy Spirit's γέγραπται, 'written', ἡ γραφή, 'oracle', προεῖπον, 'foretold', that Judas' home would be deserted and no one would live in it and that another would occupy Judas' vacant position (1.16, 20). In Luke's view this prophetic oracle was 'fulfilled', πληρωθῆναι, in Judas' purchase of property, his subsequent death, and the subsequent naming of his property as 'Field of Blood'.

Prior to the fulfillment of this oracle, Judas had 'received his position', ἔλαχεν τὸν κλῆρον (1.17). His position as a follower of Jesus enabled him, 'to be the one who lead those who arrested Jesus'. His reward money allowed him to buy the property that fulfilled the oracle when it became deserted.

For Luke, Judas' actions, death, and replacement fulfilled scriptural prophecy. A Greco-Roman audience would have noted both the parallels and differences between Acts 1.15–26 and kleromantic oracles. Read in strictly Greco-Roman terms, the vocabulary that Luke uses to describe Judas' death, actions, and replacement corresponds to the language of lotteries and fate in *Pal. Anth.* 9.158. I do not posit direct literary dependence in either direction between this epigram and Luke's narrative. The linguistic parallels suggest that Luke's symbolic universe was, at least in part, Hellenized and in partial agreement with first-century Greco-Roman religious perspectives.[25] Both Judas and the young girl receive their κλῆρος, 'lot', which was 'foretold [προεῖπεν] by the Holy Spirit' for Judas and by 'the fall [ἔβαλον] of the die' for the young girl. Judas τῆς διακονίας ταύτης, 'received his share [or 'obtained his lot', ἔλαχεν τὸν κλῆρον] of this service [membership in the Twelve]'. The young girl 'went into Hades as her lot [or 'as she was fated', ὡς ἔλαχεν]'. Both Judas and the young girl die by falling; he by 'falling forward'; she by 'slipping and falling'. For both, this was their pre-ordained fate. The scriptures foretell the death of Judas, 'For it is written in the book of Psalms [Ps. 69.25], "Let his home be deserted and let no one live in it".' The young girl's death is foretold by the roll of the dice: 'three times they threw

---

25. One implication of two recent studies is that Luke seems to participate in the 'middlebrow' segment (that of architects, merchants, physicians, scholars, etc.) of first-century Mediterranean Hellenistic society: Vernon K. Robbins, 'The Social Location of the Implied Author of Luke-Acts', in Jerome H. Neyrey (ed.), *The Social World of Luke-Acts: Models for Interpretation* (Peabody, MA: Hendrikson, 1991), pp. 305–32; Loveday Alexander, 'Luke's Prefaces in the Context of Greek Preface-Writing', *NovT* 28 (1986), pp. 48–74; *eadem, The Preface to Luke's Gospel: Literary Convention and Social Context in Luke 1.1–4 and Acts. 1.1* (SNTSMS, 78; Cambridge: Cambridge University Press, 1993).

[ἔβαλον] the die from their hands, but every time it fell to one girl'. For a Greco-Roman reader, the language of divination is present in both Acts and in the epigram. For that same reader, the difference between the two accounts is that Judas' death is ultimately under the control of God while the young girl's death is not attributable to the Greco-Roman gods nor to the Judean-Christian God, but only to her κλῆρος, 'her lot'.

After Jesus' ascension, his disciples use a lottery to choose Matthias as Judas' replacement (Acts 1.15–26). The exact procedure for the lottery is unclear. Pesch, following Lindblom, plausibly reconstructs the lottery as follows: marked stones are placed in a clay pot or cloth bag, and the pot or bag is shaken until one lot falls out, with the marked stone or lot indicating the person chosen for a particular task.[26] Pesch rightly concludes that the use of the lottery demonstrates the absolute absence of human intervention in the choice of Matthias. The choice is made without human manipulation or control; God alone controls the choice.[27]

The Greek understanding of kleromancy paralleled Luke's understanding of the lottery to replace Judas: the Greco-Roman gods (Apollo or Zeus) or the God of the Christians (and Judeans) controls fate and chance.[28] God alone determined Matthias' succession to Judas' office of apostle. Luke's Greco-Roman readers or auditors, unfamiliar with Judean traditions of fulfilled scriptural prophecy, would make sense of Acts 1.25–26 within their cultural context.

How does the repeated use κλῆρος affect the overall narrative of Acts 1.15–26? Witherington briefly comments that the use of κλῆρος in 1.17 'foreshadows' its use in 1.25–26 and that this use 'may be connected' to the following material in 1.18–19, 25.[29] I suggest that the Greco-Roman kleromantic parallels strengthen these narrative connections. According to Luke, the Psalm (109.8) prophesies that there will be someone whose property and position become vacant and who must be replaced. In fulfillment of this prophecy, Judas receives his apportioned κλῆρος or 'position' as an apostle. His divinely προεῖπεν, 'foretold', vacancy of this position requires his replacement in order to fulfill the 'mission to Israel'.[30] The kleromantic choice of Matthias insures that Matthias is *God's choice* to replace Judas. Luke's threefold repetition of κλῆρος in 1.15–26 in contexts of prophecy and kleromantic divination indicates that God is entirely in control of the church's

---

26. Rudolf Pesch, *Die Apostlegeschichte* (EKKNT, 5; Zürich: Neukirchener, 1986), I, pp. 97–98. For the Judean backgrounds to lot casting, see Zwiep, *Judas and the Choice of Matthias*, pp. 168–71 and the references cited therein. My emphasis is upon the Greco-Roman parallels and the ways that Greco-Roman readers/auditors may have understood Luke.

27. Pesch, *Apostelgeschichte*, I, pp. 91.

28. Both John O. York (*The Last Shall Be First: The Rhetoric of Reversal in Luke* [JSNTSup, 46; Sheffield: JSOT Press, 1991] pp. 176–84) and John T. Squires (*The Plan of God in Luke-Acts*; SNTSMS, 76 [New York: Cambridge University Press, 1993], pp. 121–94) reach similar conclusions by different means. York analyzes Luke's use of the literary motif of bi-polar reversal and its relationship to τύχη, εἱμαρμένη, and *fortuna*. Squires traces the motif of ἡ βουλὴ τοῦ θεοῦ, 'the plan of God', in Luke-Acts and its relationship to providence, portents, epiphanies, prophecy, and fate.

29. Witherington, *Acts*, p. 122.

30. See n. 5 above for bibliography and discussion.

growth and mission despite outward appearance. Whatever Luke's intention, his use of kleromantic language would have reinforced that point for his Greco-Roman audience.

The Πνεῦμα Πύθων

Luke narrates Paul's exorcism of a mantic female slave in Acts 16.16–18.[31] This text narrates a *unique* kind of exorcism; not the exorcism of a demon, but a πνεῦμα, 'spirit', somehow related to Apollo and Greek oracles.[32] This exorcism narrative demonstrated to Greco-Roman auditors/readers the power and authority of Christians over such πνεύματα. This narrative may have also demarcated the boundary between the Christian God and 'look-alike' Greco-Roman divinities. In order to exegete this text, one must address three issues: Is the text an exorcism? What is the nature of the πνεῦμα πύθων, 'the oracular spirit'? Why does Paul exorcise this spirit?

Acts 16.16–18 as an 'Exorcism'
Most scholars understand this text as an exorcism.[33] As it stands, Acts 16.16–18, as an exorcism, is *sui generis*.[34] Rudolf Bultmann listed the common form-critical

31. Werner Foerster, 'Πύθων', *TDNT* VI, pp. 917–20; Paul R. Trebilco, 'Paul and Silas–Servants of the "Most High God" Acts 16.16–18', *JSNT* 36 (1989), pp. 51–73; Ivoni Richter Reimer, *Women in the Acts of the Apostles: A Feminist Liberation Perspective* (Minneapolis: Fortress Press, 1995), pp. 151–94; Christopher Forbes, *Prophecy and Inspired Speech in Early Christianity and its Hellenistic Environment* (WUNT, 75; Tübingen: Mohr-Siebeck, 1995; Peabody, MA: Hendrickson, 1997), pp. 295–97; Stefan Schreiber, *Paulus als Wundertäter: Redaktionsgeschichtlich Untersuchungen zur Apostelgeschichte und den authentischen Paulusbriefen* (BZNW, 79; Berlin: Walter de Gruyter, 1996), pp. 83–99; Adriana Destro and Mauro Pesce, 'Exorcism, Magic, and Public Activities of the Preachers', in *The Anthropology of Christian Origins*, provisional, unpublished English translation of *Antropologia delle origini cristiane* (Bari, Italy: Laterza, 2nd edn, 1997); F. Scott Spencer, 'Out of Mind, Out of Voice: Slave-girls and Prophetic Daughters in Luke-Acts', *BibInt* 7 (1999), pp. 133–55, esp. 146–50; *idem*, *Journeying Through Acts: A Literary-Cultural Reading* (Peabody, MA: Hendrickson, 2004), pp. 176–77; and Eric Sorensen, *Possession and Exorcism in the New Testament and Early Christianity* (WUNT, 2/157; Tübingen: Mohr-Siebeck, 2002), p.150 n. 187. Reimer performs an extensive and thorough feminist and liberation analysis that greatly informs my comparative religions discussion. Using performance theory as developed by Victor Turner (*From Ritual to Theatre: The Human Seriousness of Play* [New York: Performing Arts Journal Publications, 1982]), Destro and Pesce parallel my own conclusions.
32. On New Testament demonology and exorcism, see Graham H. Twelftree, *Jesus the Exorcist: A Contribution to the Study of the Historical Jesus* (WUNT, 54; Tübingen: Mohr-Siebeck, 1993; repr. Peabody, MA: Hendrikson, 1994), esp. p. 11 n. 41 and pp. 143–56; and Sorensen, *Possession and Exorcism in the New Testament*, pp. 118–67.
33. E.g. Ernst Haenchen, *The Acts of the Apostles: A Commentary* (Philadelphia: Westminster, 1971), pp. 495–96; Hans Conzelmann, *Acts* (Hermeneia; Philadelphia: Fortress Press, 1987), p. 131; Bruce, *Acts*, p. 361; Johnson, *Acts*, pp. 297–98 and C.K. Barrett, *Acts* (ICC; Edinburgh: T&T Clark, 1998), II, 784–88; and the authors they cite; thorough review of research in Reimer (*Women in the Acts of the Apostles*, pp. 168–74).
34. See Reimer's useful, but diffuse, discussion, *Women in the Acts of the Apostles*, pp. 171–73. Also, Destro and Pesce, 'Exorcism, Magic', n.p.

features of exorcism narratives.[35] Table 1 compares his list of characteristics (nos. 1–6) and one additional characteristic (no. 7) of exorcisms to Acts 16.16–18.[36] As Reimer points out, Luke's brief summary of Philip's exorcisms shows that Luke did use the characteristics of a 'typical' exorcism elsewhere (Acts 8.6–7).[37] Of the seven characteristics: Two appear (1, 4), two partially appear (3, 5), one is reversed (6), and the remaining two are not used (2, 7) in Acts 16.16–18. The spirit's recognition of Paul, the expulsion vocabulary (παραγγέλλω and ἐξέρχομαι), and the spirit's departure all support the idea that Luke was narrating an exorcism. Because there is no struggle or outcry from the exorcised spirit (characteristics 3b and 5b), no seeming danger to the woman (characteristic 2), no indication that the spirit is 'unclean' (characteristic 7), and the reversal of the spectator's usual role (bringing charges against Paul instead of being impressed with his power; characteristic 6) Luke is narrating the expulsion of something other than a demon that *does not* hurt the girl it possesses.[38]

Table 1. *Characteristics of Exorcism Narratives and Acts 16.16–18.*

Characteristics	Acts 16.16–18
1. Meeting the demon(s)	Paul and his co-workers encounter the 'oracular spirit' [πνεῦμα πύθων] (v. 16)
2. Description of the danger to the possessed	Absent

35. Rudolf Bultmann, *History of the Synoptic Tradition* (New York: Harper & Row, rev. edn, 1963), pp. 209–10; also, somewhat differently, Gerd Theissen, *The Miracle Stories of the Early Christian Tradition* (Philadelphia: Fortress Press, 1983), pp. 85–90, esp. pp. 87–89.

36. Characteristic 7 is from Reimer, *Women in the Acts of the Apostles*, 160. She also discusses Luke's use of the verbs ὑπαντάω, κράζω, and ἀνακράζω in relation to exorcism narratives, pp. 157–160. See also, Destro and Pesce, 'Exorcism, Magic', n.p.

37. Reimer, *Women in the Acts of the Apostles*, p. 171.

38. According to Theissen's criteria (*The Miracle Stories* pp. 87–89), Acts 16.16–18 *does not* narrate an exorcism because: (1) The oracular slave shows, as narrated in the text, no physical distress. (2) Neither the slave nor Paul exhibit violence. (3) The spirit does not 'adjure' or command Paul. (4) There is no *battle royale* between Paul and the pythonic spirit. (5) The πνεῦμα is not destructive. This only reinforces the point that this text narrates a unique exorcism, the exorcism of a nondemonic spirit.

Sorensen understands this passage as a possible exception 'to the maleficent nature of demonic possession' because the woman brings profits to her owners (*Possession and Exorcism in the New Testament*, p. 146, n.166). As I have already argued, the slave woman *is not* demonically possessed. Also, at least to modern sensibilities, her situation is maleficent because she is a slave.

As Reimer indicates, the narrative's conclusion is also unusual because the slave is not restored to her right mind or to health nor is she reunited with her family and society (cf. Lk. 8.26–39, 9.37–43a, 11.14–23). Reimer discusses the possibility of the woman's socio-economic liberation in light of epigraphy, sacral manumissions and Phil. 4.22, and ambiguously concludes that either the woman experienced such liberation or was worse off than before (*Women in the Acts of the Apostles*, pp. 174–75, 180–84). However, against Reimer, the woman was a *slave* and could not expect such reunification with her family.

Reimer's review of research conclusively demonstrates the prevalence of eisegetical readings of Acts 16.16–18 (*Women in the Acts of the Apostles*, pp. 168–69, 173–74). Researchers persistently interpret the woman as suffering all the ill effects of demonic possession despite the absence of any indication of disease and the absence of the words δαίμων or ἀκάθαρτον.

Characteristics	Acts 16.16–18
3. Demon (a) recognizes exorcist and (b) struggles	(a) The spirit 'cries out', ἔκραζεν, and recognizes Paul (but not by name) and his co-workers as 'servants of the most high God' who 'declare a road of rescue'. (b) Absent
4. The exorcism	Paul expels the oracular spirit, 'I command [παραγγέλλω] you in the name of Jesus Christ to come out [ἐξελθεῖν] of her'.
5. The demon (a) departs while (b) making a demonstration	(a) 'And it came out [ἐξῆλθεν] of her that hour'. (b) Absent
6. The spectators are impressed	Inverted. The spectators are not impressed but offended; Paul and Silas are brought up on charges.
7. Possessing spirit is called ἀκάθαρτον, 'unclean', or δαίμων, 'demon'.	Absent. Possessing spirit is called πνεῦμα πύθων

πύθωνες

Luke calls the spirit that possesses the young girl a πνεῦμα πύθων, a 'spirit of divination' or a 'pythonic spirit'. What is a πύθων? Does the appositional πύθων refer or allude to the Delphic oracle? I suggest that Luke's Greco-Roman readership would have understood πύθων as an allusion to Greek oracles in general, to necromancy (especially by women), and possibly as a specific allusion to the Delphic oracle and Apollo.

There are scattered references to πύθωνες and cognate forms in Greek literature.[39] According to J.W. van Henton, late sources indicate that there was a 'semantic development from the specific Delphic oracle to an oracular spirit in general'.[40] The original Πύθων was both a snake and a δαιμόνιον μαντικόν, 'mantic spirit', that inhabited Delphi and was killed by Apollo when he forcefully took the shrine for his own (*h. Ap.* 300–310, 370–74). In turn, the woman who pronounced the oracles at Delphi was the Πυθία and was called a μάντις or a πρόμαντις. Philo used the term πυθόχρηστος, meaning 'oracular saying' (*Omn. Prob. Lib.* 19). The Vulgate uses *pythonicus spiritus* to translate the Hebrew אוב, 'soothsayer' (Lev. 20.27). On the basis of this evidence, van Henton concludes that Acts 16.16 refers to a 'predicting demon'. In light of the anomalies of the exorcism in 16.16–18 and the Greek uses of πύθων and πύθωνες, it is perhaps more accurate to conclude that Acts 16.16 refers to a 'predicting spirit'.

The Greeks considered πύθωνες to be persons possessed by prophesying spirits, most likely the spirits of the dead. Fifth-century BCE Athenians believed in *Eurykles*, a prophetic spirit or power that made its residence in the stomach of an individual, and muttered prophecies after taking partial possession of the

---

39. Forbes, *Prophecy and Inspired Speech*, pp. 296–97.
40. J.W. van Henton, 'Python', *DDD* (2nd edn), pp. 669–71, esp. pp. 670–71; also Sorensen, *Possession and Exorcism in the New Testament*, p. 150 n. 187.

individual's voice (Aristophanes, *Vesp.* 1019–20; Plato, *Soph.* 252C).⁴¹ Philocorus, third century BCE Athenian historian, mentioned that those possessed by
Eurykles were called 'belly talkers', ἐγγαστρίμυθοι, and were commonly
women who summoned the spirits of the dead.⁴² A scholiast on the grammarian
Erotianus Grammaticus (*c.* 50–60 CE) stated that some people referred to the
ἐγγαστρίμυθοι, as πύθωνες.⁴³ Plutarch mentions both ἐγγαστρίμυθοι and
πύθωνες :

> It is foolish, indeed childish, to believe that the god himself, like the ventriloquists
> [ἐγγαστρίμυθους] (who used to take the name Eurykles and now take the name Python
> [Πύθων]), enters into the prophets' bodies and uses their mouths and voices as his
> instruments. (*Def. Orac.* 9 [= *Mor.* 414E])⁴⁴

The Pseudo-Clementine literature also mentions πύθωνες in an extended discussion of demonic possession and exorcism, 'pythons prophesy [πύθωνες
μαντεύονται], but by us are exorcised [ὁρκιζόμενοι] and put to flight as demons
[ὡς δαίμονες]' (*Ps.-Cl. Hom.* 9.16.3, see also *Ps.-Cl. Rec.* 4.20.4).⁴⁵ Matthew
W. Dickie has further traced ἐγγαστρίμυθοι and πύθωνες into the later Empire,
e.g. the sixth century Leontius of Byzantium mentions the 'muzzling of the
ἐγγαστρίμυθοι'.⁴⁶ On the basis of this evidence, I tentatively, because of its

41. Daniel Ogden, *Greek and Roman Necromancy* (Princeton: Princeton University Press, 2001),
p. 112. Ogden has provided helpful translations of these texts in his *Magic, Witchcraft, and Ghosts in
the Greek and Roman Worlds: A Sourcebook* (Oxford: Oxford University Press, 2002), pp. 30–31 nn.
32–33. Sarah Iles Johnston has harshly criticized Ogden's methodology in his *Greek and Roman
Necromancy*, see her review, *BMCR* (online), http.//ccat.sas.upenn.edu/bmcr/2002/2002–06–19.html;
and later concluded that necromancy, or consultation with the dead was only a literary *topos* in
archaic and classical Greece, *eadem*, 'Delphi and the Dead', in Johnston and Struck (eds), *Mantikê*,
pp. 283–306, esp. p. 292. Cf. Christopher Faraone who traces the development of necromantic spells
from ancient Mesopotamia to late antiquity: 'Necromancy Goes Underground: The Disguise of
Corpse and Skull Divination in the Paris Magical Papyri *PGM* IV 1928–2144)', in Johnston and
Struck (eds), *Mantikê*, pp. 255–82. Whatever the reality of necromancy in archaic and classical
Greece, it appears to be known by the first century CE.

42. Karl Müller, FHG (Paris: Didot, 1872; repr. Frankfurt: Minerva, 1975), I, p. 416 frg. 192; Ada
Adler (ed.), *Suidae Lexicon* (Leipzig: Teubner, 1928–38); ET Ogden, *Magic, Witchcraft, and Ghosts*,
p. 31 n. 34.

43. Ernst Nachmanson (ed.), *Erotiani Vocum Hippocraticarum Collectio cum Fragmentis*
(Collectio Scriptorum Veterum Upsaliensis; Göteburg: Eranos, 1918), p. 105 frg. 21.

44. Donald Russell (trans.), *Plutarch: Selected Essays and Dialogues* (World's Classics; Oxford:
Oxford University Press, 1993).

45. In personal conversation, Chris Forbes stated that that the *Pseudo-Clement* text is dependent
upon Acts 16.16–18. Because of the use of Πύθων to indicate various forms of manticism in earlier
Greek literature, the use of πύθωνες to indicate mantics in later Greek literature, and the very poor
correlation between the narrative context of *Ps.-Clem.* 9.16.3 and Acts 16–16–18, I remain convinced
that Pseudo-Clement speaks of a reality in his time.

46. Mathew W. Dickie, *Magic and Magicians in the Greco-Roman World* (London: Routledge,
2001), pp. 238–39, 247, 290, 355 n. 146.

Additional primary sources: Hippocrates vaguely refers to ἐγγαστρίμυθοι but only in comparison
to the symptoms of a certain stomach disease (*Epid.* 5.62–63). The LXX uses the term to translate the
Hebrew אוֹב, 'witch' or 'necromancer' (1 Sam. 28, the witch of Endor narrative). Both Philo (*Somn.*
1.220) and Josephus (*Ant.* 6.327–36) adopt the LXX usage to describe Greco-Roman divination. There

sparse nature, conclude that in the first century CE, πύθωνες were individuals, mostly women, who engaged in necromantic divination.

These few references are directly parallel to the slave girl with the πνεῦμα πύθων in Acts 16.16–18. These references show that both the ancient Greek world and early Christianity recognized πύθωνες as some sort of spirit, most likely the spirit of a someone deceased, that could possess a person and make prophetic oracles.[47] Among early Christians of the third century CE, the πύθωνες were classed separately from demons but were exorcized *as if* they were demons. For a Greco-Roman auditor or reader, Luke's narrative accurately reflects contemporary cultural experiences: an oracular spirit or πνεῦμα πύθων possesses the slave girl, allows her to prophesy, μαντεύεται, and Paul was able to exorcise this πνεῦμα πύθων.

A Delphic Allusion?

Luke does not *necessarily* allude to the Delphic oracle by describing the slave girl in Acts 16.16 as having a πνεῦμα πύθων. The highly ambiguous evidence is not conclusive, but Luke did refer to a specific type of mantic or oracular behavior known in the Greco-Roman world. Possibly *some* of his audience may have associated this general reference to Delphi in particular.

Several recent exegetes, most notably Reimer (the only one who attempts in detail to prove a Lukan allusion to the Delphic oracle), associate the mantic slave girl with Delphi because Luke uses the word πύθων.[48] According to Reimer, Luke's use of the verb μαντεύομαι, the historical dispersal of the Delphic Pythias, his use of the phrase πνεῦμα πύθων, and the linguistic history of derived forms of *πυθ- all show that Luke was associating the slave girl with the Delphic oracle.[49] Unfortunately, Reimer's detailed examination is not convincing because

---

are additional vague references in Julius Pollux, *Onomasticon* 2.168; Lucian, *Lex.* 20; the *Historia Alexandri Magni* 1.4.12; and various scholia and Byzantine lexicographers. Further sources and discussion in Forbes (*Prophecy and Inspired Speech*, pp. 295–98), Ogden (*Greek and Roman Necromancy*, pp. 112–15), and Dickie (*Magic, Witchcraft, and Ghosts*, p. 355 n. 146). See also, Aune, *Prophecy in Early Christianity*, pp. 40–41; and van Henton, 'Python', pp. 1263–66. Sorensen synoptically arranges the Hebrew אוב with its Akkadian origin and to its translation in Old Greek (*Possession and Exorcism in the New Testament*, p. 58, Table 4). Cf. Foerster's arbitrary statement that the ἐγγαστρίμυθοι were 'ventriloquists' ('Πύθων', *TDNT* VI, p. 918). Though the Greeks equated ἐγγαστρίμυθοι with πύθωνες, there is no reason to suspect that Luke described a 'ventriloquist' in Acts 16.16–18. I thank Chris Forbes for discussing these issues with me.

47. Ogden (*Greek and Roman Necromancy*, p. 115) and Dickie (*Magic and Magicians*, p. 247) reach the same conclusion.

48. Werner Foerster vehemently denied any relationship between the Delphic oracle and the πνεῦμα that possessed the slave girl (*TDNT*, 'Πύθων', vol. 6, pp. 917–20 esp. p. 918). Despite his demurral, several recent exegetes have connected Acts 16.16–18 to the Delphic oracle: Johnson, *Acts*, pp. 293–94 (but cf. pp. 297–98); Reimer, *Women in the Acts of the Apostles*, pp. 154–56; Howard Clark Kee, *To Every Nation under Heaven: The Acts of the Apostles* (The New Testament in Context; Harrisburg, PA: Trinity, 1997), pp. 195–97; Talbert, *Reading Acts*, pp. 150–51; Witherington, *Acts*, pp. 493–94; and Spencer, *Journeying through Acts*, pp. 176–77; *idem*, 'Out of Mind', p. 146.

49. Reimer, *Women in the Acts of the Apostles*, pp. 154–56.

she goes well beyond her secondary sources in making this assertion.[50] The use of
the verb μαντεύομαι itself proves nothing since the verb is used in non-Delphic
contexts (Homer, *Il.* 2.300, 16.859, 19.420; *Od.* 2.170, 2.178, 9.510; Herodotus,
4.67, etc.) to describe the act of prophesying.

Reimer also argues that, by Plutarch's time, 'the oracle culture had spread over
a wider area and was present even in places where there were no oracle shrines',
citing Plutarch in support, 'the Pythia can no longer approach the region where the
god is' (*Pyth. Orac.* 17 [= *Mor.* 17B]).[51] The simplest reading of this passage is
that the Pythia cannot enter the inner sanctuary [ἄδυτον], where she pronounced
her oracles; Plutarch *does not* mention 'itinerant Pythias'. Similarly, 'oracle culture' was widespread long before and during Luke's time: Dodona in Asia Minor;
Delphi, Olympia, and Bura in Greece, Ammon in Egypt, and Praeneste in Italy.
Further, John Dillery has recently discussed the role of independent mantics
throughout the history of ancient Greece.[52]

Reimer understands Luke's use of the phrase πνεῦμα πύθων as a direct reference to the Delphic Pythia and her social situation.[53] She infers parallels between
the Delphic Pythia and the slave girl in Philippi: their common gender, their
anonymity, the Pythia's peasant origins (Plutarch *Pyth. Orac.* 22 [=*Mor.* 405C-
D]), and the girl's slavery. She also cites the Pythia's virginity or old age and
widowhood but never produces a corresponding parallel for the slave girl.[54] Since
Luke provides absolutely no information about the slave other than her gender,
possible age, and enslavement, Reimer's assumptions that the slave girl is a
virgin descended from a poor peasant family are unconvincing and tendentious.

Reimer also argues that derived forms of *πυθ- are always used in reference
to the Delphic oracle.[55] But, as shown above, the word πύθωνες was also associated with non-Delphic manticism and with female necromancy according to
Philocorus (above); thus, connection with the oracle is not proved.

In light of van Henton's discussion (above), I suggest that Luke alludes to
Greco-Roman oracles in general and to the πύθωνες, individuals who uttered
oracles after being possessed by non-demonic spirits (probably the spirits of the
dead), in particular. Because of the linguistic connection between πύθων and
Πύθια and the fact that both the possessed Philippian slave and the Delphic

50. Reimer, *Women in the Acts of the Apostles*, pp. 155 and p. 187 n. 33, citing Wolfgang Fauth,
'Pythia', PW 24 (1963), cols 515–47, esp. cols 516–17.

51. Reimer, *Women in the Acts of the Apostles*, pp. 154, 156, 186 n. 23, and 187 n. 36; citing
Fauth who merely summarizes Plutarch without providing detailed commentary on this passage
('Pythia', p. 535); cf. Stephan Schröder, *Plutarchs Schrift, 'De Pythiae Oraculis': Text, Einleitung
und Kommentar* (Beiträge zur Altertumskunde, 8; Stuttgart: Teubner, 1990), pp. 307–308.

52. John Dillery, 'Chresmologues and *Manteis*: Independent Diviners and the Problems of
Authority', in Johnston and Struck (eds), *Mantikê*, pp. 167–232.

53. Reimer, *Women in the Acts of the Apostles*, pp. 154–55, 186–87 nn. 24–31, 156, 187 n. 34.

54. Reimer, *Women in the Acts of the Apostles*, pp. 155; 186 n. 29; citing O. Höfer, 'Pythia,
Pythios, Python', *ALGRM* III/2 (1902–1909), cols 3370–412, esp. cols 3381–82; and Fauth, 'Pythia',
PW 24/2 (1963), cols 542–44.

55. Reimer, *Women in the Acts of the Apostles*, p. 187 n. 32; citing (and misinterpreting) Siegfried
Lauffer, 'Pytho', PW 24 (1963), cols 569–80, esp. col. 571.

Pythia were oracular women, Luke's audience *may* have understood an allusion to the Delphic oracle, but more likely understood a reference to a commonly used means of necromantic divination.

Why Does Paul Exorcise the Πνεῦμα Πύθων?

Since the mantic slave persistently proclaims that Paul and his co-workers are 'servants of the most high God' [τοῦ θεοῦ τοῦ ὑψίστου], who 'declare a road of rescue to you' (Acts 16.17), why does Paul 'become irritated', and exorcise a spirit that tells the truth? What is the nature of the girl's oracle that so offends Paul? There are two parts to this question. First, what type of oracle did the girl give? Second, what was the nature of the oracle's content?

The girl utters an unsolicited oracle of recognition and commendation, which emphasizes the divine legitimation of Paul and his co-workers and validates their message.[56] Unsolicited oracles were not responses to inquiries but spontaneous utterances made while in a presumed state of trance.[57] The legitimation oracle is supernatural assurance and validation of a reliable source of divine revelation.[58] The recognition form of a legitimation oracle supernaturally identifies someone with divine parentage or someone who will become king. A commendation oracle recommended the oracle's recipients to another trustworthy source of divine revelation apart from the speaker.

Nearly five per cent of the extant Delphic oracles are spontaneous pronouncements.[59] Several spontaneous oracles are found in Lucian (*Alex.* 29, 36, 43, 47) and in Philostratus (*Vit. Apoll.* 1.9, 4.1). Probably the most famous series of spontaneous oracles are the oracles from Siwah and Didyma recognizing Alexander the Great's divine descent (Strabo 17.1.43). In Acts 16.17, the girl sees Paul and his entourage and spontaneously pronounces a two-element oracle: (1) She recognizes (recognition oracle) Paul and his companions as 'servants of the most high God' and (2) validates their message as of divine origin (commendation oracle), 'They declare the way of rescue to you'.

Despite this seeming commendation of Paul, the Pythonic slave girl's oracle about 'the highest God' [ὁ θεὸς ὁ ὕψιστος] was highly ambiguous within its religious context. At least as a literary topos, Greek oracles were famed for their ambiguity.[60] According to the pre-Socratic philosopher Heraclitus (*c.* 500 BCE),

56. Aune, *Prophecy in Early Christianity*, pp. 66–70, 268–69.
57. Luke *may* suggest that the girl entered into an ecstatic trance state. The relevant data from Delphi do not necessarily indicate that the Pythia entered into an ecstatic trance state (discussion and bibliography in Aune, *Prophecy in Early Christianity*, pp. 33–34, 41, 59, 354–55, nn. 128–373, 359 n. 209). However, Jelle Zeilinga de Boer and John R. Hale report that recent geological studies at Delphi confirm the presence of an ancient source of natural gas fumes that could have produced a calm trance-like state in the Pythia ('Was She Really Stoned? The Oracle of Delphi', *Archaeology Odyssey* 5.6 [Nov/Dec 2002], pp. 46–53, 58). For my purposes, the state of the slave girl's consciousness is irrelevant.
58. Aune, *Prophecy in Early Christianity*, p. 68.
59. Aune, cites 28 oracles from Parke and Wormell's, *The Delphic Oracle*, as probable spontaneous oracles *(Prophecy in Early Christianity*, pp. 66, 365 n. 101).
60. Fontenrose denies both the historicity of Delphic ambiguity and the ancient perception of

'The [god] whose oracle is in Delphi neither declares nor conceals, but gives a sign' (Plutarch, *Pyth. Orac.* 21 [= *Mor.* 404D]).[61] According to Aune, the ancient Greek literary treatment of ambiguous oracles reveals three aspects of the Greek religious outlook. (1) Oracular speech, despite its difficult nature, was *an absolutely reliable means* for the gods to reveal their implacable will to humanity, (2) the divine-human relationship is a 'game' that requires the use of wit and cleverness by the latter and (3) the gods and fate could act capriciously and unpredictably despite human attempts to control the gods through religious ritual.[62]

One example of such Delphic ambiguity is the story of Croesus (Herodotus 1.53). He inquired from both Delphi and the oracle at Amphiaraos whether or not to send an army against the Persians. Delphi responded that if Croesus proceeded against the Persians he would destroy a great empire. Croesus fought the Persians and destroyed a great empire, his own.

In a second example, Aristomense and Theolkus, both from Messene, inquired at Delphi about the safety of their homeland. The Pythia responded:

> When a goat [τράγος] drinks of the winding stream of Neda,
> No longer do I protect Messene, for destruction is at hand. (Pausanias 4.20.1)[63]

Theolkus understood that τράγος also referred to a distinctive kind of wild Messenian fig tree, some of which were bent over into the waters of the Nebo River. Therefore, despite the oracle's ambiguity, Theokus and Aristomenes knew that the days of their homeland were numbered.

Pausanius relates two more examples. The Delphic oracle cautioned Epanimondas to beware 'the ocean' [πέλαγος]. Therefore, Epanimondas refused to travel by ship. However, he did not avoid going through a grove of trees known as πέλαγος and consequently suffered catastrophe (8.11.10). Because the oracle at Ammon warned Hannibal that when he died he would be buried in Libyan soil (Λιβύσσης), he believed that he would die at home in his old age (8.11.10). However, he accidentally wounded himself while campaigning, contracted a fever and died. He was then buried at a place called Libyssa (Λίβυσσα) by the local inhabitants.

Why was the slave girl's oracle about Paul and his co-workers ambiguous? First, her oracle used the epithet 'the highest God' without elaborating its precise meaning. This epithet was found in a variety of ancient religious contexts including both Greco-Roman and Judean and could possibly have had multiple meanings

---

oracular ambiguity at Delphi (*Delphic Oracle*, pp. 236–37). Even if his argument is *historically* true for Delphi, there is both a *literary* perception of Delphic ambiguity and extensive evidence for ambiguity in other oracles: Dodona, Didyma, Alexander of Abonuteichos, and others (Aune, *Prophecy in Early Christianity*, pp. 44, 51–52, 57, 60–62, 139–40, 153, 163).

61. Charles H. Kahn (ed. and trans.), *The Art and Thought of Heraclitus: An Edition of the Fragments with Translation and Commentary* (Cambridge: Cambridge University Press, 1979), pp. 42–43, frg. 33 (= Hermann Diels, *Die Fragmente der Vorsokratiker*, [6th edn by Walther Kranz; Berlin: Weidmann, 1951], frg. 93).

62. Aune, *Prophecy in Early Christianity*, p. 51, my emphasis.

63. Trans. Aune, *Prophecy in Early Christianity*, p. 51.

to the girl's listeners. The oracle's content was also ambiguous. Are Paul and his associates servants of the Judean God or are they acting on behalf of θεὸς ὕψιστος?

Scholars fiercely debate the historical origins of θεὸς ὕψιστος.[64] Most argue that the phrase reflects syncretistic or henotheistic tendencies in Greco-Roman religion.[65] Reimer and Irina Levinskaya posit a direct influence of Judean theology upon Greco-Roman religion with Levinskaya suggesting on epigraphic grounds that Greco-Roman listeners would have associated the slave girl's oracle with the Judean God.[66]

Alternatively, Peter Pilhofer has argued that θεὸς ὕψιστος or Ζεὺς ὕψιστος was a regional Thracian and Macedonian divinity not traceable to Judean influence.[67] This divinity was worshipped in the immediate environs of Philippi but not in Philippi itself. When listening to the slave girl's oracle, first-century inhabitants of Philippi would have associated θεὸς ὕψιστος with the nearby Thracian and Macedonian divinity while Judeans and Christians would have heard the oracular slave as referring to their own god.

In a substantial survey of the epigraphic literature, Ustivona has conclusively shown that θεὸς ὕψιστος was a phrase employed by various Greco-Roman cults, Jews, and Christians. Instead of a consistent origin in Judaism, the θεὸς ὕψιστος cult reflects rather the contemporary tendency towards henotheism, monotheism, and anonymous characterizations of the gods.[68] Therefore, θεὸς ὕψιστος could

---

64. From a substantial literature see Arthur Darby Nock, Colin Roberts, and Theodore C. Skeat, 'The Guild of Zeus Hypsistos', *HTR* 9 (1936), pp. 9–88; repr. Arthur Darby Nock, *Essays on Religion and the Ancient World* (ed. Zeph Stewart; Oxford: Clarendon Press, Oxford University Press, 1986), I, pp.414–43; W.C. van Unnik, 'Die Anklage gegen die Apostel in Philippi, Apostelgeschichte xvi 20f', in Alfred Stuiber and Alfred Hermann (eds), *Mullus: Für Theodor Klauser* (Jahrbuch für Antike und Christentum Ergänzungsband 1; Münster: Aschendorff, 1964); repr. *Sparsa Collecta: The Collected Essays of W. C. Van Unnik* (NovTSup, 29; Leiden: Brill, 1973), I, pp. 374–86; Margareta Tatscheva-Hitova, 'Dem Hypsistos geweihte Denkmäler in Thrakien. Untersuchungen zur Geschichte der antiken Religionen, III', *Thracia* 4 (1977), pp. 274–90; *eadem, Eastern Cults in Moesia Inferior and Thracia (5th Century BC-4th Century AD)* (EPRO, 95; Leiden: Brill, 1983), pp. 190–218; Trebilco, 'Paul and Silas'; Peter Pilhofer, *Philippi*, vol. 1, *Die erste christliche Gemeinde Europas* (WUNT, 87; Tübingen: Mohr-Siebeck, 1995), pp. 182–87; Reimer, *Women in the Acts of the Apostles*, pp. 160–66; Irina Levinskaya, *The Book of Acts in Its Diaspora Setting*, vol. 5 of Bruce W. Winter (ed.), *The Book of Acts in its First Century Setting* (Grand Rapids: Eerdmanns, 1996), pp. 83–104; and most recently Yulia Ustinova, *The Supreme Gods of the Bosporan Kingdom: Celestial Aphrodite and the Most High God* (RGRW, 135; Leiden: Brill, 1999), pp. 178–83, 216–28, 238–39, 282–83.

65. Nock, Roberts and Skeat, 'Guild of Zeus Hypsistos', pp. 59–60, repr. edn, pp. 420–21; van Unnik, 'Die Anklage', p. 384; Tatscheva-Hitova, 'Dem Hypsistos geweihte Denkmäler', throughout; and Trebilco, 'Paul and Silas', throughout.

66. Reimer, *Women in the Acts of the Apostles*, p. 161; Levinskaya, *Diaspora Setting*, pp. 98–100.

67. Pilhofer, *Philippi*, pp. 182–88, based on and furthering Trebilco, 'Paul and Silas', throughout.

68. Ustinova, *The Supreme Gods*, pp. 217–21, 228. Reimer (pp. 161–64) bases part of her argument on the Bosporan epigraphic usage of θεὸς ὕψιστος, precisely the subject of Ustinova's investigation. Ustinova's closely argued epigraphic investigation negates Reimer's arguments and demonstrates that the Jewish θεὸς ὕψιστος παντοκράτωρ εὐλογητός and the θεὸς ὕψιστος of the Tanais *thiasoi* are different and unrelated gods (pp. 229–38). Further, Ustinova all but demolishes

have easily be interpreted as a Greco-Roman deity by Luke's authorial audience. Both Reimer and Levinskaya make strongly compelling arguments. But Ustinova's discussion vitiates their arguments. Even if further evidence should counter Ustinova's conclusions and conclusively demonstrate a Jewish origin for all θεὸς ὕψιστος cults, it cannot be argued that members of Luke's first-century audience would have *necessarily* recognized any connection to the Jewish deity. Instead they could have easily interpreted the slave girl's cry of θεὸς ὕψιστος as a reference to non-Jewish cults.

Additionally, on narrative grounds, the slave girl's oracle about θεὸς ὕψιστος is both ambiguous and ironic. An attentive auditor/reader of Luke-Acts is aware that the phrase is a decidedly Lukan title for God. It appears seven times in Luke-Acts (Lk. 1.32, 35, 76; 6.35; 8.28; Acts 7.48; 16.17).[69] Luke 1.32 and 8.28 (taken from Mk 5.7) refer to Jesus as 'son of the most high God'. In 1.76, Jesus is called a 'prophet of the most high'. Luke 1.35 refers to God as 'the most high'. In 6.35, those who follow Jesus' teaching are 'sons of the most high'. Acts 7.48 states, 'the most high does not live in handmade [shrines]'.

Additionally, Luke makes a very subtle contextual distinction in using the title.[70] In decidedly Judean contexts (the birth narratives, Jesus' ministry in Galilee, Stephen's speech in Jerusalem) Luke uses ὕψιστος without θεὸς in three anarthrous constructions (Luke 1.32, 35, 76; 6.35) and one arthrous (Acts 7.48). In every case, the speaker and the audience are Judean.

In contrast, when the setting is non-Judean (the Decapolis and Philippi) Luke uses the construction ὁ θεὸς ὁ ὕψιστος. In both cases, a person possessed by a spirit uses the phrase to acclaim the status or function of God's messenger(s). The Gerasene demoniac (Lk. 8.28) calls Jesus, 'son of the most high God' [υἱὲ τοῦ θεοῦ τοῦ ὑψίστου]. The slave girl calls Paul and his co-workers, 'servants of the most high God' [δοῦλοι τοῦ θεοῦ τοῦ ὑψίστου]. Luke appears to understand or prefer the substantival use of ὕψιστος as a positive title for God in non-Judean contexts.

He seems to have a more nuanced understanding of ὕψιστος when used as an attributive adjective. For Luke, or at least for his readers, this title was appropriate for polytheistic Greco-Roman settings (Gerasa and Philippi) as a title of divinity.[71] In Luke 8.28 the Greco-Roman demoniac used the title as part of an

---

Levinskaya's assertion that the widely dispersed cult of θεὸς ὕψιστος was a single cult, with local features and generally linked with Judaism (Levinskaya, *Diaspora Setting*, p. 27).

69. Following Trebilco, 'Paul and Silas', pp. 58–59.

Spencer allows that θεὸς ὕψιστος was ambiguous within historic first-century Philippi ('Out of Mind', p. 148 n. 23; citing Trebilco, 'Paul and Silas', pp. 51–58; and *idem, Jewish Communities*, pp. 127–44). However, he insists that Acts 16.17 refers to the Judeo-Christian deity through its intertextual relationships to Lk. 1.76–77, 3.3–6, and 8.28 ('Out of Mind', p. 148 n. 23); cf. the discussion below.

70. Following Trebilco, 'Paul and Silas', p. 59.

71. Religious setting of Gerasa, Gadara, and the Decapolis: Jean-Paul Rey-Coquais, 'Decapolis', *ABD* II, pp. 116–21, esp. p. 119; Ute Wanger-Lux, K.J.H. Vriezen, and Svend Holm Nielsen, 'Gadara', *ABD* II, pp. 866–68; and John McRay 'Gerasenes', *ABD* 2, pp. 991–92.

Religious setting of ancient Philippi: Paul Collart, 'Le sanctuaire des dieux égyptiens à Philippes', *BCH* 53 (1929), pp. 69–100; *idem*, 'Inscriptions de Philippes', *BCH* 56 (1932), pp. 93–231; *idem*,

exorcistic struggle. The demon hoped to defeat Jesus by using a standard ritual formula that referred to the god of Jesus the Judean.[72] Luke has a Greco-Roman use the attributive adjective to refer to Jesus' god.

In Acts, the oracular spirit recognizes Paul's function 'for many days' [ἐπὶ πολλὰ ἡμέρας] within this polytheistic Greco-Roman setting.[73] Paul has already made contact with the Philippian God-fearer Lydia (Acts 16.13–15), but not a resident community of Judeans.[74] The title ὁ θεὸς ὁ ὕψιστος proclaimed by the oracular slave-girl thus has an ambiguous ring. It recalls the failure of the Gerasene demoniac to control Jesus by calling him ὁ θεὸς ὁ ὕψιστος (Lk. 8.28). Luke uses ὁ θεὸς ὁ ὕψιστος in Acts 16.16–18 to indicate the god of the Judeans and God-fearers as considered by Greco-Romans in Philippi, just one god among many. The slave girl pronounced an oracle that was *true*. Paul, Silas, and coworkers proclaimed the most high God, the God of the Judeans and God-fearers. Nevertheless, following Pilhofer, the oracle was *ambiguous*. In the polytheistic context of ancient Philippi, the 'most high God' is just another regional deity.[75] Pressing the

'Inscriptions de Philippes', *BCH* 57 (1933), pp. 313–79; *idem*, 'Philippes', *DACL* 14 (1939), pp. 712–42; *idem*, *Philippes: Ville de Macédoine depuis ses origines jusqu'à le fin de l'époque romaine* (Paris: E. de Boccard, 1937), pp. 388–486; Paul Collart and Pierre Ducrey, *Philippes I: Les reliefs rupestres* (Bulletin de Correspondance Hellénique Supplément, 2; Athens: École Française d'Athénes, 1975); Lilian Portefaix, *Sisters Rejoice: Paul's Letter to the Philippians and Luke-Acts as Received by First-Century Philippian Women* (ConBNT, 20; Stockholm: Almqvist & Wiksell, 1988), pp. 65, 70–74; Valerie A. Abrahamsen, *Women and Worship at Philippi: Diana/Artemis and Other Cults in the Early Christian Era* (Portland, ME: Astarte Shell, 1995) throughout, esp. pp. 16–18, Table 1; and Pilhofer, *Philippi*, pp. 92–112, 182–88. Pilhofer notes that no inscriptions or temples have been found in Philippi or its environs that are devoted to θεὸς ὕψιστος.

72. Twelftree, *Jesus the Exorcist*, pp. 38–39, 82–83.

73. The girl κατακολουθοῦσα (present participle) 'simultaneously follows' Paul and ἔκραζεν (imperfect tense) 'keeps on shouting' her oracle about Paul and his companions.

74. Both Reimer and Levinskaya are forced to search outside of Philippi to discuss the nature of its Judean community. Outside of Acts 16.13–15, 40 and possibly Phil. 3.2–10, 17–21, there is no independent epigraphic, archaeological, or literary evidence for Judean presence in Philippi (Portefaix, *Sisters Rejoice*, p. 73; and especially Pilhofer, *Philippi*, pp. 231–33). If Luke's account of Lydia (Acts 16.13–15, 40) is historical, then the Judean community must have been so small as to leave no impact upon the historical or archaeological record. There is only one inscription from Philippi that indicates the presence of a Judean community and it is from the late imperial era, between the third and fifth centuries CE (Pilhofer, *Philippi*, p. 232 and 232 n. 3; and Chaido Koukouli-Chrysantaki, 'Colonia Iulia Augusta Philippensis', in Charalambos Bakirtzis and Helmut Koester [eds], *Philippi at the Time of Paul and after His Death*, [Harrisburg, PA: Trinity, 1998] pp. 5–35, esp. 28–35). In any reading, Phil 3.17–21 is not evidence for a diaspora Judean community in Philippi at the time of either Paul or Luke.

75. Pilhofer, *Philippi*, pp. 182–87. Destro and Pesce similarly conclude that the spirit's exorcism was socially positive for the Christian community because it ended practices of the past now considered incompatible with the preaching of the apostles and that such a spirit is subordinate to the power of Jesus Christ (Destro and Pesce, 'Exorcism, Magic', n.p.).

Also, the anarthous ὁδός σωτηρίας, 'way of salvation', is, as Klauck points out, in itself ambiguous; it could refer to Zeus, Asclepius, the emperor, or many other deities (Klauck, *Magic and Paganism*, p. 69).

analysis further, in light of Ustinova's work, the 'most high God' is just another deity of the first century Mediterranean world.

Conclusions

Luke's Greco-Roman readers may have understood kleromantic allusions in Acts 1.15–26, a possible allusion to the Delphic oracle and oracular ambiguity in 16.16–18, and noted the unusual 'exorcism' of the slave girl in 16.16–18. What would these readers have made of these allusions?

To my understanding, Luke's audience would have viewed the kleromantic oracle of 1.26 positively for two reasons. (1) The community leadership is in part determined by kleromantic procedure, i.e., strictly by God's choice alone and (2) the kleromantic choice of Matthias reinforces (in Luke's narrative) the fulfillment of God's plan even in the exigency of Judas' betrayal and death.[76] This kleromantic procedure compares favorably with Greco-Roman kleromancy known to a Greco-Roman audience because God(s) alone makes a choice for the reestablishment of a religious institution and because the kleromantic oracle reveals the will of God(s). Though these statements are true for parallel Judean practices, a Greco-Roman audience would have interpreted Luke's text in light of their own experiences.

Despite this positive assessment, we must acknowledge that Luke refers to early Christian kleromancy only once in Acts at the very beginning of his narrative where Luke places Matthias' kleromantic election immediately before the Pentecost narrative (Acts 2). From Pentecost on, Luke substitutes direct inspiration by the πνεῦμα ἅγιον, 'holy spirit', for any form of divinatory procedure.[77] Though Luke's audience would have understood a favorable reference to kleromancy (probably because of similar practices in the LXX, i.e., the Urim and Thummin [Exod. 28.30; Lev. 8.8; Num. 27.21; 1 Sam. 28.6; Ezra 2.63]), they may have relegated it to the church's past in light of Luke's narrative. After Pentecost, the church relies upon the direct inspiration of the spirit as promised in Jesus' ascension speech (Acts 1.8).

Though Acts 16.16–18 is the only example of Greco-Roman oracular ambiguity in Acts, Luke's audience may have viewed the messages of Greek oracles as ambiguous and misinformative in contrast to Christian prophecy. In Acts 16.16–18, the slave girl's oracular spirit produces a spontaneous oracle that recognizes

---

76. Exegetes have noted other reasons for Luke's positive assessment of the kleromantic choice of Matthias: L.S. Thornton, 'The Choice of Matthias', *JTS* 46 (1945), pp. 51–59; William A. Beardslee, 'The Casting of Lots at Qumran and in the Book of Acts', *NovT* 4 (1960–61), pp. 245–62; Haenchen, *Acts of the Apostles*, pp. 162–63, esp. 163; Phillipe H. Menoud, 'The Additions to the Twelve Apostles According to the Book of Acts', in *Jesus Christ and the Faith: A Collection of Studies* (PTMS, 18; Pittsburgh: Pickwick, 1978), pp. 133–48; Pesch, *Apostlegeschichte*, I, p. 91; Johnson, *Acts*, pp. 37, 38–40; Talbert, *Reading Acts*, pp. 38–39, esp. p. 39; Witherington, *Acts of the Apostles*, pp. 126–27; and Spencer, *Journeying Through Acts*, p. 29.

77. Noted by Forbes: 'It can hardly be chance that this lone case of inductive divination falls before Pentecost' (*Prophecy and Inspired Speech*, p. 301).

the divine validation of Paul and Silas. But this divinity is ambiguous; it could refer to one deity alone or it could refer to one deity among many. Therefore, Paul exorcises the 'oracular spirit' from the slave girl.

In contrast to the ambiguity of the slave girl's oracle, Luke seems to emphasize the clarity of Christian prophecy throughout Acts. Luke mentions at least seven Christian prophecies in Acts: 11.28; 13.1–2; 13.9–11; 18.9–10; 21.11; 23.11; and 27.23–24.[78]

In 11.28, the Christian prophet Agabus predicts a world-wide famine, 'Agabus foretold through the Spirit [διὰ τοῦ πνεύματος] that there was about to be a severe famine over the whole world [or "empire"], and this happened in the reign of Claudius'.[79] Whatever the *exact* historical circumstances of this famine, this predictive prophecy is clear to the listener. The prophecy is fulfilled (11.29–39) when Paul and Barnabas take a gift of money to Jerusalem for famine relief among the Christian community there.[80] Not only is Agabus' prophecy unambiguous, it is under the control of 'the Spirit' [τὸ πνεῦμα] in contrast to being given by a πνεῦμα πύθων or 'oracular spirit'.

In 13.1–2 five men (Barnabas, Simeon Niger, Lucius of Cyrene, Manaen, and Saul) are worshipping and, 'The Holy Spirit said [εἶπεν τὸ πνεῦμα τὸ ἅγιον], "Set aside Barnabas and Saul for me for the task to which I have called them".' These men commission Barnabas and Saul (Paul) for missionary work because of this prophetic command by the Holy Spirit. The prophecy is fulfilled throughout the rest of Acts because Barnabas is a missionary through to 15.39 and Paul through to the end of Acts.

Paul proclaims a prophetic judgment against the magician and pseudo-prophet Bar-Jesus in 13.9–11 that is immediately fulfilled with the magician's blinding:

> [9]Paul, full of the holy spirit [πνεύματος ἁγίου] stared at him [Bar-Jesus] [10]and said, 'O you son of the devil, enemy of all righteousness, full of all deceit and fraud, will you not stop making the straight paths of the Lord crooked? [11]And see! From now the hand of the Lord is against you and you will be blind and not able to see the sun for a while!' At

---

78. Form-critical discussion and bibliography in Aune, who informs my discussion throughout, *Prophecy in Early Christianity*, pp. 263–70, and pp. 429–31 nn. 94–143. However, Aune uses both 'oracle' and 'prophecy' to refer to similar phenomena in Acts. I consistently use 'oracle' for Greco-Roman 'messages from the gods in human language' and 'prophecy' for Christian messages from God in human language. This is not a modern Christianizing interpretation because Greco-Roman oracles were, as discussed above, ambiguous and usually a response to a request, while Christian prophecies were, at least in Acts, spontaneous and straightforward in interpretation.

M. Eugene Boring makes similar contrasts between the ambiguity of Greco-Roman prophecy and the clarity of early Christian prophecy (*The Continuing Voice of Jesus: Christian Prophecy and the Gospel Tradition* [Louisville, KY: Westminster/John Knox, 1991], pp. 48–51; 'Early Christian Prophecy', *ABD* V, pp. 495–502, esp. 496).

79. The prophecy in its present form appears to be a predictive prophecy. Any additional structural elements have dropped out making further discussion of its form impossible (Aune, *Prophecy in Early Christianity*, p. 265).

80. For the famine's historical background, see Bruce W. Winter, 'Acts and Food Shortages', in Gill and Gempf (eds), *The Book of Acts in its Graeco-Roman Setting*, pp. 59–78; also, Robert Funk, 'The Enigma of the Famine Visit', *JBL* 75 (1956), pp. 130–36.

once mist and darkness fell upon him and he was looking around searching for people to
lead him by the hand.

The prophecies of 18.9–10; 23.11 and 27.23–24 are prophecies of divine assurance given to Paul by ὁ κύριος, 'the Lord' [God or Jesus?] in a vision: 'Do not be
afraid, but speak and do not keep silent, because I am with you , and no one will
attack you to hurt you, because I have many people in this city' (18.9–10). This
prophecy is fulfilled in v. 11 because Paul stayed a year and a half (in Corinth)
teaching the word of God among them. In 23.11, the Lord reassures Paul of his
current safety in Jerusalem because Paul must go to Rome in the future, 'The
Lord said, Take courage! For as you have testified about me in Jerusalem, so it is
necessary also for you to witness in Rome'. While en route to Rome, Paul has a
vision in which an angel gives him a prophecy of reassurance (27.23–24), 'For an
angel of the Lord ... stood by me during the night saying, "Do not be afraid,
Paul! It is necessary for you to stand before Caesar, and, see, God has given you
to those sailing with you".' In both 23.11 and 27.23–24, the prophecies are fulfilled in Acts 28 when Paul arrives safely in Rome and preaches to the Judean
and Christian communities in there.

In 21.10–11, Agabus speaks a prophecy about Paul's future, 'The Holy Spirit
[τὸ πνεῦμα τὸ ἅγιον] says that the Jews in Jerusalem will tie up the man to
whom this belongs and hand him over to the Gentiles'. This prophecy comes to
fulfillment beginning with 21.27 where Judeans riot over Paul's appearance
in the Jerusalem Temple and make various accusations against him before the
Romans. By the end of Acts (28.31), Paul is under house arrest in Rome awaiting
trial before the emperor. Agabus' unambiguous prophecy is fulfilled within Luke's
narrative.

All seven of these prophecies are fulfilled within or by the end of the narrative
of Acts. The message of each is clear and unambiguous in contrast to the traditional ambiguity attributed to Greco-Roman oracles. Additionally, four of the
seven involve the Holy Spirit (11.28; 13.1–2, 9–11; 21.10–11). The remaining
three (18.9–10; 23.11; 27.23–24) are visions or auditions directly from ὁ κύριος,
'the Lord' (God or Jesus?) to Paul.

For a Greco-Roman audience, Luke's narrative description of early Christianity seems to implicitly contrast Christian prophecy with Greco-Roman oracles
and divination. For this audience, Christian kleromancy becomes a thing of the
past, the ambiguity of Greco-Roman oracles is implicitly rejected, and the direct
unambiguous inspiration of Christian prophecies is contrasted to oracles in the
Greco-Roman world.

This Greco-Roman audience may have also seen an implicit contrast between
inspired Christian prophecies and the inspired oracle of the Philippian slave girl.
Both Luke and this putative audience accepted the existence of various spiritual
beings: demons, the 'holy spirit' and the 'spirit of divination'. This spirit of divination pronounces an ambiguous oracle about 'the Most High God' that is analogous to the traditionally ambiguous Greek oracles. When reading Acts in light of
their own cultural experiences and assumptions, Luke's Greco-Roman audience
would have understood Christian prophecies as very clear and unambiguous and

under the direct control of the Holy Spirit or the Christian God. Therefore, even if Greco-Roman oracles seemed to support the message of the early Church, Luke's Christian Greco-Roman audience may have understood their rejection as necessary.

Chapter 3

ACTS 12.20–23: RULER CULT

In this chapter, I argue that, because of Agrippa's death following acceptance or toleration of divine honors as narrated in Acts 12.20–23, Luke's Greco-Roman readers could have interpreted Agrippa's acclamation by a crowd and subsequent death in this passage as an allusion to Roman imperial cult ritual and its inherent hybris.[1] Luke's audience may have made intertextual allusions to earlier episodes in the narrative of Luke-Acts: Lk. 3.21–22; 9.2–30; 24.5–51 and Acts 1.0-11. After briefly discussing 'ruler cult' and 'imperial cult', I will analyze the ritual elements

---

1.   Walter Radl interprets Acts 12 in light of the Exodus narratives and concludes that the account of Agrippa's death connects Peter's release from prison to both Agrippa's persecution of the church and his blasphemous behavior as a warning to other blasphemers and persecutors ('Befreiung aus dem Gefängnis: die Darstellung eines biblischen Grundthemas in Apg 12', *BZ* 27 [1983], pp. 81–96, esp. pp. 85–86). He also asserts, with minimal analysis, that the narrative of Agrippa's death is a polemic against ruler cults (p. 86).

O. Wesley Allen notes the scholarly inattention to this passage and performs a monograph-length literary analysis of 12.20–23 (*The Death of Herod: The Narrative and Theological Function of Retribution in Luke-Acts* [SBLDS 158; Atlanta: Scholars Press and The Society of Biblical Literature, 1997]). He concludes that Luke used the ancient 'Death of a Tyrant' type scene in which a tyrant is brought to account by a gruesome illness and miserable death for offending the Divine. Allen is persuasive but denigrates historical analysis to the point of missing important allusions.

Hans-Josef Klauck understands Herod's θεοῦ φωνή, 'voice of a god', as a specific reference to Nero's cult of the divine voice ('Des Kaisers schöne Stimme. Herrscherkritik in Apg 12,20–23', in H.J. Klauck, *Religion und Gesellschaft im frühen Christentum* [WUNT, 152; Tübingen: Mohr-Siebeck], pp. 251–67). Regarding the θεοῦ φωνή, see the excursus below.

Allen Brent parallels my conclusions about Acts 12.20–23 while using both a substantially different methodology and substantially different data (*The Imperial Cult and the Development of Church Order: Concepts and Images of Authority in Paganism and Early Christianity before the Age of Cyprian* [Vigiliae Christianae Supplements, 45; Leiden: Brill, 1999], pp. 11–16, 73–139).

There are two significant monographs about Herod Agrippa I: Wolf Wirgin, *Herod Agrippa I: King of the Jews* (2 vols; Leeds University Oriental Society Monograph Series, 10; Leeds: Leeds University Oriental Society, 1968); and Daniel R. Schwartz, *Agrippa I: Last King of Judea* (Texte und Studien zum antiken Judentum, 23; Tübingen: Mohr-Siebeck, 1990). Wirgin is tendentious and speculative, but provides a useful review of research from 1847–1958, which illustrates the vicious anti-Semitic tone of most previous scholarship (vol. 1, pp. 31–49, esp. pp. 34–48). Schwartz is poorly organized and (over)emphasizes source criticism (see Nina L. Collins' review, *NovT* 34 [1992], pp. 90–101).

On the Herodian dynasty, see Richard D. Sullivan, 'The Dynasty of Judaea in the First Century', *ANRW* II/8 (1978), pp. 296–354, esp. pp. 322–29; and Nikos Kokkinos' comprehensive in-depth study, *The Herodian Dynasty: Origins, Role in Society and Eclipse* (JSPSup, 30; Sheffield: Sheffield Academic Press, 1998), pp. 271–304.

of Acts 12.2–23: (1) τακτῇ δὲ ἡμέρᾳ, a designated festival day, (2) ἐσθῆς βασιλική, 'royal clothing', and (3) the acclamation of Agrippa as θεός. Additionally, I will analyze the possible contrasts that Greco-Roman readers may have made between Agrippa's power and the powerlessness of the Christian community in Acts 12, the use of ritual, divine intervention, and Luke's earlier narratives of Jesus' baptism, transfiguration, and ascension.

I will reinforce my argument by referring to Josephus' parallel account of Agrippa's would-be divinization and death (*Ant.* 19.343–50) to develop and explain the ruler cult allusions contained in Acts 12.2–23.[2] In all other passages Josephus consistently portrays Agrippa in glowing colors (e.g., *Ant.* 19.32–31). God's punishment of Agrippa is, according to Josephus, tragic because of the ruler's noble attributes.[3]

What is 'Ruler Cult?'

'Ruler cult' refers to the entire complex of ritual, literature, art and architecture associated with the worship of the divinized Mediterranean rulers in the Hellenistic and Roman imperial periods. According to S.R.F. Price, Hellenistic ruler cult originated as a ritually embodied reaction by the formerly independent Greek city states to the 'otherwise unmanageable power' of Alexander and his successors.[4] The various monarchs that succeeded Alexander produced tensions within these traditionally independent city-states. The cities had to negotiate their rights and freedoms with the new cultural institution of monarch. Ruler cult resolved these tensions when it developed from the sacrifices, processions, rituals, and images adapted from traditional Greek cultic practice. This resulted in the Greeks conceptualizing their rulers as ἰσόθεος or 'equal to god'. For example, in 290 BCE the

---

2. I follow Schwartz in understanding Josephus' narrative as a description of a ruler cult ritual (*Agrippa I*, pp. 145–49) for several reasons: (1) The parallels between Agrippa's divinization ritual and Hellenistic ruler and Roman imperial cult rituals in the celebration of imperial festivals (*Ant.* 19.343), opulent royal apparel made with precious metals (*Ant.* 19.344), and an acclamation as θεός (*Ant.* 19.345). (2) Agrippa's assembly of five Roman client kings (*Ant.* 19.338–42) and the construction of an additional fortified wall for Jerusalem (*War* 2.218–19, 5.147–60; *Ant.* 19.326–27; also, Tacitus *Hist.* 5.12.2); actions suspiciously similar to Roman imperial behavior. (3) His adoption of Persian royal epithets, ὁ μέγας (the Great), and symbols, a royal parasol, on his coinage. See Schwartz, *Agrippa I*, pp. 134–44; also, Kokkinos, *The Herodian Dynasty*, pp. 303–304.

3. Following Allen, *The Death of Herod*, pp. 66–69, 198.

4. Price, *Rituals and Power*, pp. 1–100, esp. pp. 1–22, quoting p. 52. Price's monograph profoundly informs my discussion.

The following works are foundational for the study of the Roman imperial cult: Lily Ross Taylor, *The Divinity of the Roman Emperor* (American Philological Association Philological Monographs, 1; Middletown, CT: American Philological Association, 1931); Kenneth Scott, *The Imperial Cult Under the Flavians* (Stuttgart: W. Kohlhammer, 1936; repr. Ancient Religion and Mythology; New York: Arno, 1975); Fritz Taeger, *Charisma. Studien zur Geschichte des antiken Herrscherkultes* (Stuttgart: W. Kohlhammer, 1957); Price, *Rituals and Power*; Friesen, *Twice Neokoros*; Manfred Claus, *Kaiser und Gott: Herrscherkult im römischen Reich* (Stuttgart: Teubner, 1999); and Ittai Gradel, *Emperor Worship and Roman Religion* (Oxford Classical Monographs; Oxford: Clarendon Press, 2002).

Athenians greeted the conquering general Demetrius Poliorketes and his wife as, 'the greatest and most beloved of the gods' (Athenaus, *Deipn.* 6.253).

When Rome began to dominate the Hellenistic world in the third to second centuries BCE, a similar development took place. Cults of collective Roman bene-factors and individual Romans appeared as early as the third century BCE and became common by the first century BCE.[5] By using these traditional Hellenistic religious symbolic systems the citizens of Asia Minor and Greece created a subject–ruler power relationship in which the subjects conceptualized the emperor (or Roman governor) in the familiar terms of divine power.[6] A 'web of power', symbolized in the ritual of the imperial cult, linked the gods, the ruler (the Roman emperor) and the ruled.[7] Imperial cult stabilized the religious order of the world and provided a definition of the world.[8] Its ritual symbolism included festivals, temple architecture, images of the emperors and the gods, and sacrifices.[9]

Such practices soon extended to Hellenistic Palestine.[10] For example, in the Seleucid era (201–125 BCE) some Tyrian coin legends read ΒΑΣΙΛΕΩΣ ΑΝΤΙ-ΟΧΟΥ ΕΠΙΦΑΝΟΥ ΘΕΟΥ ΝΙΚΗΦΟΡΟΥ, '[Coinage] of the King of Antioch Visible God Victorious'.[11]

---

5. Price, *Rituals and Power*, pp. 25–52.

6. Price, *Rituals and Power*, p. 52.

7. In his *Emperor Worship and Roman Religion,* Gradel has closely refined Price's analysis with specific reference to the imperial cult in Rome and Italy. He concludes that the complexities of the Roman imperial state under the early emperors facilitated the positioning of the emperor in an ambiguous state between the gods and humanity while alive, the expression of 'a superhuman status of absolute power, divinity in a relative sense' (*Emperor Worship and Roman Religion*, p. 69). He also demonstrates in great detail that the 'mad' emperor Caligula did not understand himself as a god and was a fully rational, but monumentally ineffective, emperor (pp. 140–59). Similarly he argues that Domitian neither demanded nor understood himself as one of the gods. Instead, his status as *dominus et deus* ('lord and god') was attributed to him by the imperial court's freedmen (pp. 159–61).

In a brief aside, Gradel also makes the significant observation that the Roman imperial cult mani-fested itself in the eastern empire by worshiping the emperor as a divinity *while he was alive*; and in the Italy and Rome by the divinization of the emperor *after death* (*Emperor Worship and Roman Religion*, p. 261, citing Appian, *Bell. Civ.* 2.148).

Gradel's analysis of the Roman imperial cult as it was manifested within Rome and Italy is beyond the scope of this investigation.

8. Price, *Rituals and Power*, pp. 52, 247–48.

9. Price, *Rituals and Power*, pp. 101–233. Price's table of contents makes clear that he considers imperial cultic festivals part of the cult's 'context' while architecture, images, and sacrifices are 'evo-cations' of the cult (*Rituals and Power*, p. vii). I do not grasp this difference and, for my purposes, consider festivals to be physical manifestations or 'evocations' of the ruler cult. Cf. Friesen's cogent criticisms, *Twice Neokoros*, pp. 50, 73–74, 142–50, 154.

10. Martin Hengel provides extensive bibliography for ruler cult in Hellenistic Palestine (*Judaism and Hellenism: Studies in Their Encounter in Palestine During the Early Hellenistic Period* [2 vols in one; Philadelphia: Fortress Press, 1992], I, pp. 285–86; and II, pp. 189–92 nn. 175–96; and *The 'Hel-lenization' of Judea in the First Century After Christ* [London: SCM Press; Philadelphia: Trinity Press International, 1989]).

11. Richard S. Hanson, *Tyrian Influence in the Upper Galilee* (Meiron Excavation Project, 2; Cam-bridge, MA: American Schools of Oriental Research, 1980), p. 22; citing E.T. Newell, *The First Seleucid Coinage of Tyre* (Numismatic Notes and Monographs, 10; New York: American Numismatic Society, 1921); *idem, The Seleucid Coinages of Tyre* (Numismatic Notes and Monographs, 36; New

The Roman imperial cult developed in Palestine once Augustus had become emperor. After he awarded Herod the Great new territories, Herod erected temples to Augustus and Roma, i.e., temples for the imperial cult at Caesarea Maritima (Josephus, *Ant.* 15.339; *War* 1.414), Sebaste (Josephus, *Ant.* 15.298), and at Panion (Josephus, *Ant.* 15.363–64).[12]

Ruler-Cult Ritual in Acts 20.23

In Acts 12.20–23, Luke describes a festival or other public event that includes three ritual elements: (1) a designated festival day, τακτῇ δὲ ἡμέρᾳ, (2) the use of *sacra* – ritual objects or symbols – in this case, the royal robes, ἐνδυσάμενος ἐσθῆς βασιλική, and (3) an acclamation of Agrippa's divinity, ὁ δὲ δῆμος ἐπεφώνει· Θεοῦ φωνὴ καὶ οὐκ ἀνθρώπου.[13] I analyze each of these elements in light of Hellenistic ruler cult and Roman imperial cult ritual familiar to Greco-Roman readers in order to isolate possible parallels such readers may have drawn between Acts 12.20–23 and Greco-Roman ruler cult.[14]

The Designated Day: τακτῇ ἡμέρᾳ

The first ruler cult ritual element mentioned in Acts 12.20–23 is the 'the designated day', τακτῇ δὲ ἡμέρᾳ'. Josephus probably refers to the same event, 'spectacles in honor of the emperor', θεωρία εἰς τὴν Καίσαρος τιμὴν, in his account of Agrippa's death (*Ant.* 19.343–50). The emperor in question would have been

York: American Numismatic Society, 1936); and E. Rogers, *The Second and Third Seleucid Coinages of Tyre* (Numismatic Notes and Monographs, 34; New York: American Numismatic Society, 1927).

12. J. Andrew Overman, Jack Olive and Michael Nelson have convincingly argued that the sanctuary at Panion was actually a temple dedicated to Pan and that they have excavated the third Augusteum, temple to Augustus, at Omrit in northern Galilee ('Discovering Herod's Shrine to Augustus: Mystery Temple Found at Omri', *BARev* 29 [no. 2, March/April; 2003], pp. 40–49, 67–68).

13. According to Acts 12.20, Agrippa was furious with the cities of Tyre and Sidon. In response the two cities sent a delegation to Agrippa through the intervention of his chamberlain, Blastus, on the occasion of a festival. E. Mary Smallwood has plausibly reconstructed the background this dispute (*The Jews Under Roman Rule From Pompey to Diocletian: A Study in Political Relations* (corrected edn; Studies in Judaism in Late Antiquity, 20; Leiden: Brill, 1981), pp. 188 n. 30, 198, and 198 n. 67).

14. My argumentation in this section is potentially flawed by the inherent terminological, architectural, and ritual ambiguity within and between Greek and Roman ruler cult (S.R.F. Price, 'Gods and Emperors: The Greek Language of the Roman Imperial Cult', *JHS* 104 [1984], pp. 79–85; *idem*, 'Between Man and God: Sacrifice in the Roman Imperial Cult', *JRS* 70 [1980], pp. 28–43; and *idem*, *Rituals and Power*, pp. 133–233). Because of these ambiguities Price concludes that the emperor was a θεὸς ἐπιφανής, a god 'present in the world like one of the traditional gods'; but 'located in an ambivalent position, higher than mortals but not fully the equal of the gods' ('Gods and Emperors', pp. 86–94, quoting pp. 87, 94).

Friesen answers these arguments from epigraphic and archaeological evidence determining that the emperor's divinity was not ambiguous, 'The decisive question was not divine nature, but rather godlike authority in the context of a specific hierarchical relationship' (Friesen, *Twice Neokoros*, pp. 146–52, quoting p. 150). Daniel N. Schowalter argues similarly from numismatics, triumphal reliefs, literature, and other primary sources (*The Emperor and the Gods: Images From the Time of Trajan* [HDR, 28; Minneapolis: Fortress Press, 1993]).

either Augustus or Claudius.[15] In Josephus, Agrippa addresses the crowd 'on the second day of the games'. Games, festivals, and literary and music competitions frequently honored the emperor in the context of the imperial cult. A choir from the province of Asia gathered at Pergamum 'to hymn' the Emperor Tiberius 'on [his] birthday' while 'performing sacrifices and celebrating banquets and festivals'.[16]

An inscription honoring the benefactions of Epaminondas of Acraephia (in Boeotia in mainland Greece) mentions such a festival.

> ... *times at which he entertained all the city*, and again after sacrificing a bull to Hermes and Heracles and *the Augusti at the festival of these gods an athletic contest*,
> ... And *he entertained the city* at breakfast on the same day in the gymnasium after publishing a proclamation; he did not omit anyone not only of the local residents but even of the visiting strangers along with free children and the slaves of citizens ...[17]

In light of this evidence from Josephus and contemporary imperial cult festivals, I tentatively suggest that Luke's reference to a τακτῇ δὲ ἡμέρα in Acts 12.21 is not only a historical incident at the end of Herod Agrippa I's reign, but that Luke's audience may have interpreted this phrase as not only refering to this event but also as alluding to a Roman imperial-cult festival.

The Sacred Apparel: Agrippa's ἐσθῆτα βασιλικὴν

The second ruler-cult ritual element that Luke mentions is that Agrippa 'was wearing royal robes', ἐνδυσάμενος ἐσθῆτα βασιλικὴν, 'on the festival day', τακτῇ δὲ ἡμέρα (12.21). Lösch noted that for Luke ἐσθής always has connotations of royal or angelic robes.[18] Outside of Acts 12.21, ἐσθής occurs seven other times in the

---

15. Two different sets of games have been proposed: games founded by Agrippa I in honor of Claudius' conquest of Britain in 44 or the quadrennial games founded by Herod the Great in 10–9 BCE in honor of Augustus (Josephus *Ant.* 19.343). The games of Herod the Great continued after Augustus' death in 14 CE. Claudius began ruling in 41 CE and installed Herod Agrippa I as the client king of Judea that same year. Agrippa's death in Acts 12.23 occurred in 44 CE. Discussion and bibliography in Schwartz (*Agrippa I*, pp. 107–11, 203–207; and Kokkinos, (*The Herodian Dynasty*, pp. 378–80). Cf. Emil Schürer, *The History of the Jewish People in the Age of Jesus Christ (175 B.C.- 135 A.D.)*, [rev. English edn; ed. Geza Vermes, Fergus Millar, and Matthew Black; Edinburgh: T. & T. Clark, 1973], I, p. 452 n. 43). Manfred Lämmer has extensively analyzed the Greek games in Judea and the games of Herod the Great in particular ('Griechische Wettkampfe in Jerusalem und ihre politischen Hintergrunde', *KBS* 2 [1973], pp. 182–227; 'Die Kaiserspiele von Caesarea im Dienste der Politik des Königs Herodes', *KBS* 3 [1974], pp. 95–164; and 'Griechische Wettkampfe in Galilea unter der herrschaft des herodes Antipas', *KBS* 3 [1976], pp. 36–67; all unavailable to me). For a discussion of Greek games in first century CE Palestine, see H.A. Harris (*Greek Athletics and the Jews* [Cardiff, Wales: University of Wales Press, 1976], pp. 35–50).

Friesen discusses the archaeological and epigraphic evidence for the incorporation of existing Ephesian Olympics into games honoring Domitian (*Twice Neokoros*, pp. 117–41).

16. *IGR* 4.1608C = *I.Eph.* 7.2.3801 restored. Trans. Price, *Rituals and Power*, p. 105.

17. *IG* 7.2112, ll. 21–28. James H. Oliver (trans.), 'Epaminondas of Acraephia', *GRBS* 12 (1971), pp. 221–37 (233); emphasis mine.

18. Stephan Lösch, *Deitas Jesu und Antike Apotheose: Ein Beitrag zur Exegese und Religionsgeschichte* (Rottenburg, Germany: Bader, 1933), pp. 6–38; citing p. 16. Lösch is dated and at times excessively speculative but remains one of the lengthiest and most significant analyses of the text.

New Testament. James contrasts the 'elegant clothes', ἐσθὴς λαμπρά, of the rich to the 'dirty clothes', ἐσθὴς ῥυπαρά, of the poor (Jas. 2.2–3). By contrast, a careful reader may have noted that Luke consistently modifies ἐσθής with an adjective indicating royalty or the status of a divine emissary: ἐσθῆ τα λαμπρά, 'elegant cloak' (Lk. 23.11), ἐσθης ἀστραπτούσα, 'clothes that flash like lightning' (Lk. 24.4), ἐσθῆς λευκή, 'gleaming clothes' (Acts 1.10), and ἐσθῆς λαμπρά, 'shining clothes' (Acts 10.30).

In Josephus, Agrippa enters the theater 'wearing a robe made entirely from silver', which 'enveloped by the sun's first rays glittered brightly and flashed, striking fear and terror upon everyone who gazed at it' (*Ant.* 19.344).

Greco-Roman literature contains similar traditions about royal clothing.[19] Claudius wore a golden robe (Tacitus *Ann.* 12.51). Suetonius relates that Nero returned to Rome from Greece in 68 in triumphal procession wearing 'a purple robe and a Greek cloak adorned with gold stars' (*Nero* 25.1).[20] Cassius Dio commented that Nero, '[was] wearing a gold covered purple robe' (*Hist. Rom.* Ep. 52.20.3).

Lösch traced similar parallel passages in Greco-Roman literature, and concluded that such representations of the emperor were ancient and 'long remained traditional'.[21] Somewhat after this period Lucian describes the brilliant gleaming apparel found on a statue of Aphrodite in a Syrian temple (*Syr. D.* 32). Statues of the gods were clothed with similar robes from the classical period through the Roman era.[22]

On the basis of these citations, Lösch concluded that, despite Luke's brief comments about the royal robes, Luke had clearly characterized the festival at Caesarea as a ritual that had completely absorbed the rituals of the contemporary Roman court.[23] However, the literature Lösch cites does not necessarily refer to 'ruler cult ceremonial' or 'imperial cult ceremonial'.

Despite this objection, I conclude that a Greco-Roman audience may have interpreted the description of Agrippa's royal apparel in Acts 12.20–23 as alluding to Mediterranean ruler-cult dress and ritual on two grounds. First, at what point do we demarcate ruler or imperial cult ritual from other activities and ceremonials of a ruler's court? Can we sharply distinguish between the use of elaborate or sumptuous robes and clothes in the everyday affairs of a ruler's court and the use of such robes and clothes in ceremonies specifically signifying the ruler's divinity?

---

19. Andreas Alföldi has studied Roman imperial costume in detail ('Insignien und Tracht der Römischen Kaiser', *Mitteilungen der römischen Abteilung des Deutschen Archäologischen Institutes* 50 (1935), pp. 1–158; repr., *idem, Die monarchische Repräsentation im römischen Kaiserreiche* [Darmstadt: Wissenschaftliche Buchgesellschaft, 1980], pp. 121–276). I cite the reprint edition.

20. J.C. Rolfe (trans.), *Suetonius* (LCL; London: Heinemann, 1920).

21. Lösch, *Deitas Jesu*, pp. 13–16, quoting 14, 'blieb lange Sitte'; who cites Apollonius Rhodius *Argon.* 1.279; Virgil *Aen.* 5.250–52; and Ovid *Metam.* 6.1–8 as parallels. His citations of Catullus 68.50ff and Claudian *Carm.* 22 appear to be in error.

22. Elizabeth Wayland Barber, *Women's Work: The First 20,000 Years: Women, Cloth, and Society in Early Times* (New York: Norton, 1994), pp. 153–54, 281–83.

23. Lösch, *Deitas Jesu*, p. 16.

Could Claudius' golden robe described by Tacitus be a symbol of his imperial power in the same way that the purple edged toga symbolized the Roman aristocracy?[24] Similarly, for emperors given to excess, such as Nero, any occasion could become an expression of imperial divinity as with his triumphant return from Greece in 67–68 CE. Therefore, although Lösch ignores the fact that his citations of primary sources are not related specifically to rituals that either deify a ruler or acknowledge a ruler's divinity, I still follow his contention that Luke refers to a constituent element of ruler cult by mentioning Agrippa's ἐσθῆτα βασιλική. More precisely, I conclude that Luke's audience may have understood Agrippa's ἐσθῆτα βασιλική in light of ruler cult imagery.[25]

Agrippa's Acclamation as θεός

When hearing or reading Acts 12.23, a Greco-Roman audience may have noted a third element of ruler-cult ritual, the acclamation as θεός: 'The crowd kept shouting, "The voice of a god and not of a man!", ὁ δὲ δῆμος ἐπεφώνει· Θεοῦ φωνὴ καὶ οὐκ ἀνθρώπου!'[26] This acclamation parallels both epigraphic and ritualized acclamations of Greek rulers and the Roman emperor as θεός.[27]

An 'acclamation' was the rhythmically formulized recitation of a short statement of praise or condemnation often performed by a 'speech choir'.[28] Historically, acclamations originated in Persian court ceremonial, Greek civic cult during the hellenistic era, and greetings given to Roman aristocrats by the populace.[29] Because of these influences, acclamations became not only greetings, praises, or criticism but near or absolute attributions of divinity. As already mentioned, the Athenians greeted Demetrius Poliorketes as θεός with the hymn:

24. See Alföldi, 'Insignien und Tracht der Römischen Kaiser', pp. 143–61. Alföldi cites Josephus' *Ant.* 19.344 to argue that Agrippa's use of a *silver* robe indicated both his sovereignty over his small kingdom and his subservience to Rome because the emperor wore gold robes (p. 146).

25. Cf. Allen, 'As Peter's obedient robing and rising [Acts 12.8] leads to his rescue, Herod's robing and sitting upon his throne leads to his downfall' (*The Death of Herod*, p. 88). Allen notices neither Luke's intratextual use of ἐσθής nor a Greco-Roman audience's possible interpretation of Acts 12.21 as a reference to ruler cult. The contrast between Peter's 'street clothes' and Agrippa's cultic apparel strengthens the case for and expands the literary parallelism noted by Allen.

26. On the Θεου φωνή, 'the sacred voice', see Excursus.

27. 'Acclamation' covered a wide semantic field in antiquity, including cultic responses, wedding toasts, responses to victorious Roman generals celebrating their triumph, etc. (Alföldi, 'Die Ausgestaltung des Monarchischen Zeremoniells am Römischen Kaiserhofe', *Mitteilungen der römischen Abteilung des Deutschen Archäologischen Institutes* 49 [1934], pp. 3–118; repr. *idem*, *Die monarchische Repräsentation*, pp. 3–118, esp. pp. 79–88, all citations from the reprint edn; and Theodor Klauser, 'Akklamation', *RAC* [1950], I, pp. 216–33). For my purposes, I limit the use of acclamation to the ritualized public, literary or epigraphic attribution or near-attribution of divinity to a human being.

28. Klauser, 'Akklamation', p. 216.

29. Klauser, 'Akklamation', pp. 217, 219–22; Alföldi, 'Die Ausgestaltung des Monarchischen Zeremoniells', p. 82.

For the greatest and most regarded of the gods
comes to the city;

....

He comes full of joy, nobility,
and laughter.
He seems to be someone solemn and majestic, all his friends encircling,
but he is in their midst,
his friends the stars,
while he is the sun.
Child of the most noble god Poseidon
and Aphrodite, Welcome!
For other gods are very far away,
have no ears,
do not exist, or give not one thought to us;
but you we see here and now,
not as wood, not as stone, but truly present.
Therefore, we pray to you,
First, most esteemed, make peace!
For you are Lord! (Athenaus, *Deipn.* 6.253)[30]

Though not strictly an acclamation, this hymn contains lines that may been accla-
mations, 'Child of the most noble god Poseidon/and Aphrodite, Welcome!', ὦ
τοῦ κρατίστου παῖ Ποσειδῶνος θεοῦ, χαῖρε, καφροδίτης, or, 'For you are
Lord!' κύριος γὰρ εἶ σύ. During the Second Macedonian War (200–194 BCE),
T. Quinctius Flamininus freed Greece from Philip V of Macedonia and announced
Greece's liberation to the crowd at the Isthmian Games in 196. In response, the
Greeks 'acclaimed [his] words' (Livy 34.50.2), 'as if the voice was an oracle'
(Livy 34.50.4), and acclaimed Flamininus as or 'savior', σωτήρ (Plutarch, *Flam.*
10.5).[31]

Acclamations continued to develop and evolve in the late Republic and through-
out the imperial period and eventually became part of court ritual.[32] In 19 CE,
Germanicus became angry at the Alexandrians because, 'you call [me] equal to
God', ἰσόθεους ἐκφώνησεις, and prohibited the practice.[33] Choristers in the

---

30. For Demetrius' deification and the advent of ruler cult in Hellenistic cities against the background of the traditional Greek pantheon, see Robert Parker, *Athenian Religion: A History* (Oxford:
Clarendon Press, Oxford University Press, 1996), pp. 258–62 and Jon D. Mikalson, *Religion in
Hellenistic Athens* (Hellenistic Culture and Society; Berkeley: University of California Press, 1998),
pp. 75–104. Both Parker and Mikalson rightly emphasize that Demetrius' deification was a blend of
both politics *and* religion and that Demetrius *did not* replace the traditional deities.

31. Translated and adapted from Foster *et al.* (trans.), *Livy* (LCL, 9; trans. Evan T. Sage;
Cambridge, MA: Harvard University Press, 1961 [1935]).

32. Klauser, 'Akklamation', pp. 221–26; Alföldi, 'Die Ausgestaltung des Monarchischen Zeremoniells', pp. 79–88. Both Klauser and Alföldi present numerous primary literary sources.

33. This account is known from a papyrus published by Ulrich von Wilamowitz-Moellendorf and
Fr. Zucker ('Zwei Edickte des Germanicus auf einem Papyrus des Berliner Museums', Siztungbericht
der preussischen Akademie der Wissenschaften (Berlin) 33 [1911], pp. 794–821; further discussion in
Conrad Cichorius, *Römische Studien: Historisches, Epigraphisches, Literargeschichtliches aus vier
Jahrhundertes Roms* [Leipzig: Teubner, 1922], pp. 377–88; Erik Peterson, 'Εἷς Θεός' [FRLANT,
n.s., 24. Göttingen: Vandenhoeck & Ruprecht, 1926], pp. 177–80; and Klauser, 'Akklamation', pp.
220–221.

province of Asia 'hymned the god Augustus [θεὸς Σεβαστός] and the goddess Roma'.[34] Nero appointed a corps of 'Augustiani', young Roman equestrians who performed acts of *acclamatio* or acclamation making Nero ἰσόθεος, 'Days and nights they thundered applause, conferred the epithets reserved for deity [*deum*] upon the imperial form and voice' (Tacitus, *Ann.* 14.15).[35] In 68 CE he was acclaimed as one of the traditional gods, 'Hail to Nero our Hercules! Hail to Nero our Apollo!' (Cassius Dio, *Hist. Rom.* 62.20.5). By the time of Trajan, the Roman Senate loudly acclaimed the emperor and his decrees in an adulatory manner during sessions of the Senate (Pliny the Younger, *Pan.* 75).[36]

Josephus hints at similar acclamations made by court officials (court encomiasts?) who acclaim Agrippa as θεός at, 'spectacles in honor of the emperor', εἰς τὴν Καίσαρος τιμήν (*Ant.* 19.343):

> a large crowd of high officials and those who had attained high rank gathered for this event.
> ....
> Immediately the toadies and yes-men raised their voices, not at all for Agrippa's own good, from various sides addressing him as a god, 'May you be favorable!' adding, 'If up until now we have feared you as a human, from now on we agree that you are by nature superior to mortals'. (*Ant.* 19.343, 345).

To Luke's readers, the crowd's acclamation of Agrippa may have suggested a standard response within the setting of contemporary ruler cult.[37] Such readers may have seen two parallels between Luke's narrative and ruler cult acclamations: The acclamation of Agrippa as θεός occurs in a public setting after he has settled a dispute with Tyre and Sidon (12.20–21). Also, Luke uses a verb typical of acclamations, ἐπιφωνέω, 'to call out loudly', in 12.20 when the crowd acclaims Agrippa divine.[38]

A Perceived Critique of Ruler Cult

A Greco-Roman audience may have interpreted Luke's highly condensed mention of an 'appointed day', his depiction of Agrippa's clothing, and use of terminology that refers to royalty or divinity as an allusion to a contemporary ruler-cult ritual (and possibly to Roman imperial cult).[39] How would this audience

---

34. *IGR* 4.353. Additional examples in Price, 'Gods and Emperors', p. 90, nn. 90–94.

35. Trans. adapted from John Jackson (ed. and trans.), *Tacitus' Annals* (LCL; Cambridge: Harvard University Press, 1931).

36. See discussion in Alföldi, 'Die Ausgestaltung des Monarchischen Zeremoniells', pp. 84–86.

37. Allen's literary analysis misses the overtones of ruler cult possibly noted by the ancient audience: 'the reader has suspicions concerning the *sincerity* of the crowd's praise. If no reconciliation has been achieved [between Tyre, Sidon, and Agrippa] their acclamation *must be motivated by a desire* to placate the tyrant' (*The Death of Herod*, p. 88, my emphasis). The claque's acclamation both recognizes the ruler's god-like power *and* attempts to placate the infuriated ruler.

38. Klauser, 'Akklamation', p. 216; and Erik Peterson, 'Die Einholung des Kyrios', *ZST* 7 (1929–30), pp. 682–702, esp. 697.

39. Because of the parallels between Acts 12.20–23 and Josephus (*Ant.* 19.343–50), there was indeed an *historical cultic divinization* of Agrippa I. However, I address a Greco-Roman audience's understanding of the reference to that event within Luke's narrative.

have understood the point of this putative allusion? In Acts 12.20–23, Luke's readers may have seen an indirect indictment of the ruler and emperor cult through the narrative castigation of Agrippa's toleration for divine honors. By reading a severely castigating allusion to ruler and imperial cult in the text, Luke's audience may have drawn a sharp distinction between the Christian community and the religious and political world of Mediterranean ruler cult in at least three ways: the exercise of power, the use of ritual, and the notion of divine intervention.

Luke's Indictment of the Emperor Cult

Luke states that Agrippa died a particularly gruesome death: 'Immediately an angel of the Lord struck him because he had not given the glory to God [οὐκ ἔδωκεν τὴν δόξαν τῷ θεῷ]. He was eaten by parasitic worms and died' [γενόμε- νος σκωληκόβρωτος ἐξέψυξεν] (Acts 12.23). In ancient literature, death by worms was the traditional punishment assigned to the worst of villains (e.g., Herodotus, *Persian Wars* 4.205; Pliny, *Nat.* 7.172; Lucian, *Alex.* 59; Jdt 16.17; 2 Macc 9.9; Josephus, *Ant.* 17.169 and *War* 1.656).[40]

What was Agrippa's villainy? Luke claims that Agrippa 'did not give the glory to God', οὐκ ἔδωκεν τὴν δόξαν τῷ θεῷ. As shown above, Agrippa accepts an acclamation that makes him ἰσόθεος, 'equal to God'. Luke consistently uses δόξα to mean 'reputation', 'honor' or 'brilliance' in the 12 times he attributes the concept to God or Jesus: Lk. 2.9, 14; 9.26, 32; 17.18; 19.38; 21.27; 24.26; Acts 7.2, 55; and 12.23.[41] For Luke and a 'friendly' audience, Agrippa usurped the reputation or honor properly attributable only to God and to Jesus. If Luke's audience understood an allusion to ruler or imperial cult in his description of Agrippa's

Bruce W. Winter, in his discussion of the imperial cult and Acts, never cites 12.20–23 ('Acts and Roman Religion, B. The Imperial Cult', in *The Book of Acts in Its Graeco-Roman Setting*, David W. J. Gill and Conrad Gempf (eds), vol. 2 of *The Book of Acts in Its First Century Setting*, Bruce W. Winter (ed.) [Grand Rapids: Eerdmanns, 1994], pp. 93–104). He concludes 'the imperial cult was firmly established and flourished in all the areas where the Christian missionary endeavors were active. As far as Acts records, no actual confrontation with [the imperial cult] appears to have arisen in the Julio-Claudian era …' (p. 103). Even if there was no direct confrontation between the imperial cult and early Christianity in the Julio-Claudian era, Luke's Greco-Roman audience possibly understood Luke as writing a literary allusion that condemns ruler cult. If Luke wrote *circa* 80 CE, then he may have reflected the circumstances of his own time of writing. Throughout the imperial era, a Greco-Roman audience could potentially have seen an allusion to Roman imperial cult.

40. Wilhelm Nestle provides comparative background materials for this literary topos, 'Legenden vom Tod der Gottesverächter', *ARW* 33 (1936), pp. 246–69. For more recent discussion and bibliography: Thomas Africa, 'Worms and the Death of Kings: A Cautionary Note on Disease and History', *Classical Antiquity* 1 (1982), pp. 1–17; Schwartz, *Agrippa I*, pp. 217–18; and Kokkinos, *The Herodian Dynasty*, pp. 303–304; 303, n.142. Africa traces the theme throughout history citing similar statements made about King George III and President Woodrow Wilson by political opponents and historians (p. 16 nn. 89–95). In light of this long literary history, there is no historically credible way of determining the exact nature of Agrippa's death. Cf. Kokkinos who plausibly suggests that Agrippa was poisoned without being able to prove his suggestion (*The Herodian Dynasty*, pp. 303–304).

41. Luke also associates δόξα with God's people Israel (Lk. 2.32), with the nations of the world (Lk. 4.6), angels (Lk. 9.26), Elijah and Moses (Lk. 9.31), Solomon (Lk. 12.27), personal honor (Lk. 14.10), and to describe a visionary experience (Acts 22.11).

divinization ritual, they may have concluded that not only was Agrippa's acceptance of divine honors to be condemned but also the acceptance of divine honors
by rulers (including the Roman emperor) who in turn did not properly render
δόξα to God.

Distinctions Between the Emperor Cult and the Christian Community

Luke's Greco-Roman audience may not have only read a sharp condemnation of
ruler emperor cult in Luke's narrative; they may have also implicitly defined the
boundaries between Christianity and ruler cult. The short narrative of Agrippa's
death is the penultimate point in Acts 12. The chapter ends with the continued
spread of the Christian message (12.24).[42] The subtle allusions to the Roman
imperial cult in 12.20–23 stand in sharp contrast to the narrative material in 12.1–
19 (James' execution, Peter's imprisonment, his miraculous release, the celebration of Passover). Agrippa's political power contrasts with the political weakness
of the Jerusalem community. Agrippa accepts divine honors in a ritual centered on
the recognition of his powerful, 'more than human status'. The Jerusalem community participates in celebrating the Passover recognizing God's power and
deliverance in the exodus event. Agrippa intervenes in the lives of his subjects.
God intervenes in both the lives of the Christian community and the supposedly
'divine' Agrippa. These contrasts between 12.1–19 and 12.20–23 establish boundaries between Luke's conception of Christianity (or at least his audience's understanding of his conception of Christianity) and the underlying social, economic,
and political assumptions of Greco-Roman imperial cult in three areas: expressions
of power, the use of ritual, and divine intervention.

Expressions of Power. Agrippa expresses his political power four times in Acts
12: (1) in 12.1–2 he sets out to persecute the early church and has James, one of
Jesus' first followers (Lk. 5.10, 6.14, and Acts 1.13), beheaded. (2) In 12.3–4,
Agrippa has Peter seized and imprisoned, intending to have him executed. (3) In
12.19 he summoned the guards who failed in their duty to guard Peter and
possibly ordered their torture and execution, 12.19.[43] (4) In 12.20–23, Agrippa
exerts autocratic economic authority over Tyre and Sidon and expresses that
authority in ritual that is imitative of Greco-Roman ruler cult ritual.

   How would Luke's audience have understood the exertion of power by the
early Christian community? The community itself exerts no power in response to
Agrippa's persecution beyond its own intercessory prayer, 'But urgent prayers
[προσευχη ἐκτενῶς] were continually[44] being offered by the church on his
[Peter's] behalf' (Acts 12.5). For the audience there is a clear contrast: Agrippa is

---

42. I take 12.25 as a narratival bridging device that serves as a transition between the imprisonment and release of Peter and Agrippa's death in Acts 12 and the developing outreach of Paul and his
associates in Acts 13. Therefore, 1.25 is not the conclusion to the narratives in Acts 12.

43. On the verbs ἀνακρίνω and ἀπάγω, see Bruce, *Acts*, p. 287; and Johnson, *Acts*, p. 214. Ms.
D, the Syriac versions, and the Bohairic Coptic understand the context as requring a verb for murder
and thus replace ἀπάγω with ἀποκτείνω.

44. Because ἦν … γινομένη is an imperfect periphrasis, I translate as, 'were continually being
offered'. Bruce suggests the emphasis is upon 'the continuousness [*sic*] of the praying', *Acts*, p. 282.

able to behead one of the Twelve and imprison another; the church has divinely enabled power in prayer to effect Peter's miraculous escape.[45]

Prayer *is* the expression of power for the Christian community according to Luke.[46] Luke's three parables on prayer (Lk. 11.5–8; 18.1–8, 9–14) demonstrate themes seen again in Acts 12: persistence, faithfulness in prayer during difficult circumstances and true dependence on God.[47] The Jerusalem community persists continually in prayer in the same way as the man persistently asking his friend for bread in the middle of the night (11.5–8). The community prays in a state of humility, as did the tax collector (18.9–14.) The community remains faithful in prayer, '[prayers] were continually being offered by the assembly', ἦν... γινομένη ὑπὸ τῆς ἐκκλησίας (Acts 12.5) in the same way the widow remains persistent and faithful in petitioning the unjust judge (Lk. 18.1–8).

Luke's readers would conclude that Agrippa's *hybris* resulted in his death. Reading the wider context of Acts 12, they would probably also conclude that Agrippa's continued practice of autocratic power was also responsible for his death.[48] Luke 'demonstrate[s] the final impotence of this seemingly powerful ruler'.[49] Acts 12.24 proclaims that the Christian community and its message continued to flourish despite opposition. James' death at the hands of Agrippa (Acts 12.1–2) and the political powerlessness of the Christians (Acts 12.1–19) results not in the dissolution of the Christian community but in continued growth. Luke's readers could conceivably compare the contrast between Agrippa and the early Jerusalem community to the contrast between the established powers (client kings, Roman governors, and the emperor) and the Christian communities in their own particular local setting.

45. Cf. Tannehill, 'In Acts 12 it is primarily Peter and the church who fail to understand [divine power] and are taken by surprise' (*The Narrative Unity of Luke-Acts: A Literary Interpretation*, Vol. 2. *The Acts of the Apostles* [Minneapolis: Fortress, 1990], pp. 155–56, quoting 155).

46. From a substantial literature: P.T. O'Brien, 'Prayer in Luke-Acts', *TynBul* 23 (1973), pp. 111–27; Allison A. Trites, 'The Prayer Motif in Luke-Acts', in Charles H. Talbert (ed.), *Perspectives on Luke-Acts* (Perspectives in Religious Studies Special Studies Series, 5; Danville, VA: Association of Baptist Professors of Religion, 1978), pp. 168–86; David Michael Crump, *Jesus the Intercessor: Prayer and Christology in Luke-Acts* (WUNT 2/49; Tübingen: Mohr-Siebeck, 1992); Joel B. Green, 'Persevering Together in Prayer: The Significance of Prayer in the Acts of the Apostles', in Richard N. Longenecker (ed.), *Into God's Presence: Prayer in the New Testament* (McMaster New Testament Studies; Grand Rapids: Eerdmans, 2001), pp. 183–202.

O'Brien and Trites both provide vocabulary statistics for Luke's use of προσευχή and semantically related words (O'Brien, 'Prayer in Luke-Acts', pp. 112–13, 121; Trites, 'Prayer Motif', pp. 169–70. None of these scholars connect prayer to the power of Lukan Christianity as opposed to the power of Rome and the emperor and local governments.

47. O'Brien, 'Prayer in Luke-Acts', pp. 117–18. O'Brien interprets, without detailed exegesis, the parable of the widow and the unjust judge, as referring to intense persecution of the Lukan community. Since he has not substantiated this claim, which is specious at best, I prefer to relate the parable to 'difficult circumstances' that can occur in the absence of persecution.

48. As Allen convincingly demonstrates (*The Death of Herod*). Allen's narrative analysis also demonstrates that 12.20–23 is not merely an awkward digression but serves as an important transition in the narrative of Acts, is intimately connected to the rest of Acts 12, and contributes to Luke's theology of retribution.

49. Tannehill, *The Narrative Unity of Luke-Acts*, p. 152.

The Use of Ritual. As shown above, Greco-Roman readers may have understood Acts 12 as an allusion to a ruler-cult ritual complete with actors, costumes, an orally performed 'liturgy' (the acclamations) and a 'mythology' of power and hierarchy. Within the immediate context of Acts 12, Luke portrays the Christian community as having only two rituals: the Passover and prayer. While Agrippa's imperial-cult ritual may allude to an entire complex of involved contemporary rituals, the two Christian rituals are simple and have God as the only power figure.

For a Greco-Roman audience, Agrippa was the central focus of the ruler cult ritual. He has proved his political dominance through his ability to execute James, imprison Peter, and bend Tyre and Sidon to his will. The actors (the flattering crowd), Agrippa's royal costume (ἐσθῆτα βασιλική), his acclamations, and his political power cultically elevate him above mere humans, ἄνθρωποι and make him ἰσοθεός, 'equal to God', i.e., positioned among the gods.

In contrast, an attentive Greco-Roman reader would note that Luke presents the two Christian rituals apart from human political power, 'It was Passover', αἱ ἡμέραι τῶν ἀζύμων (12.3), and 'Peter was guarded in prison. But urgent prayers [προσευχὴ δὲ ἦν ἐκτενῶς] were offered by the church on his behalf' (12.5). In Acts 12.3 Luke mentions that the Jerusalem community celebrated the Passover at the home of Mary (John Mark's mother, 12.12).[50] Contrary to Agrippa, the Christian community does not develop a ritually enacted hierarchy of human power. Instead they perform an ancient ritual that unifies the community, in an egalitarian fashion, through a cultic meal and the cultic recitation of a foundation myth (the Passover story).[51] Cultic recitation is the only hierarchical conception of power that emerges; the Christian community recounts the power and mercy

50. As various commentators observe, Luke dissolves any distinction between αἱ ἡμέραι τῶν ἀζύμων, the days of unleavened bread, and the Passover itself, τὸ πάσχα (12.4); e.g. Conzelmann, *Acts*, p. 93; Bruce, *Acts*, p. 282; Johnson, *Acts*, p. 211.

Exegetes consistently notice the Passover allusions in Acts 12: Mark R. Strom, 'An Old Testament Background to Acts 12.20–23', *NTS* 32 (1986), pp. 289–92; Radl, 'Befreiung aus dem Gefängnis', and Susan R. Garrett, 'Exodus from Bondage: Luke 9.31 and Acts 12.1–24', *CBQ* 52 (1990), pp. 656–80. However, no one seems to have noted contrasts between Agrippa's acclamation and the Jerusalem community's Passover observance in terms of ritual *as* ritual. The theological concepts and intertextual allusions are analyzed while entirely ignoring the performative dimension.

For the observance of Passover in the first century, see *JewEnc*, vol. 9, pp. 553–56; J.B. Segal, *The Hebrew Passover From the Earliest Times to A.D 70* (London Oriental Series 12; London: Oxford University Press, 1963), pp. 240–47; *EncJud*, vol. 13, cols 153–64, esp. cols 169–71; Baruch M. Bokser, 'Unleavened Bread and Passover, Feasts of', *ABD* VI, pp. 755–65, esp. pp. 761–63; and Joseph Tabory, 'Towards a History of the Passover Meal', in *Passover and Easter: Origin and History to New Testament Times*, ed. Paul F. Bradshaw and Lawrence Hoffman (Two Liturgical Traditions, 5; Notre Dame, IN: University of Notre Dame Press, 1999), pp. 62–81, esp. p. 63.

51. Recently feminist biblical scholars have argued that Luke is not as egalitarian as he seems at first glance. Concerning this issue in Acts 12.12–14: Richter Reimer, *Women in the Acts of the Apostles*, pp. 238, 241; Gail R. O'Day, 'Acts', in Carol A. Newsom and Sharon H. Ringe (eds), *Women's Bible Commentary* (expanded edn; Louisville, KY: Westminster John Knox, 1998), pp. 394–402, esp. pp. 399–400; and Albert Harrill, 'The Dramatic Function of the Running Slave Rhoda (Acts 12.12–16): A Piece of Greco-Roman Comedy', *NTS* 46 (2000), pp. 150–57. However, from the perspective of Luke and his first-century readership, Luke portrays a high level of egalitarianism in early Christian ritual as opposed to Agrippa's self-divinizing court ritual.

of God to God's people. No human transcends the boundary between the divine and human; no human becomes ἰσόθεος by means of cult.

Secondly, this attentive reader might note that while Agrippa wields both the might of the sword (12.3) and superior economic power (12.20) the Christians, as mentioned above, can only respond with the ritual of prayer (12.5) and the power of God. Luke provides no specifics; the ritual is quickly mentioned in 12.5. He sets the ritual of προσευχὴ ἐκτενῶς γινομένη, 'impassioned prayer', within the Passover celebration at Mary's home.[52] They do not ritually appeal to any socio-politically or socioeconomically powerful human; only to the Christian God, the creator of heaven and earth.

Divine intervention. Luke seems to contrast God's intervention in Agrippa's rituals and God's intervention in the Jerusalem community's rituals. Agrippa usurps the δόξα reserved for God and faces the consequent judgment, 'Immediately an angel of the Lord struck him because he had not given the glory to God. He was eaten by parasitic worms and died', παραχρῆμα δὲ ἐπάταξεν αὐτὸν ἄγγελος κυρίου ἀνθ᾽ ὧν οὐκ ἔδωκεν τὴν δόξαν τῷ θεῷ, καὶ γενόμενος σκωληκόβρωτος ἐξέψυξεν (Acts 12.23). The Jerusalem community is at Agrippa's mercy: one member has been killed, a second is imprisoned and awaits execution. Through prayer, within the Passover ritual, the community intercedes to God for Peter. God intervenes by sending an angel to free Peter from prison. Luke's audience would grasp a simple narratival point. By depending upon God and not upon human political power, the Jerusalem community gives the glory where it right-fully belongs: to God.

Textual Connections: Acts 12.20–23, Rituals, and Lukan Christology
Luke seems to sharply contrast his portrayal of Jesus' 'rituals' to the ritual of the Greco-Roman ruler cult, as represented by Agrippa in Acts 12.20–23. In Lk. 3.2–22; 9.2–36; 24.5–51 and Acts 1.0–11 Jesus participates in a variety of rituals which in some way define his character and/or mission. Jesus' baptism (Lk. 3.21–22) is a rite of consecration, God's identification and approval of Jesus as God's son.[53]

> [21]When all the people had been baptized, Jesus had also been baptized. While he was praying, heaven opened (ἀνεῳχθῆναι τὸν οὐρανόν) [22]and he saw the holy spirit descending (καταβῆναι τὸ πνεῦμα τὸ ἅγιον) upon him in the bodily form of a dove.

52. It is a false assertion to claim at this point that Luke differentiates between the simple earnest prayers of the Christians and the verbose flattering self-interested prayers of the Greco-Roman world. See the examples cited by H.S. Versnel ('Religious Mentality in Ancient Prayer', in H.S. Versnel (ed.), *Faith, Hope, and Worship: Aspects of Religious Mentality in the Ancient World* [SGRR, 2; Leiden: Brill, 1981], pp. 1–64).
53. Bultmann, *History of the Synoptic Tradition*, pp. 247–53, esp. 247–48; 428–29; Joseph Fitzmyer, SJ, *The Gospel According to Luke* (AB, 28–28A; Garden City, NY: Doubleday, 1981–85), I, pp. 479–87, esp. 480–83; and Luke Timothy Johnson, *The Gospel According to Luke* (Sacra pagina, 3; A Michael Glazier book; Collegeville, MN.: Liturgical Press, 1991), pp. 69–70. Fitzmyer provides a thorough bibliography through to 1980; Johnson through to 1990.

There was a voice out of heaven (φωνὴν ἐξ οὐρανοῦ γενέσθαι), 'You are my beloved son (ὁ υἱός μου ὁ ἀγαπητός). In you I have delighted.'

In the transfiguration, 9.28–36, Jesus is again designated as God's son and also as a chosen servant:[54]

[28]Eight days after these words, he [Jesus] ascended the mountain in order to pray, taking along Peter, John, and James. [29]While he was praying the form of his face became altered and his cloak was shining like white flashing lightning. [30]There were two men speaking with him. They were Moses and Elijah. [31]They appeared in glory (οἱ ὀφθέντες ἐν δόξῃ) and were speaking about his exodus (ἔξοδος),[55] which he was about to fulfill in Jerusalem. [32]But Peter and those who were with him were weighed down by sleep. After waking up they saw his glory and the two men standing with him. [33]After they left him, Peter said to Jesus, 'Master, it is good for us to be here. Let us make three tents. One for you, one for Moses, and one for Elijah.' He did not know what he was saying. [34]While he was still speaking, a cloud came and overshadowed them. They were terrified as they entered the cloud. [35]A voice came from the cloud, 'This is my son, the chosen one (ὁ υἱός μου ὁ ἐκλελεγμένος). Listen to him.' [36]While the voice was speaking, they saw that Jesus was alone. They were silent and reported nothing of what they had seen at that time to anyone.

Jesus' ascension, Lk. 24.50–53 and Acts 1.9–11, shows Jesus going to live with God, his Father, in glory:[56]

[50]He led them out as far as Bethany, lifted his hands, and blessed them. [51]While he as blessing them, he parted from them and was carried into heaven (ἀνεφέρετο εἰς τὸν οὐρανόν). [52]After worshipping him they returned to Jerusalem with great joy. [53]They were regularly in the temple blessing God. (Luke 24.50–53)

[9]After he said these things, they saw him lifted up and a cloud carried him from their sight. [10]While he was going and they were gazing into heaven, two men dressed in white clothes were suddenly standing by them. [11]They said, 'Men of Galilee! Why do you stand looking into heaven [εἰς τὸν οὐρανόν]? This Jesus who was carried away [ὁ ἀναλημφθείς] from you into heaven [εἰς τὸν οὐρανόν] will come in the same way that you saw him go into heaven [εἰς τὸν οὐρανόν]. (Acts 1.9–11)

These four texts are rituals of 'divine filiation', i.e., rituals that disclose the participant's filial relationship with the gods. Jesus' divine-filiation rituals stand in contrast to Agrippa's ruler-cult ritual, which either divinizes him or acknowledges his (already existing) divinity. Luke's Greco-Roman readers may have contrasted

54. Fitzmyer, *Gospel According to Luke*, pp. 791–804, esp. 792–94; Johnson, *Gospel According to Luke*, pp. 150–56, esp. 156; and Barbara E. Reid, OP, *The Transfiguration: A Source- and Redaction-Critical Study of Luke 9.28–36* (Cahiers de la Revue Biblique, 32; Paris: J. Gabalda, 1993), esp. pp. 98–148.

55. The precise meaning of ἔξοδος in this passage is debated. Both Fitzmyer (*Gospel According to Luke*, p. 800) and Reid (*The Transfiguration*, p. 126) understand the word as not only referring to Israel's exodus in the Hebrew Scriptures but also Jesus' entire death, resurrection, and ascension. Since this discussion is beyond this monograph, I translate literally with 'exodus'. Further bibliography in Fitzmyer and Reid.

Interestingly, both Radl ('Befreiung aus dem Gefängnis') and Garrett ('Exodus from Bondage') found an allusion to Israel's exodus in Acts 12.20–23. Garrett explicitly connects Lk. 9.31 and Acts 12.1–24.

56. Fitzmyer, *Gospel According to Luke*, pp. 1586–93, esp. 1588–90.

the ritual terminology, ritual actions, and ritual participants between Jesus' and Agrippa's divine-filiation rituals (Table 2).

Luke's description of Agrippa's filiation ritual shows Agrippa wearing ritual or 'royal' clothing, possessing a 'divine voice', being addressed as 'god', and passively receiving acclamation of divine status. Implicit in Luke's mention of Agrippa's dispute with Tyre and Sidon is Agrippa's active use of political power which qualifies him for divine status. The other active participant in the ritual is the crowd which acclaims Agrippa divine. Luke's description does not use assumption language nor the terms νεφέλη and οὐρανός. The result of Agrippa's divine-filiation ritual is Agrippa's macabre death. Jesus' clothing is never described by Luke in the three divine-filiation rituals Luke associates with him: his baptism, transfiguration, and ascension.[57] Jesus does not have a 'divine voice', instead he is twice addressed or referred to by the (implied) voice of God (Lk. 3.21–22; 9.28–36). Jesus is not addressed as 'god'; rather he is the 'son of God' and the 'chosen one'.[58] Indirectly these terms imply a relational status, filiation, between Jesus and God. This status is clarified when the disciples worship Jesus and then bless God in the temple afterwards (Lk. 24.52–53): Jesus is divinized. These three rituals bear parallels to Greco-Roman 'assumption rituals' in which a man is bodily 'assumed' into the realm of the gods by being carried into the sky, e.g., an anonymous god, (Dionysius of Halicarnassus *Ant. Rom.* 1.77.2; Hercules, Apollodorus *Bibl.* 2.7.7; and Romulus, Plutarch *Numa* 2.2; *Rom.* 27.7–8).[59] Jesus is enveloped by a cloud in his transfiguration and ascends to heaven on a cloud. Similar rituals also take place on a mountain. In the baptism, instead of a comet (Caesar's apotheosis: Pliny, *Nat.* 2.94; Dio Chrysostom, *Def.* 6.4–7.1(= *Or.* 45); Suetonius, *Jul.* 88; Ovid, *Metam.* 15.746–50 and 15.840–50) or an eagle ascending to the gods (Augustus' apotheosis: Cassius Dio 56.42.3;

57. Does Luke's seeming subtle contrast between Jesus (Lk. 3.21–22; 9.28–36; 24.50–51; Acts 1.9–11) and Agrippa (Acts 12.20–23) account for the understated mention of Agrippa's robes in Acts in comparison to Josephus' account (*Ant.* 19.344)?

58. Luke is here not using υἱός as technical Greco-Roman ruler-cult vocabulary since he does not use the phrase θεοῦ υἱός. By calling Jesus both ὁ ἐκλελεγμένος, 'elected' or 'chosen', and ὁ υἱός μου ὁ ἀγαπητός, 'my beloved son', Luke emphasizes the divine election of Jesus in his use of υἱός (Eduard Schweizer, 'υἱός', *TDNT* VIII [1972], pp; 363–92, esp. pp. 380–82). Peter Wülfing von Martitz briefly discusses θεοῦ υἱός and the imperial cult ('υἱός', *TDNT* VIII [1972], pp. 334–40, esp. 336–37 with citations of primary sources). Interestingly, Luke refers to Agrippa solely as a θεός, possibly reflecting Agrippa's actual historical ruler-cult ritual.

59. Gerhard Lohfink, *Die Himmelfahrt Jesu: Untersuchungen zu den Himmelfahrts- und Erhöhungstexten bei Lukas* (SANT, 26; Munich: Kösel, 1971), pp. 32–50. Cf. Mikeal Parsons who concludes that Luke's imagery is based on Greco-Roman assumption narratives while his language derives from Jewish assumption narratives, *The Departure of Jesus in Luke-Acts* (JSNTSup, 21; Sheffield: JSOT Press, 1987), pp. 135–44, esp. p. 136, Table 12; p. 138, Table 13; p. 139, Tables 14–15; and p. 140.

I do not deny the importance of the Hebrew Scriptures and intertestamental literature upon Luke's narratives in Lk. 3.21–22; 9.28–36; 24.50–51 and Acts 1.9–11. I am merely emphasizing that Luke's educated Greco-Roman audience would have noted the parallels between these narratives in Luke-Acts and Greco-Roman literature.

see also, Suetonius, *Aug.* 100), the Holy Spirit (in the form of a dove) descends from God in heaven to Jesus on earth.[60] Jesus and all other participants are passive throughout the rituals, Jesus is chosen (Lk. 9.35); he does not choose himself. God alone is active. Agrippa achieves only a horrible death; Jesus' body is ultimately resurrected and ascended after his death.

For Greco-Romans there may have been an ironic note to these contrasts between Agrippa and Jesus. Luke may describe Agrippa's divinization in terms of Greco-Roman ruler cult. Luke seems to depict much of the imagery of Jesus baptism, transfiguration and ascension using Greco-Roman imagery from mythological narratives of bodily assumption and apotheosis (Table 2, opposite): clouds, bodily assumption or ascension into the sky, accompanying natural signs, etc. Consequently his Greco-Roman readers may have drawn distinctions between Agrippa and Jesus in light of Luke's use of this Greco-Roman mythological imagery. For this readership, Luke's use of this Greco-Roman mythological imagery may have served to indict and condemn the Greco-Roman religious thought world for *hybris* and inappropriate conferrals of divinity upon mere humans.

Conclusions

Greco-Roman readers may have noticed parallels between Acts 12.20–23 and contemporary Greco-Roman ruler cult because of references to: (1) τακτῇ ἡμέρα, an appointed festival day; (2) ἐσθῆς βασιλική, Agrippa's costume; and (3) the crowd's acclamation of Agrippa as θεός. These readers may have also noticed contrasts between the early Jerusalem-Christian community's powerlessness, rituals and divine aid for their community and Agrippa's *hybris* and power, his divinization ritual and divine punishment in the context of Acts 12. These contrasts serve to form distinctions between Lukan Christianity and the Greco-Roman world. The Roman emperor's (or local political leader's) (ab)use of power, expressed and maintained by imperial-cult ritual, is antithetical to God's proper use of power. Ritual should not transgress the human and divine realms by the divinization of any human agent (except God's anointed, Jesus). Instead, ritual serves to express the dependence of the Christian community upon divine (and not divinized human) intervention. Expressing such dependence properly attributes δοξά to God and not to human social, economic, or political agency.[61]

60. For a thorough discussion of the comet related to Caesar's apotheosis, see John T. Ramsey and A. Lewis Licht, *The Comet of 44 B.C. and Caesar's Funeral Games* (American Classical Studies 39; Atlanta: American Philological Association, Scholars Press, 1997). Ramsey and Licht print the texts cited above with facing page translations, pp. 158–67, pp. 174–77.

61. John H. Elliott has derived a set of contrasts parallel to my own between the Jerusalem temple and the early Christian private household or οἶκος in Luke-Acts ('Temple versus Household in Luke-Acts: A Contrast in Social Institutions', in Neyrey (ed.), *The Social World of Luke-Acts*, esp. p. 231, fig. 8–1; p. 234, fig. 8–2). Though Elliot contrasts 'symbolic features' between the Jerusalem temple and the οἶκος and uses a wider spectrum of social relations than in my analysis, he does not contrast rituals.

Table 2. *Elements of Divine-Filiation Rituals in Luke-Acts*

	Agrippa's Divinization	Jesus' Baptism	Jesus' Transfiguration	Jesus' Ascension
Ritual Clothing	ἐσθῆτα βασιλικὴν (Acts 12.21) στολὴν...ἐξ ἀργύρου πεποιημένην πᾶσαν (*Ant.* 19.344).	absent	absent	Absent for Jesus. Two men dressed ἐν ἐσθήσεσι λευκαῖς, 'in white clothing',
Voice	φωνὴ θεοῦ	φωνὴν ἐξ οὐρανοῦ	φωνὴ ... ἐκ τῆς νεφέλης	absent
Relationship to θεός	Agrippa is θεός	Jesus is ὁ υἱός μου ὁ ἀγαπητός, 'my beloved son'.	Jesus is ὁ υἱός μου ὁ ἐκλελεγμένος, 'my son, the chosen one'.	Jesus is (now) θεός.†
Assumption‡ language and imagery	absent	οὐρανός and inverted imagery*	ὄρος, νεφέλη	ὄρος, **νεφέλη οὐρανός ὑπολαμβάνω ἀναλαμβάνω
Fate of ritual participant's body	dies	baptized	transformed τὸ εἶδος τοῦ προσώπου αὐτοῦ ἕτερον	resurrected and ascended
Participants	Agrippa overtly passive, covertly active. Crowd active.	Jesus passive. God and Holy Spirit active.	Jesus passive? Moses, Elijah, and disciples passive. God active.	Jesus, God, and two men active. Disciples passive.

† Implied by the disciple's *proskyneisis* to the ascended Jesus (Luke 24.52).
‡ Language and imagery found in Greco-Roman assumption stories
* *Descending* dove instead of *ascending* eagle or comet
** Implied by the setting of the narrative (Kirsopp Lake, 'The Ascension', in Kirsopp Lake and Henry J. Cadbury (eds) *Additional Notes to the Commentary*, vol. 5 in F.J. Foakes-Jackson and Kirsopp Lake (eds), *The Beginnings of Christianity*, Part I, *The Acts of the Apostles* (London: MacMillan, 1933), pp. 16–22; and *eadem*, 'Localities in and Near Jerusalem Mentioned in Acts', in Lake and Cadbury, *Beginnings*, V, pp. 474–86, esp. 475–76).

Reading Luke's account of Agrippa's imitation ruler-cult ritual, Greco-Romans would possibly contrast both the Christian community and Jesus to Herod Agrippa I and by implication to the Roman emperor as well. Because Jesus fulfilled his commission, which was narrated in Lk. 4.16–21, he is divinized following his death through his ascension. This divinization is foreshadowed in both Jesus' baptism and transfiguration. After divinization, Jesus is worthy of worship by the Christian community. In turn the Christian community is to use rituals that acknowledge Jesus and God his father, as well as acknowledge their power as mediated through the acts described in Lk. 4.16–21.

A Greco-Roman audience may have also seen that the abuse of power, the worship of political leaders, and the rituals associated with such worship, i.e., the ruler cult, leads only to certain retributive death at the hands of God.

Excursus: Agrippa's θεοῦ φωνή

In Acts 12.22, the crowd declares that Agrippa has a divine voice, 'The crowd kept shouting, "The voice of a god and not of a man!"', ὁ δὲ δῆμος ἐπεφώνει· Θεοῦ φωνὴ καὶ οὐκ ἀνθρώπου! Both Lösch and Klauck find a parallel in his construction of a hypothetical cult dedicated to Nero's voice.[62] Cassius Dio wrote that upon his return to Rome in 68 Nero was hailed by populace and the senators, 'Sacred Voice! Blessed are those that hear you!', ἱερὰ φωνή· μακάριοι οἵ σου ἀκούοντες (*Hist. Rom.* 62.20.5). The *Augustiani*, equestrian choristers, accompanied Nero and applauded and cheered his sacred voice (Suetonius, *Nero* 20). As already noted above of these *Augustiani*, 'Days and nights they thundered applause, bestowed the epithets reserved for deity upon the imperial form and *voice*' (Tacitus, *Ann.* 14.15; my emphasis).[63] Tacitus also records that Nero brought charges against Thrasea Paetos, a Stoic philosopher, 'he had never offered a sacrifice for the welfare of the emperor or for his celestial voice [*caelesti voce*]' (Tacitus, *Ann.* 16.22).[64] Philostratus mentions two incidents from Apollonius' life about Nero's divine voice. A drunken harpist is hired to sing songs composed by Nero and is empowered to arrest individuals who express disinterest in Nero's

62. Lösch, *Deitas Jesu*, pp. 16–26; Klauck, 'Des Kaisers schöne Stimme'. Lösch also attempts to find historical precedents for Agrippa's capabilities as an orator, pp. 17–18. In addition to the primary sources quoted below, Klauck also cites Seneca, *Apocolocyntosis* 4; Lucan, *Pharsalia* 1.33–66; the Einsidlen declogues; Dio Chrysostom, *Or.* 66; and Plutarch, *Sera* (=*Mor.* 32F). For reasons of space, I do not discuss these texts here.

C. Kavin Rowe argues against Klauck's interpretation because: (1) by Luke's time it was possible to openly criticize Nero, (2) thus Luke had no need to implicitly criticize Nero and (3) if Luke's target is not Nero, then the point about the 'divine voice' is lost and also the implicit critique of the imperial cult (p. 282 n. 15). Instead Rowe understands the Cornelius episode in Acts 10 as an allusion to the imperial cult ('Luke-Acts and the Imperial Cult: A Way Through the Conundrum', *JSNT* 27 [2005], pp. 279–300). Against Rowe, is my argument in this chapter that the ritual elements in Acts 12.20–23 and Agrippa's own behavior, all shared cultural assumptions of Luke's readers, would have constituted a Lukan allusion to the imperial cult as understood by his readers.

63. Trans. Jackson, *Tacitus' Annals*.
64. Trans. Jackson, *Tacitus' Annals*.

lyrics for 'irreverence', ἀσέβεια. 'He said that they were irreverent [ἀσεβέω] to Nero by listening with indifference and that they were enemies of the divine voice' [ἡ θεία φωνή] (*Vit. Apoll.* 4.39). Later Apollonius reflects upon the disastrous consequences of Nero's visit to Greece, 'You [the Greeks] did not sacrifice to the voice [ἡ φωνή] so that it would shine brilliantly at the Pythiad' (*Vit. Apoll.* 5.7).[65]

There is no evidence that this supposed cult persisted after Nero's death, but it is possible that Luke alluded to (or that a Greco-Roman audience would have understood an allusion to) a notorious and idiosyncratic feature of Nero's egocentric cultic practice. Luke uses φωνή forty-one times, of which twelve refer to the voice of a divinity: Lk. 3.22 (Jesus' baptism), Lk. 9.35 (Jesus' transfiguration), Acts 9.4, 7; 22.7, 9, 14; 26.14 (Paul's call/conversion), Acts 10.15; 11.7, 9 (Peter's vision about clean and unclean food), and 12.22 (Agrippa's acclamation as Θεός). Luke makes a very subtle contrast between the voice of the living God (and the resurrected Jesus) and Agrippa. All of the voices that refer to the living God are contained in or refer to visionary experiences. The spectators present at Agrippa's non-visionary, purely human, divinization ritual declared his voice divine. Luke's mention of Agrippa's φωνή may be an allusion to Nero's practice; however, it did not refer to a 'standard' part of Roman imperial cult.[66]

Most likely Luke relied upon long-held contemporary understandings about divine voices as being terrifying, loud, and sounding like thunder or a trumpet. Gerard Mussies has briefly noted the 'loud and far-reaching sound' of a god's voice as one of the distinguishing characteristics by which the gods were recognized.[67] Apollo's voice frightens Hector during the Trojan war:

> [Apollo said,] 'Hector, no longer stand as a champion against Achilles, but wait for him in the crowd and in the confusion of battle, lest he strike you with his spear or a sword'…
> Hector, terrified, then fell back into the crowd of men, when he heard the god's voice.
> (Homer *Il.* 20.375–80)

Athena's voice similarly frightens the people of Ithaca when she commands them to stop their civil war:

---

65. Lösch concluded on the basis of these texts and contemporary Roman law that the cult of the ruler's voice had become a substantial part of ruler cult during and after Nero's reign. There are two problems with this conclusion: (1) as Conzelmann pointedly observed, 'the analogy is only apparent because…[here] we do not have the veneration of the voice, but of the person (who is recognized as 'divine' by his voice)' (Conzelmann, *Acts*, 96); (2) Suetonius does not report that the cult of the emperor's divine voice continued but only that Vitellius performed one of Nero's compositions (*Vit.* 11). From this passage in Suetonius, Lösch concluded, 'The memory of the *caelestis vox* of the emperor-poet once more had become imprinted upon contemporaries in word and song' ('Den Zeitgenossen wird damit die Erinnerung an die *caelestis vox* des Kaiser-Poeten nochmals in Wort und Lied eingeprägt worden sein').

66. Tannehill suggests that the mention of Agrippa's voice is an allusion to Nero, because (1) Nero encouraged the honors Agrippa accepts in 12.22, (2) Nero falls under the same divine judgment as Agrippa and (3) Paul will appear before Nero in Acts 27.24 (*Narrative Unity*, vol. 2, p. 157 n. 18).

67. Gerard Mussies, 'Identification and Self-Identification of Gods in Classical and Hellenistic Times', in R. van den Broek, T. Baarda, and J. Mansfeld (eds), *Knowledge of God in the Graeco-Roman World* (EPRO 112; Leiden: Brill, 1988), pp. 1–18, esp. 7.

[Athena] shouted loudly and held back all of the fighters. 'Stop the harsh slaughter
Ithacans so that you may quickly be parted without bloodshed'. So Athena spoke, and
pale horror seized them. Then in terror the weapons flew from their hands and they all
fell on the ground while the goddess spoke. They turned toward the city anxious for
their lives (Homer *Od.* 24.529–35).

Hera's voice sounds like thunder and frightens Jason and the Argonauts when she
demands they stop their expedition:

But Hera leaping from heaven cried out from the lookout on the Hercynian rock. All of
them together were shaking with fear at her cry because the great sky roared ferociously
(Apollonius Rhodius, *Argon.* 4.640–42).

Sophocles has Odysseus compare Athena's voice to a bronze gong or trumpet:

Voice of Athena, dearest of the gods to me, how easily do I hear your words and grasp
them with my mind, even if I cannot see you, as though a Tyrrhenian trumpet spoke
with a bronze mouth. (*Aj.* 14–17)[68]

The early Christian world also knew the loud divine voice. When God answers
Jesus' prayer, the spectators believe they have heard a thunderclap or the voice of
an angel:

[28][Jesus said], 'Father, glorify your name'. Then a voice came out of heaven [ἦλθεν οὖν
φωνὴ ἐκ τοῦ οὐρανοῦ], 'I have glorified it and I will glorify it again'. [29]The crowd standing there also heard it and said that it had thundered [ἔλεγεν βροντὴν γεγονέναι], but
others said, 'An angel has spoken to him [Ἄγγελος αὐτῷ λελάληκεν]' (Jn 12.28–29).

John of Patmos describes the voice of the cosmic Christ as the loud sound of a
trumpet, 'I was in the spirit on the Lord's day and heard a loud voice like a trumpet [φωνὴν μεγάλην ὡς σάλπιγγος]' (Rev. 1.10–11). In 22 other passages, he
describes the voices of various heavenly beings as μεγάλη or ἰσχυρά, 'loud',
sounding like a σάλπιγξ, 'trumpet', a φωνὴ βροντῆς, 'voice of thunder', or a
φωνὴ ὑδάτων πολλῶν, 'sound of many waters'.[69]

Paul shows this same tradition when he connects the voice of the heavenly
Christ, commands, the voice of an angel, and the trumpet of God, 'For the Lord
himself, with a cry of command [ἐν κελεύσματι], with the voice of an archangel
[ἐν φωνῇ Ἀρχαγγέλου], and the trumpet of God [ἐν σάλπιγγι θεου] will
descend from heaven' (1 Thess. 4.16).

Similarly, the writer of Hebrews, relying on traditions from Exodus, describes
the terrifying nature of God's voice: 'and the sound of a trumpet and the sound of
spoken words [καὶ σάλπιγγος ἤχῳ φωνῇ ῥημάτων], which the hearers will
beg not to hear another word' (Heb. 12.19); 'whose voice then shook the earth
[οὗ ἡ φωνὴ τὴν γῆν ἐσάλευσεν τότε]'(Heb. 12.26).

---

68. Translation slightly adapted from Hugh Lloyd-Jones, trans., *Sophocles* (LCL; Cambridge:
Harvard University Press, 1994).

69. μεγάλη φωνή: Rev. 5.2, 12; 7.2; 10.3; 11.12, 15; 12.10; 14.7, 9, 15, 18; 16.1, 17; 19.17; 21.3.
ἰσχρὰ φωνή: Rev. 18.2. σάλπιγξ: Rev. 4.1. φωνή βροντῆ ς: Rev. 6.1, 10.4. φωνὴ ὑδάτων
πολλῶν: Rev. 1.12; 14.2; 19.6.

Moreover, the LXX had already established the tradition of God's powerful voice: Pss. 28.3–9 (29.3–9 HB) and 45.6 (46.7 HB) describe God's voice as, 'powerful' and 'full of majesty', capable of 'breaking the giant cedar trees of Lebanon', 'bursting into flames of fire', 'shaking the wilderness', 'causing the deer to calve', 'strips the forest bare' and 'the earth melts' at its sound.

Luke may have used pre-existing LXX and Greek traditions about the terrifyingly loud sound of the divine voice in describing Agrippa's voice as a θεοῦ φωνή and may have combined them with an allusion to Nero's divine voice.[70]

Alternatively, the text may reflect not a 'cult of the divine voice', but rather the giving of divine honors to Agrippa for his rhetorical abilities. It is almost impossible to underestimate the importance of and regard for rhetorical ability in the ancient Greco-Roman world.[71] Throughout Acts, Luke consistently portrays Paul, Peter, and other early Christian leaders as making speeches modelled on Greco-Roman rhetorical technique.[72]

70. Additional primary sources including rabbinic and early Christian texts in Otto Betz, 'φωνή', *TDNT* IX (1974), pp. 279–301, esp. pp. 279–80, 282–90, 293–300.

There is also the highly speculative possibility that Luke alludes to a mechanical amplification of Agrippa's voice. About such amplification , see William W. Klein, 'Noisy Gong or Acoustic Vase: a Note on 1 Corinthians 13.1', *NTS* 32 (1986), pp. 286–89; and William Harris, ' "Brass" and Hellenistic Technology', *BARev* 8 (Jan–Feb 1982), pp. 38–41; cf. Todd K. Sanders, 'A New Approach to 1 Corinthians 13.1', *NTS* 36 (1990), pp. 614–18.

71. Donald Andrew Frank Moore, 'Rhetoric, Greek', *OCD* (3rd edn), pp. 1312–14; Michael Winterbottom, 'Rhetoric, Latin', *OCD* (3rd edn), p. 1314; Ruth Majercik, 'Rhetoric and Oratory in the Greco-Roman World', *ABD* V (1992), pp. 710–12; Benjamin Fiore, 'New Testament Rhetoric and Rhetorical Criticism', *ABD* V (1992), pp. 715–19.

72. See both Marion Soards, *The Speeches of Acts: Their Content, Context and Concerns* (Louisville, KY: Westminster/John Knox Press, 1994), throughout; and Witherington, *Acts of the Apostles*, pp. 39–51 and his discussion of individual speeches.

Similarly, both 2 Corinthians and Galatians reflect both a use of rhetorical technique and an intense theological discussion about the validation of Paul's orally proclaimed message based on rhetorical ability; Charles H. Talbert, *Reading Corinthians: A Literary and Theological Commentary on 1 and 2 Corinthians* (New York: Crossroad, 1987), p. xiv and passim; and Hans Dieter Betz, *Galatians: A Commentary on Paul's Letter to the Churches in Galatia* (Hermeneia; Philadelphia: Fortress Press, 1979), pp. 14–25 and throughout; *idem*, *2 Corinthians 8 and 9: A Commentary on Two Administrative Letters of the Apostle Paul* (Hermeneia; Philadelphia: Fortress Press, 1985), pp. 38–41, 88–90, and throughout.

Chapter 4

ACTS 14.8–18: PROCESSIONS AND SACRIFICES

In Acts 14.8–18, because Paul and Barnabas heal a lame man, the townspeople of Lystra hail them as Hermes and Zeus, a priest brings garlanded bulls in order to sacrifice to the two missionaries, and Paul and Barnabas struggle to keep the local Lystrans and the priest of Zeus from sacrificing to them. In this brief episode, a Greco-Roman reader may have seen Luke as parodying and reversing what was perhaps the heart of Greco-Roman religion, the sacrificial system.

For these eleven verses, scholars have devoted most of their exegetical labors to investigating a possible allusion to Baukis and Philemon in Ovid, *Metam.* 8.611–724.[1] However, both Luther H. Martin and Hans-Josef Klauck are attentive to the element of Greco-Roman sacrifice mentioned in the text.[2]

---

1. Joseph Fontenrose provides significant bibliography for this discussion ('Philemon, Lot, and Lycaon', *University of California Publications in Classical Philology* 13 [1945], pp. 93–120). Amy Lorine Wordelmann provides a detailed review of research for Acts 14.8–18 from the patristic era to the present, 'The Gods Have Come Down: Images of Historical Lycaonia and the Literary Construction of Acts 14' (PhD disseration, Princeton University, 1994), pp. 24–135. More recent discussion: Cilliers Breytenbach, 'Zeus und der Lebendige Gott: Anmerkungen zu Apostlegeschichte 14.11–17'. *NTS* 39 (1993), pp. 396–413; Daniela Flückinger-Guggenheim *Göttliche Gäste: Die Einkehr von Göttern und Heroen in der griechischen Mythologie* (European University Studies, Series 3; History and Allied Studies, 237; Bern: Peter Lang, 1984), pp. 52, 174 n. 11; and A. Denaux, 'The Theme of Divine Visits and Human (In)Hospitality in Luke-Acts: Its Old Testament and Graeco-Roman Antecedents', in J. Verheyden (ed.), *The Unity of Luke-Acts* (BETL, 142; Leuven: Leuven University Press and Peeters, 1999), pp. 255–80, esp. pp. 263–68, p. 264 nn. 27–28, and p. 265 nn. 29–310. Breytenbach includes a wider discussion of Zeus cults in the area and discusses the epigraphic association of Zeus and Hermes. Flückinger-Guggenheim surveys the theme of human hospitality to gods and heroes in Greek myth and understands the Philemon and Baukis tale as the source of Acts 14.8–18. Denaux posits a Homeric background to this text, citing Athena's visit to Odysseus' palace in *Od.* 1.

2. Luther H. Martin, 'Gods or Ambassadors of God? Barnabas and Paul in Lystra', *NTS* 41 (1995), pp. 152–56; and Klauck, *Magic and Paganism*, pp. 69–76. Martin understands Luke to be writing from a classical perspective that identifies Zeus and Hermes as the guarantors of ambassadors and their missions. Luke uses this perspective to remind his 'Hellenistic readers of customary ambassadorial prerogatives and to recommend to them traditional Hellenic obligations of hospitality' (p. 155). Klauck briefly discusses the healing miracle, the crowd's acclamation of Paul and Barnabas, the Ovidian allusion, the apostles' reaction to the acclamation, Paul's speech and the riot which results in Paul's stoning. He concludes, following Pesch, that the narrative's main point is, 'There are no gods in human form' (*Magic and Paganism*, p. 61; quoting Pesch, *Apostelgeschichte*, II, p. 60).

Klauck further argues, without support, that the riot occurred because 'the crowd, frustrated of their hope for a great sacrificial meal with meat for all, now became enraged and tried to stone those who had been their heroes a short time before' (*Magic and Paganism*, p. 75). This goes far beyond what

These various exegetes have explored the historical, cultural, and literary backgrounds of Acts 14.15–18. However, beyond merely noting their presence – as with the scholarship on Acts 12.20–23 – these scholars virtually ignore the elements of sacrificial ritual in this text: the priest, the sacrificial victim and the sacrificial ritual itself; the very elements that would have appeared most significant to a Greco-Roman audience.

There are several ritual elements in the text: the priest, ὁ ἱερεύς who conducts the ritual; the bull, ὁ ταῦρος, which is the sacrificial victim; the procession, πομπή; and the use of ritual ornamentation, τὰ στέμματα. Concentrating solely on issues of historicity, Lukan theology or narrative technique ignores these elements. Therefore, the interpreter anachronistically ignores that 'the Greeks [and Romans] in general considered what one believed to be of much less importance than what one did'.[3] In other words, Luke's Greco-Roman auditors or readers would have considered the ritual of sacrifice itself as an essential component of the text.

In this chapter, I will examine the four aspects of sacrificial ritual found in Acts 14.8–18 in their Greco-Roman setting and Luke's narrative treatment of them to show that Luke's audience may have seen humorous ironic reversals and an implicit condemnation of Greco-Roman sacrifice.

Greco-Roman Sacrifice

In a very real sense, sacrifice was at the heart of Greco-Roman religion.[4] Animal sacrifice persisted as the major religious rite of the Greeks and the Romans in

the text specifically narrates and grossly underestimates the level of sacrality and εὐσέβεια Greco-Romans brought to sacrificial ritual.

3. Vincent J. Rosivach, *The System of Public Sacrifice in Fourth-Century Athens* (American Classical Studies, 34; Atlanta: American Philological Association, Scholars Press, 1994), p. 1.

4. Royden Keith Yerkes, *Sacrifice in Greek and Roman Religions and Early Judaism* (The Hale Lectures; New York: Scribner's, 1952) esp. pp. 51–114; Jean Rudhardt and Olivier Reverdin, eds, *Le Sacrifice dans L'Antiquité* (Entretiens sur L'Antiquité Classique 27; Geneva: Fondation Hardt pur L'Étude de L'Antiquité Classique, 1980); Walter Burkert, *Homo Necans: The Anthropology of Greek Sacrificial Ritual and Myth* (Berkeley: University of California Press, 1983); Michael H. Jameson, 'Sacrifice and Ritual: Greece', *CAM* II, pp. 959–80; *idem*, 'Sacrifice and Animal Husbandry in Classical Greece', in C.R. Whittaker (ed.), *Pastoral Economics in Classical Antiquity* (Proceedings of the Cambridge Philological Society, 14; Cambridge: Cambridge Philological Society, 1988), pp. 87–119; John North, 'Sacrifice and Ritual: Rome', *CAM* II, pp. 981–86; Marcel Detienne, *et al.*, *The Cuisine of Sacrifice Among the Greeks* (Chicago: University of Chicago Press, 1989); Mary Beard, 'Priesthood in the Roman Republic', in Beard and North (eds), *Pagan Priests*, pp. 17–48; Richard Gordon, 'From Republic to Principate: Priesthood, Religion and Ideology', in Beard and North (eds), *Pagan Priests*, pp. 177–198; *idem*, 'The Veil of Power: Emperors, Sacrificers and Benefactors', in Beard and North (eds), *Pagan Priests*, pp. 199–232; *idem*, 'Religion in the Roman Empire: the Civic Compromise and its Limits', in Beard and North (eds), *Pagan Priests*, pp. 233–56; Dennis D. Hughes, *Human Sacrifice in Ancient Greece* (London and New York: Routledge, 1991), esp. pp. 1–12; Froma I. Zeitlin (ed.), *Mortals and Immortals* (Princeton: Princeton University Press, 1991), pp. 291–302; Louise Bruit Zaidman and Pauline Schmitt Pantel, *Religion in the Ancient Greek City* (Cambridge: Cambridge University Press, 1992), pp. 28–39; Stanley K. Stowers, 'Greeks Who Sacrifice and Those Who Do

essentially the same form from the Homeric era until the Roman emperor made it illegal in the fourth century CE.[5] Sacrifice existed in the home, kin or tribal group, private association, and civic and imperial government.[6] For example, the

Not', in L. Michael White and O. Larry Yarbrough (eds), *The Social World of the First Christians: Essays in Honor of Wayne A. Meeks* (Minneapolis: Fortress Press, 1995), pp. 293–333; F.T. van Straten, *Hierà Kalá: Images of Animal Sacrifice in Archaic and Classical Greece* (RGRW, 127; Leiden and New York: Brill, 1995); and Fritz Graf, 'What is New About Greek Sacrifice'? in H.F.J. Horstmanshoff, *et al.* (eds), *Kykeon: Studies in Honour of H.S.S. Versnel* (RGRW, 142; Leiden: Brill, 2002), pp. 113–26. G.S. Kirk discusses and critiques contemporary methods of understanding sacrifice ('Some Methodological Pitfalls in the Study of Ancient Greek Sacrifice (in Particular)', in Rudhardt and Reverdin (eds), *Le Sacrifice*, pp. 41–80). Michael Lambert persuasively argues for extreme caution in comparing sacrifice in modern pre-technological cultures to ancient Greece, 'Ancient Greek and Zulu Sacrificial Ritual: A Comparative Analysis', *Numen* 40 (1993), pp. 293–318. Recent bibliography in Hughes; van Straten; Graf; and also Derek Newton, *Deity and Diet: The Dilemma of Sacrificial Food at Corinth* (JSNTSup, 169; Sheffield: Sheffield Academic Press, 1998), pp. 175–257.

Important discussions and presentations of pictorial evidence are in Nanno Marinatos, 'The Imagery of Sacrifice: Minoan and Greek', in Robin Hägg, Nanno Marinatos and Gullög C. Nordquist (eds), *Early Greek Cult Practice: Proceedings of the Fifth International Symposium at the Swedish Institute at Athens, 26–29 June, 1986* (Skrifter Utgivna av Svenska Institutet i Athen, 4°, 38; Stockholm: Svenska Institutet i Athen, 1988), pp. 9–20; B.C. Dietrich, 'The Instrument of Sacrifice', in Hägg, Marinatos and Nordquist, (eds), *Early Greek Cult Practice*, pp. 35–40; Folkert van Straten, 'The God's Portion in Greek Sacrificial Representations: Is the Tail Doing Nicely?' in Hägg, Marinatos and Nordquist, (eds), *Early Greek Cult Practice*, pp. 51–68; *idem*, 'Greek Sacrificial Representations: Livestock Prices and Religious Mentality', in Tullia Linders and Gullög Nordquist (eds), *Gifts to the Gods: Proceedings of the Uppsala Symposium 1985* (Acta Universitatis Upsaliensis; Boreas, Uppsala Studies in Ancient Mediterranean and Near Eastern Civilizations, 15; Uppsala: Academia Upsaliensis, 1987), pp. 159–70; Jean-Louis Durand, 'Greek Animals: Toward a Topology of Edible Bodies', in Marcel Detienne, *et al.* (eds), *The Cuisine of Sacrifice among the Greeks* (Chicago: University of Chicago Press, 1989), pp. 87–118, esp. pp. 106–117, figs. 1–23; and van Straten, *Hierà Kalá*, pp. 193–332, figs. 1–168.

Summary discussion of θύω, θυσία, and θυσιαστήριον and useful citation of primary sources and older secondary literature in Johannes Behm, 'θύω', *TDNT* III (1965), pp. 180–90, esp. pp. 180–83, 187–89. However, his statement, 'Everywhere in the world around early Christianity we see the literal concept of sacrifice disappearing' (p. 189), grossly underestimates the importance of sacrificial cult in daily life in the ancient world and its persistence into the fifth century CE; cf. Beard, North, and Price, *Religions of Rome*, pp. 374, 387–88.

For a contemporary, comparative, and theoretical discussion of sacrifice in general: Joseph Henninger, 'Sacrifice', *ER* (2nd edn), XII, pp. 7997–8008; and Fritz Graf, 'Sacrifice (Further Considerations)', *ER* (2nd edn), XII, pp. 8008–10.

5. Jameson, 'Sacrifice and Ritual: Greece', *CAM* II, pp. 960–61. Despite increasing homogeneity, there were significant differences between Greek and Roman sacrificial ritual including the types of participants in the procession and the dress of the priests and assistants. The most notable difference was the Roman requirement for the sacrifice to exactly and precisely follow archaic ritual formulae. Any error on the part of the officiating priest required that the sacrifice begin over again from the beginning. See North, 'Sacrifice and Ritual: Rome', *CAM* II, pp. 981–86; Beard, North, and Price, *Religions of Rome*, p. 36.

6. Greco-Roman domestic sacrifice: H.J. Rose, 'The Religion of the Greek Household', *Euphrosyne* 1 (1957), pp. 95–116; Martin Nilsson, 'Roman and Greek Domestic Cult', *Opuscula Romana* 18 (1954), pp. 77–85; and S.C. Humphreys, *The Family, Women, and Death: Comparative Studies* (London: Routledge & Keegan Paul, 1983). For kin and tribal groups: Robert Parker, 'Festivals of the

Eleusinian mysteries were remarkable for a 'striking' number of bull sacrifices while the closely related Thesmophoria had an enormous number of piglet sacrifices.[7] Sacrifice accompanied all acts of classical Athenian government and occurred within various levels of fourth-century BCE Athenian society approximately every eight to nine days.[8] In Herodas' fourth *Mime* two women offer a cock to Asclepius and in return they want the god's comment on their present situation. At Delphi, those who requested an oracle offered sacrifices before receiving the oracle (Plutarch, *Def. Orac.* 46, 49, 51 [=*Mor.* 435B, 437B, 438B]).

The Reasons for Animal Sacrifice

Why did the Greco-Romans perform animal sacrifice? The philosophers Plato and Theophrastus argued against sacrifice but also preserved the common ancient understanding of sacrifice: it honors the gods, it thanks the gods for past benefits or deliverance, and it expresses a desire for future protection by the god.[9] Plato records a discussion between Euthyphro and Socrates about the reasons for sacrificing:

> Euthyphro: ... I say to you...that if someone knows how to say and to do what is agreeable to the gods by both praying and *sacrificing*, this is holiness, and these things save both private families and city-states. The opposite of what is gratifying to the gods is impious, which, quite obviously, overturns and destroys everything.
>
> Socrates: ... What do you say the holy and holiness are? Are you not saying that they are some sort of skilled knowledge of prayer and sacrifice?
>
> Euthyphro: Certainly.
>
> Socrates: Therefore sacrifice is giving gifts to the gods, while prayer is making requests of them?

Attic Demes', in Linders and Nordquist (eds), *Gifts to the Gods*, pp. 137–48; and Burkert, *Greek Religion*, pp. 216–75. For sacrifices and the Athenian government, see P.J. Rhodes, *The Athenian Boule* (corrected ed. with additions; Oxford: Clarendon, Oxford University Press, 1985), pp. 127–34. For the Roman imperial government and the imperial cult: Price, 'Between Man and God, 28–43; *idem, Rituals and Power*, pp. 207–33 and Friesen, *Twice Neokoros*, pp. 146–52.

7.   Kevin E. Clinton, *The Sacred Officials of the Eleusinian Mysteries* (Transactions of the American Philosophical Society, n.s., v. 64, pt. 3; Philadelphia: American Philosophical Association, 1974), pp. 82–86 and *idem*, 'Sacrifice at the Eleusinian Mysteries', in Hägg, Marinatos and Nordquist (eds), *Early Greek Cult Practice*, pp. 69–80; and Burkert, *Greek Religion*, pp. 285–90.

8.   Sacrifice accompanying government: Rhodes, *The Athenian Boule*, pp. 127–34; frequency of Athenian sacrifice: Vincent J. Rosivach, *The System of Public Sacrifice in Fourth-Century Athens* (American Classical Studies, 34; Atlanta: American Philological Association, Scholars Press, 1994), p. 66.

9.   P.A. Meijer, 'Philosophers, Intellectuals and Religion', in H.S. Versnel (ed.), *Faith, Hope, and Worship: Aspects of Religious Mentality in the Ancient World* (SGRR, 2; Leiden: Brill, 1981), pp. 245–49. Despite Socrates' devasting assault against sacrifice in *Euthyphro*, he also observed proper sacrifices, 'Krito, we owe a cock to Asklepius; make certain you offer it and do not neglect it' (Plato *Phaed.* 118A; also Xenophon *Mem.* 1.3.3). The contrast between Socrates' verbal attack on sacrifice and his insistence on fulfilling his vow to Asclepius demonstrates the complexity and ambiguity of ancient attitudes toward animal sacrifice.

Euthyphro: Precisely, Socrates.
Socrates: It would seem then that holiness, from this definition, is a skilled knowledge of asking and giving… What is this service to the gods? You say, therefore, that it making requests of them and giving to them?
Euthyphro: Exactly.
Socrates: Therefore, Euthyphro, holiness would be some sort of skilled commerce between men and gods.
Euthyphro: Commerce, if you wish to call it that.
Socrates: What happens to be the advantage of the gifts to the gods which they receive from us?… What then would these gifts of ours to the gods be, Euthyphro?
Euthyphro: What other than *honor* and *praise* and, as I was just saying, *gratitude*? (excerpts from Plato *Euthyphr.* 14B–15A).

Likewise, Theophrastus argued that:

We must sacrifice to the gods for three reasons: to honor them, to thank them, or because we need something good. It is just as if we are dealing with good men, when we consider it necessary to make sacrifices of the first fruits [to the gods]. We honor the gods when avoiding evil things, or when we seek good things for future benefit, or when we have been well treated by them, not in order just for us to acquire some benefit, or because of simple respect for their good disposition toward us. (*Peri Eusebeias* fr. 12, ll. 43–48)[10]

Five centuries later, Artemidorus expressed a similar understanding of sacrifice: 'For people sacrifice to the gods when they have received benefits or when they have escaped some evil' (*Onir.* 2.33).[11]

For a Greco-Roman reader, Luke's narrative would seem to correlate precisely with these long-standing definitions of sacrifice. Paul and Barnabas do something beneficial for the lame man by healing him (Acts 14.10). Though Theophrastus' word ἀγαθός, 'good', does not appear in Luke's description of the healing, there is a conceptual parallel between the Lystran crowd's response and both Plato's *Euthyphro* and Theophrastus. In response to the miracle, the crowd wants to recognize or 'honor' the divinity of Paul and Barnabas by offering sacrifice to them. Conceptually, if not in exact vocabulary, the crowd attempts to offer, 'honor, praise, and gratitude' (τιμὴ καὶ γέρα καὶ χάρις). For a Greco-Roman, Luke describes an act fully comprehensible within the traditional framework of Greco-Roman sacrifice.

Greco-Roman Sacrificial Ritual
What was the sacrificial ritual? G.S. Kirk has summarized Homeric sacrificial procedure detecting some thirty steps from the bringing of the animal to the distribution and removal of the sacrificial remains (Table 3).[12] One example from the *Odyssey*:

10. My translation is informed by Jameson, 'Ritual and Sacrifice: Greece', *CAM* II, p. 975. Cf. Meijer, 'Philosophers, Intellectuals and Religions', pp. 250–60.
11. Robert J. White, trans., *The Interpretation of Dreams, Oneirocritca* (Noyes Classical Studies; Park Ridge, NJ: Noyes, 1975).
12. G.S. Kirk, 'Methodological Pitfalls', p. 64. Durand provides a detailed if theoretical and prolix discussion of the butchery and distribution of the sacrificial animal's corpse ('Greek Animals', pp. 87–118).

Stratios and noble Echephron led an ox by the horns, and Aretos [brought] them…water in a flower-decked cauldron; in the other hand he held barley-meal in a basket. Thrasymedes stood by with a sharp axe in his hand to strike the ox dead. Perseus held a bowl [to receive the blood]. Old Nestor…began to pour the water and sprinkle the barley-meal. He made many prayers to Athena, setting aside as first-fruits hairs from the victim's head and tossing them in the fire. When they had prayed and sprinkled out the barley… Thrasymedes…moved up and struck: the axe cut the neck tendons and stunned the ox. The women [in attendance] let out a shrill cry… The men raised it from the ground, and Peisistratos cut its throat. Its dark blood flowed out, its life left its bones. Straightway they quartered it, and cut off all the thigh-pieces, covered them with fat, folded them double, and placed pieces of raw flesh on them. The old man burnt them on split wood, and poured sparkling wine on it. The young men, beside him, held forked spits in their hands. When both the thighs had burned up and they had tasted the intestines, they cut the rest into smaller pieces and skewered them on spits, then took the sharp spits in their hands and roasted them (*Od.* 3.439–63).[13]

We can summarize Kirk's steps into five elements: (1) the procession, πομπή, of the priests, assistants and victims to the altar; (2) various pre-sacrificial rituals; (3) the slaughtering of the animal; (4) the holocaust, or burning and (5) the distribution of meat. Additionally, the Homeric text presents the personnel and physical elements needed for the sacrifice: the priest and assistants, the victim, miscellaneous ritual items and implements (water, wine, barley-meal, fire and firewood, the ax, etc.), and ritual decorations, the flower garlands. This ritual 'format' persisted from the Homeric era until the fourth century CE.[14] Lucian conveniently summarizes second century CE sacrificial ritual in a passage parallel to the Lukan account:

But those who sacrifice [θύοντες]…crown [στεφανώσαντες] the animal with garlands, after determining well in advance if it is perfect, so that they would not slaughter something of use. Then they lead the animal to the altar and kill it before the god's eyes…' (*Sacr.* 12)

These same five elements can be found in the elaborate descriptions of sacrificial rituals by Greek novelists in the third to fifth centuries CE. The third- to fourth-century CE novelist Heliodorus described a sacrificial procession in the city of Delphi that included garlanded sacrificial animals (including exactly one hundred bulls), the animal's slaughterers, young women singing hymns and carrying baskets full of flowers, fresh fruit, sweetmeats and spices, a troop of fifty young horsemen, and a young woman dressed as Artemis. The procession wound three times around the tomb of a local hero. Then the participants cried out loudly and the animals were immediately sacrificed. The priest of Pythian Apollo poured out a libation and the leader of the sacred mission lit the altar fire. (*Aeth.* 3.1–6).[15]

13. Trans. David G. Rice and John E. Stambaugh, *Sources for the Study of Greek Religion* (SBLSBS, 14; Missoula, MT: Scholars Press, 1979), p. 107.

14. Jameson, 'Sacrifice and Ritual: Greece', *CAM* II, pp. 960–61. Some historical development of sacrificial ritual did occur. Pausanias lists six different participants in a grain, i.e., bloodless sacrifice: the *theokolos* who holds office for the month supervises, the soothsayers, the libation-bearers, the *exegetes*, the flute-player, and the wood-man (5.15.10–12). In this same text, Pausanias also mentions the use of hymns, 'traditional words', and libations offered to various gods, heroes and wives of heroes.

15. See translation by J.R. Morgan, *CAGN*, pp. 409–15.

Table 3. *Homeric Sacrificial Procedure According to G. S. Kirk*[16]

1.	Animal(s) sent for
2.	Their horns are gilded
3.	The animal(s) are led forward to the altar
4.	Sacrificial party stations itself around altar
5.	Wine mixed
6.	The animal's hair cut and distributed
7.	The hair is thrown on the fire
8.	Sacrificial party washes hands
9.	Sacrificial party picks up barley grain
10.	Sacrificer prays
11.	Sacrificer pours libation
12.	Sacrificial party throws grain
13.	The victim is stunned
14.	Women in attendance cry out in a loud shriek
15.	The animal's blood is collected in a bowl
16.	Victim's neck held back
17.	Victim's throat cut
18.	Victim skinned
19.	Victim singed
20.	Thigh bones removed
21.	Thigh bones covered with double-fat
22.	Raw meat piled on thigh bones
23.	Thighs burned on wooden spits
24.	Sacrificer pours wine
25.	*Splanchna* roasted
26.	*Splanchna* spitted
27.	Thighs burned, *splanchna* eaten
28.	Remainder of animal cut up and roasted on spits
29.	Roasted meat removed from spits
30.	The participants eat the sacrificial meat and drink
31.	The remainder of the victim is apportioned to the onlookers with one portion reserved for the gods
32.	Victim(s) carried away

Longus' narrative of two rural sacrifices by a sheepherder suggests that the pea-
santry also preserved the complexity of traditional sacrificial ritual:

> Then he sent her to fetch Dryas and Lamon and their families and to bring what they
> needed for a sacrifice. Meanwhile he caught the best of the goats and put a garland
> [στεφανώσας] of ivy on it... Then he poured a libation of milk on its horns [κεράτων],
> sacrificed [ἔθυσέ] it to the Nymphs, and after hanging it up and skinning it, he presented
> the skin as a thank-offering.
>
> * * *
>
> They put a pine garland [στεφανώσαντες] on the he-goat that was the leader of the
> herd, led him to the pine, poured a libation of wine, and shouted in celebration of the
> god, before sacrificing [ἔθυσαν], hanging up, and skinning the goat. After roasting and
> boiling the meat, they placed it nearby on the leaves in the meadow. But they tied the
> skin, together with its horns, to the pine beside the image, a pastoral offering to a pastoral

16. Adapted from Kirk, 'Methodological Pitfalls', p. 64.

god. They made the first offerings of the meat to Pan and poured out libations from a
larger mixing bowl. Chloe sang, and Daphnis played the pipes. (*Daphn.* 2.30.5, 31.2–3)[17]

Greco-Roman Sacrificial Ritual in Acts 14.8–18

Below, I will examine four specific elements of sacrificial ritual found in Acts
14.8–18: the priest or ritual leader of the sacrifice (ὁ ἱερεύς), the sacrificial
victim (ὁ ταῦρος), the ritual ornamentation (τὰ στέμματα), the sacrificial ritual
procession (ἡ πομπή), and the timing and frequency of sacrificial ritual.

ὁ ἱερεύς: *The Priest at Lystra*

In Acts 14.8–18, Luke describes two social groups who respond to the lame man's
healing: the native Lystrans and the priest of Zeus. For my purposes, the priest of
Zeus is significant because Luke's readers would probably have expected him to
officiate at the would-be sacrifice and because, for such readers, he is the Greco-
Roman 'representative' of the Greco-Roman deity Zeus.

By the imperial era, a 'homogenous' Greco-Roman 'priestly system' had spread
throughout the Mediterranean.[18] Whatever the original form of local 'religious
authority'; local civic priesthoods increasingly modeled themselves after the
Roman 'euergetic' model. Local aristocrats or Roman colonists performed the
duties of the specific priesthood, which included supervising sacrifices and providing civic benefactions. Kleanax occupied the *prytaneis*, 'council chair', of
Kyme in Asia Minor:

> He celebrated the mysteries founded by the city, and paid all the expenses necessary for
> the five-yearly celebration of the mysteries, at which time the magnitude of the sums
> involved displayed his love of honor, and reverence for the gods, sums he alone paid and
> which he was the first to engage to pay, and having summoned the citizens, Romans,
> resident aliens, and strangers to the midday meal he extravagantly and sumptuously
> entertained in the sacred precinct of Dionysis.[19]

In the Roman colonies of Asia Minor, resettled veterans promptly organized
their local religious offices parallel to that of Rome.[20] At Antioch, there were

17. Christopher Gill (trans.), 'Daphnis and Chloe', *CAGN*.

18. Following Gordon, 'The Veil of Power', pp. 224–31; *idem*, 'Religion in the Roman Empire',
pp. 240–45. Gordon notes and explains the exceptional circumstances of Roman Egypt ('Religion in
the Roman Empire', in Beard and North [eds], *Pagan Priests* pp. 241–42).

19. Trans. following Gordon, 'The Veil of Power', p. 226. Discussion and Greek text in P. Hodot,
'Décret de Kymè en l'honneur du prytane Kleanax', *The J. Paul Getty Museum Journal* 10 (1982),
pp. 165–80; and J. and L. Robert, *Bulletin Epigraphique* (1983), no. 323.

Kleanax is an example of the 'tricultural' complexity of Roman Asia Minor and its institutions that
combined native Anatolian, Greek, and Roman culture. See further P.M. Fraser, 'The Kings of Commagene', pp. 359–74; Richard D. Sullivan, 'Priesthoods of the Eastern Dynastic Aristocracy', pp. 914–39;
and Houwink ten Cate, *The Luwian Population Groups of Lycia*, esp. pp. 205, 201–203.

20. For the history of these colonies, their administration, social class, and other matters along with
Roman rule in Asia Minor generally, see A.H.M. Jones, *The Cities of the Eastern Roman Provinces*
(Oxford: Oxford University Press, 2nd, edn, 1971); David Magie, *Roman Rule in Asia Minor* (2 vols;

augurs, pontiffs, and *flamines*; at Lystra, the pontificate and a *sacerdos Mariti*, priest of Mars.[21] The same person held both the Antiochene pontificate and the office of ἀρχιερεύς for the local god Mên. The second- or third-century CE epigraphic evidence for these offices post-dates the writing of Acts. However, there is direct epigraphic evidence that the Romans instituted the pontificate in Antioch shortly after founding the city in 25 BCE.[22] The Roman colonists possibly founded the other priestly offices about the same time.

At Antioch the quaestors were responsible for the city's regular financial affairs.[23] At Kara Kuyu, the *curator arcae santuarii* was responsible for the financial affairs of the local temple of Mên. According to Strabo (12.8.14), the Romans had broken up the existing native cultic personnel.[24] Because one function of a Roman colony was to spread Roman culture and because the cult was non-Roman *and* non-Greek, the Romans assumed both financial (the *curator arcae santuarii*) and cultic (the pontifex who was also the ἀρχιερεύς or high priest of Mên) control of the cult.

Epigraphic evidence demonstrates the existence of both the pontificate and the *sacerdos* at Lystra. As mentioned above, Roman policy in the colonies of Asia

Princeton: Princeton University Press, 1950); and Barbara Levick, *Roman Colonies in Asia Minor* (Oxford: Oxford University Press, 1967).

For Lystra specifically: W.M. Ramsay, *St. Paul the Traveler and the Roman Citizen* (New York: Putnam's, 1902), pp. 114–116; *idem*, *The Cities of St. Paul: Their Influence on His Life and Thought* (The Dale Memorial Lectures; New York: George H. Doran; London: Hodder & Stoughton, 1907), pp. 407–18; Jones, *Cities*, pp. 123–46, esp. pp. 134–35; Magie, *Roman Rule*, I, pp. 462–63; vol. 2, pp. 1324; and Levick, *Roman Colonies*, pp. 14, 39, 51–53, 66 n. 8, 76–79, 94–95, 128, 134, 153–57, 159, 183, 196–97, 222 n. 3.

Wordelmann details the history of Lycaonia, 'Gods Have Come Down', pp. 102–35. William M. Ramsay collected the inscriptions pertinent to Lystra, other parts of Asia Minor, and various aspects of life and society in Roman Asia Minor (*The Social Basis of Roman Power in Asia Minor* [Aberdeen: Aberdeen University Press, 1941; repr., Amsterdam: Hakkert, 1967], pp. 36–37, no. 26; pp. 167–69, nos. 164, 180–83, 184–99).

21. Offices at Antioch: the augurs: W.M. Calder, 'Colonia Caesareia Antiocheia', *JRS* 2 (1912), pp. 79–120, 99 no. 31; David Moore Robinson, 'Greek and Latin Inscriptions from Asia Minor', *TAPA* 57 (1926), pp. 195–237; 225 n. 51; the pontificate: J.G.C. Anderson, 'Festivals of Mên Askaênos in the Roman Colonia at Antioch of Pisidia', *JRS* 3 (1913), pp. 267–300; 291, n. 20; *flamines*: W.M. Ramsay, 'Colonia Caesarea (Pisidean Antioch) in the Augustan Age', *JRS* 6 (1916), pp. 83–134; 106, fig. 10; *idem*, 'Studies in the Roman Province Galatia VI. Some Inscriptions of Colonia Caesarea Antiochea', *JRS* 14 (1924), pp. 172–205; p. 197 n. 27; *CIL* 3.6837 (=*ILS* 5081); Robinson, 'Greek and Latin Inscriptions', p. 221 n. 44. At Lystra; the pontificate: *MAMA* 8.12; the *sacerdotes*: *CIL* 3.14400.

22. Levick, *Roman Colonies*, pp. 68–91, esp. pp. 87–88 and 91. Primary sources: *ILS* 9502f.; William Ramsay, 'Studies in the Roman Province Galatia VI', p. 178 n. 5 (=*ILS* 3.6832); and p. 201 n. 39.

23. Summarizing Levick, *Roman Colonies*, pp. 85–87.

24. Strabo: 'Here there was also a temple of Mên Arkaios which had many temple slaves and sacred districts. The priesthood was destroyed after the death of Amyntas [king of Galatia, died 25 BCE] by those sent as his inheritors'. See Magie, *Roman Rule*, I, pp. 139–142; 457; and 1316 n. 22; II, pp. 1016–17 n. 62; and T. Robert S. Broughton, 'New Evidence on Temple Estates in Asia Minor', in P.R. Coleman-Norton (ed.), *Studies in Roman Economic and Social History in Honor of Allan Chester Johnson* (Princeton: Princeton University Press, 1951), pp. 236–50.

Minor tended towards replacing the native priest of local and Hellenistic cults with Roman colonists. Because of this tendency, Luke probably describes the historical *sacerdos* (a Roman colonist or a local Hellenistic aristocrat) when he uses ἱερεύς and does not refer to a local priest of Mên. Even if Luke is describing local priest of Mên, his Greco-Roman audience would probably have understood and assumed a reference to the euergetic Romanized priest. For a Greco-Roman audience, this cultural background possibly distinguished the priest of Zeus from the local Lystran population because they understood him to be either a local aristocrat or a Roman colonist.

A Greco-Roman reader may have perceived a subtle ironic contrast (see below) between the aristocratic priest and the indigenous population in Acts 14.8–18. The priest, a member of the local elite or a resettled Roman veteran, neither expresses nor confirms his political and social power in the sacrificial ritual.[25] Instead the very person who should control civic religious expressions appears to be responding 'after the fact'.

ὁ ταῦρος: *The Sacrificial Victim*

What was the significance of the bull in Greco-Roman sacrificial ritual and for Luke's Greco-Roman readership? Despite older theories about fertility and power symbolism, the probable actual significance is quite simple: the greater the quantity of meat, the more the gods are honored. In Herodas, *Mim.* 4.14–16, two women sacrifice a cock because they are poor; otherwise they would have sacrificed an ox or a pig, 'For we draw little from our wells;/sometimes nothing at all/otherwise an ox or a farm-fresh crackling pig, and not a cock'.[26] Drawing on evidence from inscriptions and votive reliefs, van Straten showed that bulls accounted for less than twelve per cent of recorded sacrificial victims.[27] Only civic cults sponsored by the deme, the entire *polis*, or elite benefactors could generally afford to sacrifice a large animal such as a bull.

Additionally, Luke and his audience probably considered bulls the most appropriate sacrificial victims for Zeus. Certain gods required certain types of sacrifice and prohibited others. Aristophanes wrote, 'but a pig is no sacrifice for Aphrodite!' (*Ach.* 793) Pausanias records a similar prohibition at Aphrodite's sanctuary in Corinth, 'but they offer the thighs of the sacrificial victims, except for pigs' (2.10.5). An inscription from Athens carefully specifies the sacrificial animal needed for various Athenian religious festivals: a sheep for Ge 'at the oracle', an ox, three sheep, and a pig for Athena Helliotis, a ram and three pigs for Kore, and

---

25. M.F.C. Bourdillon, Introduction, in M.F.C. Bourdillon and Meyer Fortes (eds), *Sacrifice* (London: Academic Press, Royal Anthropological Institute of Great Britain and Ireland, 1980), p. 21.

26. My translation follows the commentary and translation of I.C. Cunningham (ed.), *Herodas Mimiambi* (Oxford: Clarendon; Oxford University Press, 1971), pp. 131–32.

27. Van Straten, 'Greek Sacrificial Representations', pp. 164–67; *idem, Hierà Kalá*, pp. 170–86 esp. pp. 175–81 and Michael Jameson, 'Sacrifice and Animal Husbandry', in Whittaker (ed.), *Pastoral Economics*, pp. 87–119. The cheapest bull was 40 drachmae, the most expensive sheep 17, and the most expensive pig 40.

so on.[28] Some festivals closely associated bull sacrifice with Zeus. Bulls were the appropriate sacrifice at the Olympiads (Dio Chrysostom *Dei cogn.* 51 [= *Or.* 12.51]). One of the important Athenian New Year festivals was the Bouphonia. the 'ox murder', that was performed at the Akropolis in honor of Δίς Πολίευς, 'Zeus, Guardian of the City' (Porphyry *Abst.* 2.28–30).[29] A Greco-Roman may have brought such assumptions of the relationship between the type of sacrificial animal, a bull, and a sacrifice to Zeus when reading Luke's narrative.

In Acts 14.13, Luke describes the attempted sacrifice of *several bulls*, or at least more than one (masculine accusative plural, τοὺς ταύρους), to Paul and Barnabas. In terms of both piety and economics, Lystra's civic cult makes an extravagant offering by attempting to sacrifice several bulls. A benefactor, such as the priest or a local official, would sponsor such an offering or the *polis* as a whole would finance it. A Greco-Roman audience would see not only a commonly understood cultural convention, bull sacrifices, but also may have assumed governmental or euergetic sponsorship of this offering.

The mention of the bulls heightens the Lystran misapprehension of Paul and Barnabas for Greco-Romans. Elsewhere, Luke describes both apostles as tradesmen: Barnabas, a diaspora Levite, has property that he can sell on behalf of the church (Acts 4.36) and Paul is a σκηνοποιὸς τῇ τέχνῃ, 'a tent maker by trade' (Acts 18.3). The crowd and the priest offer both non-elite apostles two or more bulls as sacrificial offerings; an economic extravagance suitable for gods and perhaps heroes but most certainly not for Judean craftsmen.

τὰ στέμματα: *Ritual Ornaments*

Luke mentions 'bringing…bulls and garlands [or 'wreaths']', ταύρους καὶ στέμματα…ἐνέγκας, an essential element of Greco-Roman sacrificial ritual. Karl Baus reviewed the literary and artistic evidence and concluded that offering sacrifices and wearing wreaths were thus two closely connected activities in antiquity.[30] Lucian attests to such ritual use, 'crowning [στεφανώσαντες] the [sacrificial] animal with garlands' (*Sacr.* 12), as do the Greek novelists (Longus *Daphn.* 2.30–31, Heliodorus *Aeth.* 3.1). Numerous reliefs, vase paintings, and other art forms depict the sacrificial animal wearing garlands and being led to the sacrifice.[31]

Baus considered Luke's terminology 'ambiguous', *mehrdeutig*, because it is not clear whether Luke means 'garlands', 'wreaths' or 'wool bands'. Baus suggested

28. *IG* II² 1358, col. 2, ll. 1–53, English trans. in Rice and Stambaugh (eds), *Sources for the Study*, pp. 113–15; discussion in R.B. Richardson, 'A Sacrificial Calendar from the Epakia', *AJA* 10 (1895), pp. 209–26.

29. For the Bouphonia, see Burkert, *Homo Necans*, pp. 136–43.

30. Karl Baus, *Der Kranz in Antike und Christentum: Eine religionsgeschichtliche Untersuchung mit besonder Berüsichtigugen Tertullians* (Theophaneia: Beiträge zur Relgions und Kirchengeschichte des Altertums, 2; Bonn: Hanstein, 1940), p. 10; also, Ludwig Deubner, 'Die Bedeutung des Kranzes im klassischen Altertum', *ARW* 30 (1933), pp. 70–104; and van Straten, *Hierà Kalá*, pp. 43–45.

31. For garlands (στέμματα) in ancient Greek sacrifices: van Straten, *Hierà Kalá*, pp. 206, 208–209, 265, figs. 17, 43, 45–46; in ancient Roman sacrifices: Everett Ferguson, *Backgrounds of Early Christianity* (Grand Rapids: Eerdmanns, 3rd edn, 2003), p. 189.

that the garlands were for decorating the altar.[32] Luke's terminology is ambiguous, because, as Baus demonstrated, the semantic fields and linguistic usages of ὁ στέφανος, τὸ στέμμα, and *corona* to refer to garlands and wreaths overlapped. Further, τὸ στέμμα could also refer to 'wool bands'. According to Herodas these wool bands were a necessary ornament for the sacrificial animal, 'But we want/a wool band [στέμμα] for sacrifice. There is not the least bit of wool fleece in this house for us' (*Mim.* 8.12–13).[33] Whatever the exact nature of these ornaments, Luke is overtly mentioning an important constituent element of Greco-Roman sacrificial ritual. The ancient Greeks consistently demarcated their rituals into the sacred and profane spheres by various means, including clothing and ornamentation.[34] For Greco-Roman readers, Luke's mention of the στέμματα reinforces the crowd's misunderstanding of Paul and Barnabas as sacred and divine.

ἡ πομπή: The Procession

Most public Greco-Roman religious expressions included πομπαί, processions.[35] Sacrificial rituals included public processions of priests, assistants, sacrificial victim(s), and people carrying various ritual implements.[36] These processions had various contextual functions: displays of wealth, elite honors, promotion of shared values, the movement from profane space to ritual space, and simply the physical moving of the sacrificial victim to the place of sacrifice.[37] After Peisistratus regained control of Athens, he had Phyle, an extremely tall woman, dressed as Athena and had her processed into the city on a chariot in order to proclaim the reestablishment of the relationship between the city and the goddess (Herodotus, 1.60.2–5). Plutarch describes Demetrius Poliorketes' processional entrance (290 BCE) into Athens underscoring both the Athenians' acceptance and recognition of

32. Baus, *Der Kranz in Antike*, pp. 13–15 , esp. p. 14, n. 84. Michael Blech reached similar conclusions, calling the meaning of στέμμα *unscharf*, 'blurred, fuzzy, or unclear', *Studien zum Kranz bei den Griechen* (Religionsgeschichtliche Versuche und Vorarbeiten 38; Berlin and New York: Walter de Gruyter, 1982), pp. 30; 31 n. 31, 239 n. 144, 245, 275 n. 27, and esp. pp. 304–305, quoting p. 304.

33. My translation, following, Cunningham, *Herodas Mimiambi*, p. 198.

34. Jameson, 'Sacrifice and Ritual: Greece', *CAM* II, p. 964.

35. Martin Nilsson outlines the various types of Greek religious processions, 'Die Prozessionstypen im griechischen Kult', in *idem*, *Opuscula Selecta* (3 vols; Skrifter Utgivna av Svensak Institute I Athen, 8°, ser. 2, no. 2; Lund: Gleerup, 1951), I, pp. 166–213, esp. pp. 166–71. Also, Burkert, *Greek Religion*, pp. 99–102, 387–88; and van Straten, *Hierà Kalá*, pp. 10–11, 13–24.

36. Jameson, 'Sacrifice and Ritual: Greece', *CAM*, II, pp. 959–80; North, 'Sacrifice and Ritual: Rome', pp. 981–86; Detienne, *Cuisine of Sacrifice Among the Greeks*; and Zaidman and Schmitt Pantel, *Religion in the Ancient Greek City*, pp. 28–39.

37. On the contextual and multiple 'meanings' of Greek religious processions, see W.R. Connor, 'Tribes, Festivals and Processions', *JHS* 107 (1987), pp. 40–50; S. Goldhill, 'The Great Dionysia and Civic Ideology', *JHS* 107 (1987), pp. 58–76; Rogers, *The Sacred Identity of Ephesos*; Susan Guettel Cole, 'Procession and Celebration at the Dionysia', in Ruth Scodel (ed.), *Theater and Society in the Classical World* (Ann Arbor: The University of Michigan Press, 1993), pp. 25–38 and Lilian Portefaix, 'Ancient Ephesus: Processions as Media of Religious and Secular Propaganda', in Tore Ahlbäck (ed.), *The Problem of Ritual: Based on Papers Read at the Symposium on Religious Rites at Åbo, Finland, on the 13th-16th of August 1991* (Scripta Instituti Donneriani Aboensis, 15; Stockholm: Almqvist & Wicksell, 1993), pp. 195–210.

Demetrius' power and his hybris (*Dem*. 10). The two third century CE novelists
Xenophon of Ephesus (*Ephesiaka* 1.2) and Heliodorus (*Aeth*. 3.1–6). described
sacrificial processions in honor of Artemis that served to showcase the elite youth
and their splendid attributes and to bring the necessary sacrificial implements,
personnel, and victims to Artemis' altar for the sacrifice.

For Greco-Romans, Luke's mention of the procession would have emphasized
the attribution of divinity to Paul and Barnabas by the Lystrans. Such readers
may have also seen hints of the reciprocal relationship between the crowd and the
elite priest. The crowd shows its devotion by either witnessing the procession or
joining in it. The priest maintains elite control by providing both the procession
and the sacrificial victims in order to acknowledge the crowd's religious claims
about Paul and Barnabas.

Ritual Frequency

In Luke's portrayal of the sacrificial ritual in Acts 14.13 the sacrifice to Paul and
Barnabas appears spontaneous and instantaneous; the priest merely has to bring
the bulls and slay them on the spot at the temple of Zeus or the city gates.[38] In
reality, the complexity of the ritual itself precluded instantaneous sacrifices. When
Telemachos visits Nestor, Nestor arranges a sacrifice (*Od*. 3.418–63). To prepare
the sacrificial heifer properly, Nestor has Laerkes the goldsmith summoned, who
then gilds the heifer's horns for the sacrifice (*Od*. 3.432–35). Homer implies that
the gold must be melted and then applied to the animal's horns, a time-consuming
process. Eumaios sacrifices a hog when visited by Odysseus (*Od*. 14.414–38,
446–67).[39] In one sense, Eumaios' sacrifice is spontaneous since he performs it as
an act of welcome for an unexpected visitor. However, he must send servants to
fetch the hog while he chops wood for the hearth. After the hog arrives, Eumaios
performs the sacrifice. In Longus' third-century CE description of private rural
sacrifices, Daphnis has to catch the sacrificial victim, garland it, pour a libation,
sacrifice the animal, skin it, dedicate the skin to the gods, and roast and cook the
meat (*Daphn*. 30.5, 31.2–3). In these private sacrifices, the complexity of the
sacrificial ritual precludes instantaneous sacrifice.

For both private and civic sacrifices, time was necessary to prepare all the steps
involved in the sacrifice.[40] The στέμματα, wool bands or floral garlands, appear
carefully crafted when depicted on Greek vase paintings and Roman reliefs.[41]

38. Luke's narrative does not specify the attempted sacrifice's location. Kee suggests that the
sacrifice was at the temple of Zeus (*To Every Nation*, p. 173). Several exegetes place the sacrifice at the
city gates (Haenchen, *Acts*, p. 427 nn. 4–5, 428; Johnson, *Acts*, p. 248; Talbet, *Reading Acts*, p. 133;
Witherington, *Acts*, p. 425). Conzelmann concludes that the location is unclear (*Acts*, p. 110). Bruce
agrees that the text is unclear but suggests the temple, city gates or the door to the house where the
missionaries were staying as possibilities (*Acts*, p. 322).

39. On Eumaios' sacrifice, see Edward Kadletz, 'The Sacrifice of Eumaios the Pig Herder', *GRBS*
25 (1984), pp. 99–105.

40. An anachronistic modern parallel is the time required to plan and rehearse graduation, wedding,
and 'high church' processions.

41. Ancient Greek sacrifices: van Straten, *Hierà Kalá*, pp. 206, 208–209, 265, figs. 17, 43, 45–46;
ancient Roman sacrifices: Ferguson, *Backgrounds of Early Christianity*, p. 189.

Unless the στέμματα were immediately available – which seems doubtful – they would require prior weaving. Also time was required for the assistants in the sacrifice to assemble, decorate, and process the sacrificial animals. For example, in Xenophon's *Ephesiaka*, when Perilaus makes the necessary preparations for his wedding to Anthia he 'had sacrificial animals brought in from the countryside' (3.3). In Heliodorus, a number of pirates were 'sent out to buy cattle from the surrounding countryside' (*Aeth.* 5.27.9). A Greco-Roman reader would have noted the hurried nature of Luke's narrative and that Luke skips over the details involved in a sacrifice.[42]

Classical Athens centrally regulated public sacrifices.[43] Individuals could offer private devotions to any deity, but public cult for a specific deity occurred only after proper approval. The Athenian victory over the Persians at Marathon in 490 BCE was in part attributed to Pan.[44] Before this, Pan was essentially a rustic deity receiving cult in the Attic countryside. After 490 BCE, Pan formally received a shrine, annual sacrifices and a torch race at state expense (Herodotus 6.105.3). In 399, Socrates was charged for ἕτερα...εἰσηγούμενος, 'introducing other new gods (καινὰ δαιμόνια) [or "daimonic beings"]' (Diogenes Laertius 2.40).[45] This 'new god' seems to have been a private oracle that prompted Socrates to withdraw from participation in public life including sacrifices. This 'new god' also impinged directly upon the Demos' self-understanding that it and it alone determined the gods that Athenian democracy would recognize and worship.[46]

The Romans also carefully controlled new gods and their public cult, 'No one shall have gods to himself, either new gods or alien gods, unless recognized by the state' (Cicero *Leg.* 2.8).[47] Asclepius was not accepted at Rome until formally invited by the Roman Senate in 293 BCE to intervene on the city's behalf during a plague. In 291, the Romans built a temple and dedicated it to Asclepius on the *isola Tiberi*. From that time on, Asclepius received formal cult (Livy 10.47.6–7, *Epit.* 11; Ovid *Metam.* 15.622–743, *Fast.* 1.289–94). Spontaneous, instantaneous public sacrifices probably did not exist within the carefully regulated complexity

42. This 'narrative compression' of sacrificial ritual frequently occurs in the novelists. Examples include Achilles Tatius *Leuc. Clit.* 2.15–18, Xenophon of Ephesus *Ephesiaka* 5.15.2, and Chariton *Chaer.* 3.7–8. Presumably, the novelists' audience would have the shared cultural knowledge to form a complete image of the sacrifice in their imaginations. In his *Aethiopika*, Heliodorus plays on this very technique of narrative compression. A narrator within the story attempts to merely sum up the details of a sacrificial procession and ritual. His listener interrupts and demands the complete details about the procession and the sacrifice (*Aeth.* 3.1.1–2).

43. Rhodes, *The Athenian Boule*, pp. 127–34; Garland, *Introducing New Gods*, pp. 23–46.

44. Following Garland, *Introducing New Gods*, pp. 47–63.

45. My discussion follows Garland, *Introducing New Gods*, pp. 136–51. There are monumental interpretive difficulties surrounding the accusations against Socrates, his defense, and his trial, which are beyond this discussion; see Garland for details.

It is difficult to translate δαιμόνια. The alternate translation in brackets is Garland's (*Introducing New Gods*, p. 137).

46. Garland, *Introducing New Gods*, p. 151. Garland briefly discusses other examples of 'illicit religious innovation' in ancient Athens, p. 150.

47. Clinton Walter Keyes, trans., *Cicero De Legibus* (LCL; Cambridge, MA: Harvard University Press, 1928).

of civic cult. Greco-Roman readers would probably have noted the seemingly extra-legal nature of the attempted sacrifice in Luke's narrative.

Both private and civic sacrifices were not spontaneous, instantaneous affairs; they required planning and time to prepare. Luke has radically condensed the necessary time interval in his narrative in Acts 14.1–19 either by altering an historical account for his needs or freely creating part or all of this narrative. His Greco-Roman audience would perhaps have noted the peculiarity of the sacrificial ritual in Acts 14.1–13.

Greco-Romans Read Reversals

A Greco-Roman audience may have seen three ironic reversals in Acts 14.8-18 and possibly interpreted these reversals as a condemnation of Greco-Roman sacrifice. First, these readers may have seen an allusion to the expected social division between the local Lycaonian populace and the implied Greco-Roman priest. They may have seen a reversal of the expected norm for Greco-Roman social structure. Greco-Romans may have observed Greek social relations as being 'stood on its head'.[48] The priest does not control either the timing of the sacrifice or the intended divine recipient. The crowd supposes Paul and Barnabas to be gods because of the healing power they display. The priest comes running with victims and ornaments for the sacrifice because he 'desired (ἤθελεν) to sacrifice (θύειν) *with* (σύν) the crowd' (Acts 14.13). The crowd believes it recognizes two gods, Zeus and Hermes, in Paul and Barnabas. The logical Greco-Roman response is to offer Paul and Barnabas worship. The priest does not initiate the sacrificial procedure but, within Luke's narrative, seems to be 'breathlessly' attempting to align his duties as the civic religious officiant to the crowd's desire to offer worship. A Greco-Roman reader would have probably recognized that although the crowd is fundamentally mistaken about the nature of Paul and Barnabas, the Lycaonians properly respond, in Greco-Roman terms, to manifestations of divine power in their midst. The priest comes to this realization late (or not at all?) and brings the trappings of 'official' civic cult for use by the crowd. The irony is that the depiction of social roles that Luke's ancient audience would have expected has been reversed. The elite Greco-Roman priest does not respond to Paul and Barnabas' healing of the lame man in 14.8–10 while the non-elite

---

48. See Stowers' model, 'Greeks Who Sacrifice', pp. 325–29.

Despite Luther H. Martin's assertion to the contrary, Luke does not narrate an invitation to a civic communal meal related to a sacrifice, 'Gods or Ambassadors of God?', pp. 152–56. Martin's analysis profitably introduces the question of ambassadorship into the scholarly discussion of Acts 14.8–18. However, his argument far exceeds the Lukan text, 'Lystran hospitality is represented…by the apparently extravagant gesture of sacrifice by the priests [*sic*] of Lystra [which]…is better understood as an invitation to honour Barnabas and Paul by including these foreign dignitaries in the local civic ceremonies of the Lystrans', p. 155. Unless we accept the variant reading οἱ δὲ ἱερεῖς of D and gig, there is only one priest present in the text. Also, Luke specifically states that Paul and Barnabas *were acclaimed gods* in 14.12–13, which then leads to Paul's response in the speech of 14.15–18.

Lycaonians respond immediately. The expected religious insight and control of the elite priest and the expected incomprehension of the non-elite are reversed.

Secondly, the culturally expected imagery of a Greco-Roman sacrificial procession may have appeared ironically reversed to Greco-Romans (Table 4). The 'meaning' of sacrificial processions could include the movement from profane to sacred space. The sacrificial animals are led from their pasture in the 'mundane' world to the τέμενος or sacred space of the sacrificial altar.[49] The priest of Acts 14.13 leads the sacrificial bulls not to a τέμενος but instead directly to Paul and Barnabas. In Luke's narrative, the sacred space is apart from either the sacred compound (τέμενος) or the the temple of Zeus-before-the-city. Instead, for both the crowd and the priest, sacred space is present where Paul and Barnabas are present.[50] The sacrificial bulls are led to the direct presence of the gods. But the so-called gods, Paul and Barnabas, deny their divinity and defer the notion of sacred space away from themselves. In fact, the reader does not find sacred space defined in Paul's speech, 14.14–18. Paul points to the living God, θεὸν ζῶντα, who acted through time, ἐν ταῖς παρῳχημέναις γενεαῖς. Paul also extends sacred space to encompass God acting in history and in a very real sense to the entire κόσμος because God acts in ὁ οὐρανὸς καὶ ἡ γῆ, 'heaven and earth'.

Table 4. *Luke's Ironic Inversions of Greco-Roman Sacrificial Processions*

Greco-Roman Sacrificial Procession	Luke's Inversion
The procession honors Greco-Roman gods	The sacrificial party intends to honor Paul and Barnabas, who are merely human (14.15)
Processional heralds [εὐαγγελιζόμενοι] lead the procession	Paul and Barnabas are processional heralds [εὐαγγελιζόμενοι] for Lukan Christianity (14.15)
The procession is oriented to 'empty things' = Zeus and Hermes	Paul and Barnabas desire to turn the procession from 'empty things' to the living God (14.15)
Zeus and Hermes were created (Hesiod *Theogeny*)	The 'living God' made the cosmos (14.15)
Each ethnic group (Greeks, Romans, barbarians) has their own sacrificial procession for their own gods (14.16)	Paul and Barnabas desire to turn the procession of Lystrans and Greco-Romans to the living God (14.15)
The human procession ultimately offers sacrificial food to the gods	God provides rain from heaven, harvests, food and joyful hearts (14.17) to humanity
Participants receive the heart, καρδία, of the animal in the Greco-Roman post-sacrificial feast.	God fills human hearts with joy (14.17)

This narrative evokes, especially for a Greco-Roman reader, the image of a sacrifical procession. However, this very vocabulary and narrative reverses the system of Greco-Roman sacrificial processions. At the point of attempted sacrifice (14.13) Paul's speech (14.14–18) interrupts the narrative of the sacrificial

49. E.g., Aristophanes, *Pax* 956–60; and Euripides *Iph. taur.* 1568–72. See Jameson, 'Sacrifice and Ritual: Greece', pp. 967–68.
50. Cf. Lake and Cadbury, *Beginnings*, IV, p. 165.

procession. In this speech, Paul denies being divine: 'We are humans of the same nature [ὁμοιοπαθεῖς] as you' (14.15).[51] Paul calls both Barnabas and himself 'proclaimers' or 'heralds', εὐαγγελιζόμενοι, of 'good news', at the head of a Lystran procession (14.15). They are trying to turn [ἐπιστρέφειν] the procession around from empty [i.e.,Greco-Roman, ἀπὸ τούτων τῶν ματαίων] religious practices to the living God [ἐπὶ θεὸν ζῶντα] (14.15). This God, 'made the realm of the divine and the earth and the sea and everything in them', ἐποίησεν τὸν οὐρανὸν καὶ τὴν γῆν καὶ τὴν θάλασσαν καὶ πάντα τὰ ἐν αὐτοῖς (14.15), unlike Zeus and the other Greco-Roman gods who themselves are children of divinities, born after the creation of the universe (Hesiod *Theogeny*). Before the arrival of the heralds Paul and Barnabas, God 'permitted' [εἴασεν] each ethnic group [i.e., Greeks, Romans, barbarians, πάντα τὰ ἔθνη], 'to go their own way' or 'have their own procession' [πορεύεσθαι ταῖς ὁδοῖς αὐτῶν], 'through time' [ἐν ταῖς παρῳχημέναις γενεαῖς] (14.16).[52] Not only did the living God 'provide rain from heaven' but also 'harvests and food and joy' (14.17). Humanity does not offer food to the gods; rather the living creator God provides humanity with food. For the reader, there is a final ironic note. Humanity does not receive the heart, καρδία, of the animal, as happens in the Greco-Roman post-sacrificial feast (Table 4). Instead God fills human hearts with joy.

Greco-Roman readers may have also noted a third use of irony in the reversal of the narrative roles of Paul and Barnabas when the crowd call Barnabas Zeus and Paul Hermes (Table 5).[53] Barnabas disappears from Acts after 15.39, having separated from Paul over the dispute about John Mark. Before this controversy, he is Paul's companion but not the chief actor in the narrative. After that point, the narrative centers entirely around Paul. Barnabas is acclaimed as the chief god of the Greco-Roman pantheon but is a 'minor character' in Luke's narrative.

Table 5. *Paul and Barnabas as Narratival Inversions of Hermes and Zeus*

Greco-Roman Religion	Lukan Ironic Reversal
Zeus is leader and chief of the gods. Hermes is a lesser god, the messenger	Paul (Luke's protagonist) is hailed as the messenger. Barnabas (a secondary character) is hailed as the leader.
Hermes is the messenger of the Greco-Roman pantheon.	Paul, hailed as Hermes, is the messenger of the God of the Christians and Judeans.

Since Paul is the central character in Luke's narrative, the crowd should logically acclaim him as Zeus. However, the crowd acclaims him as Hermes, the messenger of the gods who speaks for the Greco-Roman pantheon. Ironically,

51. Both Lerle and Soards fail to connect the speech's vocabulary to the preceding attempted sacrifice (Lerle, 'Die Predigt in Lystra'; Soards, *The Speeches in Acts*, pp. 88–90).

52. These three ethnic groups are implied in the narrative. The Lycaonians, barbarians in Greco-Roman terms, are mentioned by their language in 14.11. Luke's mention of Zeus and Hermes implies Greeks. Because Lystra is a Roman colony, the priest, a community leader, may imply an upper class Roman colonist.

53. Even if this acclamation was an historical event, it appears ironic within the narrative.

Paul, acclaimed as the messenger for the Greco-Roman gods, speaks for the God of the early Christians and the Judeans.

In summary, Greco-Romans would have probably seen an inversion of the social hierarchy of Greco-Roman sacrifice. They may have noted a contrast between the processional language and imagery in the attempted sacrifice of v. 13 and the speech of vv. 15–18. They may have also observed subtle irony in the characterization of Barnabas as the head of the divine pantheon and of Paul as the pantheon's messenger. Careful readers would have most likely perceived this as an example of the theme of reversal found throughout Luke-Acts.[54] Luke explicitly declares this theme in the Magnificat (Lk. 1.46–55) and Jesus' inaugural sermon (Lk. 4.1–21). In Acts 14.8–18, this reversal seems to depict the Greco-Roman sacrificial system in satirical terms: the lower class takes the initiative, the upper class responds after the fact, cult is offered to very non-heroic human men. Reading this passage, a Greco-Roman may have concluded that humans do not provide for God through sacrificial cult. Instead God provides for humanity and is to be recognized as God through God's act as creator.[55]

Conclusions

Luke very briefly, almost as an aside, mentions Greco-Roman sacrificial procedure by referring to a priest leading garlanded bulls in procession in Acts 14.13. Reading this brief comment, a Greco-Roman audience may have understood a subtle parodying allusion to the central act of Greco-Roman religious ritual throughout the classical, Hellenistic, and early imperial Roman worlds. Furthermore, they may have seen a reversal pattern in the reactions of the crowd and the priest. The crowd immediately (mis)perceives the significance of Barnabas and Paul. Instead of providing the legitimating authority for this new cult of Zeus and Hermes, the elite Greco-Roman priest merely responds to the behavior of the non-Greco-Roman or 'barbarous' crowd.

After reading this highly condensed account of an attempted sacrifice, a Greco-Roman audience may have detected another literary reversal. Paul attempts to show in his speech that God provides 'for all nations' [πάντα τὰ ἔθνη], including those who 'he allowed...to go their way' [εἴασεν πορεύεσθαι ταῖς ὁδοῖς αὐτῶν]. Greco-Roman sacrifice was predicated on a a medium of exchange, τέχνη ἐμπορική, between the gods and humanity. For Luke's audience, Paul's speech not only condemns offering worship to mere mortals and calling them god, but also insists that there is no 'medium of exchange', only God's goodness toward humanity.

Greco-Romans may have noticed that Acts 14.8–18, as well as Acts 12.2–23, sharply divides humanity and God into two separate spheres. In contrast to Agrippa's acceptance of worship, here Paul and Barnabas refuse it. They refuse

54. See, e.g., Tannehill, *Narrative Unity*, I, pp. 29–31; Frederick W. Danker, *Luke* (Proclamation Commentaries; Philadelphia: Fortress Press, 2nd, edn, 1987), pp. 37–47; and York, *The Last Shall Be First*.

55. Following Soard's brief discussion (*The Speeches in Acts*, pp. 89–90).

sacrifice, the ritual heart of public Greco-Roman religion. Greco-Roman readers may have also understood Greco-Roman sacrifice as being condemned by the use of literary reversal and humor. Based on this understanding, they may have interpreted Acts 14.8–18 as saying that, humanity is humanity; God is God. Only God acts for humanity or acts through divinely appointed emissaries; humanity does not act for God through sacrificial ritual. Reading the account of the attempted sacrifice to Paul and Barnabas in Lystra, a Greco-Roman may have concluded that sacrifice, as the Greco-Romans understood it, is pointless and worthy only of comedic parody.

Chapter 5

ACTS 17.16–34 AND AESCHYLUS' *EUMENIDES*

Most exegetes of the Areopagus narrative in Acts 17 have emphasized natural theology, Greek philosophy, the Ἄγνωστος Θεός motif, Greco-Roman philosophical religion and historical questions.[1] I will not renew these discussions but explore a related and ususally neglected subsidiary issue. A few scholars have noted a possible relationship between the mention of ἀνάστασις in both Acts 17.18, 32 and in Aeschylus' *Eumenides* (647) without developing the parallel further.[2] In this chapter, I develop this parallel to tentatively suggest that Luke's audience may have observed an allusion to the Athenian literary tradition because of subtle parallels between Luke's narrative and that of Aeschylus' *Eumenides*.

---

1. The literature is immense and beyond the scope of this monograph. Joseph A. Fitzmyer's commentary provides basic bibliography (*The Acts of the Apostles: A New Translation with Introduction and Commentary* [AB, 31; New York: Doubleday, 1998]), pp. 613–17.
I summarize important and recent literature below.
(1) Natural theology: Most importantly, Bertil Gärtner, *The Areopagus Speech and Natural Revelation* (ASNU 21; Uppsala: Almqvist & Wiksell, 1955). Also, Dean William Zweck, 'The Function of Natural Theology in the Areopagus Speech' (ThD dissertation, Lutheran School of Theology at Chicago, 1985), esp. pp. 1–42 for a comprehensive review of research, and pp. 220–60 for an exegesis of 17.24–29.
(2) Philosophy: most recently, Balch, 'The Areopagus Speech', pp. 52–79 and Neyrey, 'Acts 17, Epicureans, and Theodicy', pp. 118–34; and N. Clayton Croy, 'Hellenistic Philosophies and the Preaching of the Resurrection (Acts 17.18, 32)', *NovT* 39 (1997), pp. 21–39. There are several Greco-Roman philosophical parallels to Acts 17: the seventh-century BCE poet and sage Epimenides (quoted in Diogenes Laertius 1.109–15), Kleanthes *Hymn to Zeus*, and the philosopher-mathematician Aratus (*Phaen.* 5). See also, from among many others, Seneca (*Ep.* 41.1–2, 44.1 and 95.47), Euripides (*Heracl.* 1345–46), Plutarch (*Stoic. Rep.* [=*Mor.* 1052D]), Dio Chrysostom (*Dei. cogn.* 83 [=*Or.* 12.83] and *Charid.* [=*Or.* 30.26]), and Cicero (*Tusc.* 1.28.68–69).
(3) Historical issues: Colin J. Hemer, *The Book of Acts in the Setting of Hellenistic History* (Tübingen: Mohr-Siebeck, 1989).
(4) Ἄγνωστος Θεός: most importantly, Eduard Norden, *Agnostos Theos: Untersuchungen zur Formengeschichte Religiöser Rede* (Leipzig: Teubner, 1913; repr. Darmstadt: Wissenschaftliche Buchgesellschaft, 1956) and P.W. van der Horst, 'The Altar of the "Unknown God" in Athens (Acts 17.23) and the Cults of "Unknown Gods" in the Graeco-Roman World', *ANRW* II/18, part 2, pp. 1426–56; repr. *idem*, *Hellenism-Judaism-Christianity: Essays on Their Interaction* (CBET, 8; Kampen: Kok Pharos, 1994), pp. 165–202.
2. Bruce, *The Book of the Acts*, p. 343; Bruce W. Winter, 'In Public and in Private: Early Christian Interactions with Religious Pluralism', in Andrew D. Clarke and Bruce W. Winter (eds), *One God One Lord in a World of Religious Pluralism* (Cambridge: Tyndale House, 1991), pp. 112–34 at 129; Talbert, *Reading Acts*, p. 165; and Witherington, *Acts*, p. 532.

Allusions to Aeschylus

Because Paul discusses resurrection in Acts 17, Luke's Greco-Roman audience may have seen parallels to Aeschylus' *Eumenides* in at least three ways: (1) the mention of ἀνάστασις, (2) the mention of the Areopagus and its examination of the central character and (3) the introduction of new gods.[3] Before exploring these parallels, I will briefly summarize the plot of Aeschylus' *Eumenides*.

Aeschylus' Eumenides

At the beginning of the play, Orestes is a suppliant before Apollo at Apollo's oracle in Delphi (*Eum.* 1–234). The Erinyes have been pursuing Orestes to obtain vengeance for murdering his mother Clytemnestra (previously described in the *Choephoroi*), which he committed at Apollo's command. At Delphi, Apollo assures Orestes that he has been ritually cleansed from the pollution of homicide and sends Orestes to Athena's temple in Athens to seek asylum. Clytemnestra's ghost appears from the dead and verbally abuses the Erinyes for not completing the task of avenging her death. Orestes flees to Athens and begs asylum from Athena, who arrives just in time to prevent the Erinyes from destroying Orestes. Both the Erinyes and Orestes present their respective cases to Athena who concludes that she cannot decide the case alone. As a consequence, Athena founds the Areopagus as a trial court to decide cases of homicide. The Erinyes, Orestes and Apollo, speaking on Orestes' behalf, present their cases to the Areopagus. The vote is split and Athena decides for Orestes by casting the tie-breaking vote. The humiliated Erinyes then threaten to destroy Athens but Athena placates them by promising them a cult in Athens as both avengers of injustice and promoters of good with the cultic site located at the east end of the Areopagus. The play concludes with a celebratory procession of the Athenian citizens and the Erinyes, who now become the Eumenides. Thus the play serves to recount the etiological myth for the formation of the Areopagus council.

Methodology

How can one plausibly suggest that Luke's Greco-Roman audience could possibly have seen these three allusive intertextual parallels of ἀνάστασις, the Areopagus' examination of the central character, and introducing new gods? First, I will closely examine the parallels between Acts and *Eumenides* to see if there are sufficient similarities between the two works to suggest that Greco-Roman readers may have seen allusions to Aeschylus.

3. Basic Aeschylus bibliography in Alan H. Sommerstein, 'Aeschylus', in *OCD*, 3rd edn, pp. 28–29. Recent thorough bibliographies in James C. Hogan, *A Commentary on the Complete Greek Tragedies: Aeschylus* (Chicago: University of Chicago Press, 1984), pp. 307–18; Alan H. Sommerstein (ed.), *Aeschylus' Eumenides* (Cambridge Greek and Latin Classics; Cambridge: Cambridge University Press, 1989), pp. ix–xi; and Alan Shapiro and Peter Burian (trans.), *The Oresteia* (The Greek Tragedy in New Translations; Oxford: Oxford University Press, 2003), pp. 281–85

Secondly, I will adapt criteria developed by Dennis Ronald MacDonald for determining intertextual dependence: accessibility, analogy, and motivation.[4] MacDonald uses these criteria to answer the following: Was an alleged source text available to the author of the dependent text (the criterion of *accessibility*)? Did the supposed source text influence other texts (the criterion of *analogy*)? Is there a reasonable explanation for the use of the allusions (the criterion of *motivation*)? For my purposes, I consider accessibility and analogy together. Also, I adapt the criteria to pose the questions from the perspective of Luke's Greco-Roman audience: Was the alleged source (*Eumenides*) available to or known by this audience and did it influence other texts (*accessibility* and *analogy*)? Could a Greco-Roman reader not only see an allusion to *Eumenides*, but also perceive a purpose for such an allusion? Positive answers to these three questions reinforce the possibility that Greco-Romans may have noted an allusion to *Eumenides* in Acts 17.16–34.

The Parallels

Ἀνάστασις

The word ἀνάστασις appears in both Aeschylus and Acts when the central character is about to appear before the Areopagus. Aeschylus uses the noun ἀνάστασις twice in his extant complete works: *Ag.* 589 and *Eum.* 647.[5] In context, the first citation refers to the 'desolation' of a city. *Eumenides* 674 reads, 'once a man is dead, there is no raising him up [ἀνάστασις]'. In this context, ἀνάστασις means 'resuscitation', i.e., the revivification of a corpse. Apollo is saying that if

---

4.   Dennis Ronald MacDonald, *Christianizing Homer: the Odyssey, Plato, and the Acts of Andrew* (Oxford: Oxford University Press, 1994), pp. 302–16. MacDonald uses seven different criteria and used them to determine the degree to which the *Acts of Andrew* is directly dependent upon Homer through citation, allusion, and structure. He later altered these criteria to evaluate the depence of both Mark and Acts upon Homer: *The Homeric Epics and the Gospel of Mark* (New Haven: Yale University Press, 2000), pp. 1–23, esp. pp. 2, 5–6, 8–9 and *Does the New Testament Imitate Homer?: Four Cases from the Acts of the Apostles* (New Haven: Yale University Press: 2003), pp. 2–5. He has stated to me that he now considers 'accessibility and analogy environmental issues somewhat difficult to apply to particular texts. I've dropped them as criteria, but use them to bolster the argument' (e-mail to author, 6 Feb. 1998).

MacDonald developed his criteria in order to study the literary dependence of one *entire* literary work on another *entire* literary work. Since I am studying the allusions to sections of one text found in a short section of another text, and a text's dependency upon not only literary works but also upon cultural phenomena, I retain MacDonald's criteria of accessibility and analogy for my purposes. I wish to thank Dr. MacDonald for discussing these issues with me and sharing early drafts of his work on Mark and Acts.

5.   Vocabulary data from Henrik Holmboe, *Concordance to Aeschylus' Supplices* (Århus: Akademisk Boghandel, 1971); *idem*, *Concordance to Aeschylus' Prometheus Vitens* (Århus: Akademisk Boghandel, 1971); *idem*, *Concordance to Aeschylus' Persiae* (Århus: Akademisk Boghandel, 1971); *idem*, *Concordance to Aeschylus' Septem Contra Thebas* (Århus: Akademisk Boghandel, 1971); *idem*, *Concordance to Aeschylus' Agamemnon* (Århus: Akademisk Boghandel, 1972); *idem*, *Concordance to Aeschylus' Choephoroi* (Århus: Akademisk Boghandel, 1973); and *idem*, *Concordance to Aeschylus' Eumenides* (Århus: Akademisk Boghandel, 1973).

the Erinyes extract their murderous vengeance upon Orestes, then Orestes' life cannot be restored because Zeus made no provision for this. For Apollo, Orestes is entitled to life because he both obeyed Apollo's command to murder Clytemnestra and was ritually purified from blood guilt at Delphi.

This statement about death's finality is part of Apollo's defense argument before the Areopagus to save Orestes from the Erinyes' murderous, vengeful wrath. For the Athenian playwright, for his characters, and for his audience, there is no resurrection. Shortly before the end of the play, both the Areopagus and Athena declare Orestes innocent, and he returns home (754–77). Orestes retains his physical life; his only hope of life beyond the grave is his oath that his spirit will avenge Athens against all the rulers of his native Argos who march in military force against Athens:

> Now I'll go home. But first I make this oath
> to your land and people for all time to come –
> never will an Argive leader march in here
> with spears arrayed against you. If he does,
> in violation of this oath of mine,
> from the grave we'll see his effort fails.
> We'll bring him bad luck, trouble on the march,
> send birds of evil omen over him. (*Eum.* 762–71).[6]

The noun ἀνάστασις appears twice in Acts 17 (vv.18, 32). In 17.31, Paul uses the aorist participle ἀναστήσας in reference to Jesus. These three uses of 'rise/raised' terminology are clustered in and around Paul's discussion with the Stoic and Epicurean philosophers and his speech to the Areopagus. Thus17.18 and 17.31, both of which mention Jesus and the resurrection, form an *inclusio* for the speech.[7] Also, the scoffing banter of the Athenian philosophers appears in the *inclusio* in 17.18 and 17.32. A reader may have noticed an emphasis on the resurrection of Jesus by observing this literary device.

Aeschylus portrays Orestes as having only a shadowy post-mortem existence as a vengeful spirit. In Acts, an attentive reader would notice a reiteration of the importance of Jesus' resurrection as the proof of God's impending judgment upon the world (17.31). This emphasis on the resurrection recalls Luke's previous mentions of Jesus' resurrection (Acts 1.22; 2.31; 4.2, 33).[8] By noting this possible allusion to *Eumenides*, a Greco-Roman reader may have contrasted the

6. Trans. Ian Johnston, public domain (2003, online), http.//www.mala.bc.ca/~johnstoi/aeschylus/ aeschylus_eumenides.htm. Accessed Dec. 16, 2005. Unless specified, all further translations *Eumenides* are by Johnston.

7. In 17.18 Luke overtly mentions Jesus by name, and in 17.30 Luke refers to Jesus by using the third person pronoun αὐτός, 'raising *him* [Jesus] from the dead'; a distinction that does not affect my overall argument. Spencer rightly concludes Christology is subordinate to theology throughout the Areopagus episode (*Acts*, 175).

8. Interestingly, all references to the resurrection before and including Acts 17.18, 32 are only about Jesus' resurrection. After Acts 17.32, there are four general references to resurrection or the hope of the resurrection (23.6, 8; 24.15, 21). The final Acts reference to the resurrection (26.23) refers to Jesus' resurrection and implicitly to the general resurrection. Does this change after Acts 17.16–34 signify a structural pattern in Acts?

emphasis on the resurrection in Acts to the blunt finality of the Athenian classical literary heritage, 'there is no resurrection' (*Eum.* 647).

The Areopagus, Social Order and the Innocence of Orestes and Paul

For Luke's audience, the references to the Areopagus in Acts 17 would have brought to mind aristocracy, respectability, antiquity and the divine establishment of the Areopagus. By writing his narrative in this way, Luke operated within the ancient mindset of 'reverence for antiquity', which assured the preservation of both social *and* religious order.[9] By the first century CE the Areopagus, composed of local Athenian aristocrats, was eight centuries old and thus had an air of sacredness, immense respectability, and aristocracy.[10] Cicero attests to the respectability of the Areopagus in the Roman period (*Nat. d.* 2.29.74, *Att.* 1.14.5, 5.11.6). Aelius Aristides called the Areopagus, 'most honorable and most holy' (*Or.* 1.367, also 46–48, 385). In imperial decrees and communications, Roman emperors consistently addressed the Areopagus: 'the council of the Areopagus, the council of the Six Hundred [or Five Hundred] and the people...'.[11] Because of its antiquity and aristocratic membership, the Roman emperor recognized the Areopagus as the first in importance among the three governing bodies of Athens.

Aeschylus connects the judgment and proclamation of Orestes' innocence to the foundation of the Areopagus. In the play Athena declares herself inadequate to judge the case alone and so appoints the Areopagus:

> This is a serious matter, too complex
> for any mortal man to think of judging.
> It's not right even for me to adjudicate
> such cases, where murder done in passion
> merits passionate swift punishment.
> ...
> Two options, each of them disastrous.
> Allow one to remain, expel the other?
> No, I see no way of resolving this.
> But since the judgment now devolves on me,
> I'll appoint human judges of this murder,
> a tribunal bound by oath – I'll set it up

9.   Ramsay MacMullen, *Paganism in the Roman Empire* (New Haven: Yale University Press, 1981), pp. 1–5; pp. 141–43 nn. 1–25.

10.   For the Areopagus' historical development, see Robert J. Bonner and Gertrude Smith, *The Administration of Justice from Homer to Aristotle* (Chicago: University of Chicago Press, 1930), I, pp. 88–107, 125–29, 163–69, 251–78, 364–65; II, pp. 167–71, 232–33, and *passim*; D.J. Geagan, *The Athenian Constitution after Sulla* (Hesperia Supplement, 12; Princeton: American School at Athens, 1967); *idem*, 'Ordo Areopagitarum Atheniensium', in Donald William Bradeen and Malcom Francis McGregor (eds), *ΦΟΡΟΣ: Tribute to Benjamin Dean Meritt*, (Locust Valley, NY: J.J. Augustin, 1974), pp. 51–56; R.W. Wallace, *The Areopagus Council to 307 BC* (Baltimore: Johns Hopkins University Press, 1985); Hubert M. Martin Jr, 'Areopagus', *ABD* I, pp. 370–72; and D.W.J. Gill, 'Achaia', in Gill and Gempf (eds), *Book of Acts in its Graeco-Roman Setting*, pp. 447–48.

11.   Among many inscriptions: *IG* II² 3500, 3501, 4104, 4129; *OGIS* 428). Also, Edward William Bodnar, SJ, *Cyriacus of Ancona and Athens* (Collection Latomus, 43; Brussels: Latomus, Revue D'Études Latines, 1960), pp. 171–73.

to last forever. So you two parties,
summon your witnesses, set out your proofs,
with sworn evidence to back your stories.
Once I've picked the finest men in Athens,
I'll return. They'll rule fairly in this case,
bound by a sworn oath to act with justice. (*Eum.* 470–74, 481–89)

After Athena appoints the members of the Areopagus, they listen to the testimony and arguments of the Erinyes, Orestes, and Apollo. Athena then decides to establish the Areopagus as a permanent court of justice: 'Now and forever/this court of judges will be set up here (*Eum.* 681–84)'. The Areopagus casts its ballots and is equally divided for and against Orestes. Athena casts the deciding vote that allows Orestes to go free. Orestes then disappears from the play in an almost anti-climactic fashion.

The philosophers take Paul before the Areopagus.[12] The narrative is highly ambiguous about whether Paul was being formally examined by the Areopagus or simply conversing with Athenian philosophers and local civic officials who are interested in hearing something 'new' (17.21).[13]

Luke's Greco-Roman audience could have read this ambiguity in two ways. First, Luke's audience could have read his narrative as depicting a friendly discussion between Paul, the Epicurean and Stoic philosophers, and the Areopagus in the Stoa Basilica on the northwest corner of the Athenian agora.[14] Secondly, Luke's audience could have interpreted his narrative as depicting a formal judicial proceeding investigating Paul's possible introduction of new gods to Athens. Viewing the narrative in this light, the readers/auditors could possibly associate the judicial functions of the Areopagus in the imperial period with its functions in Aeschylus' *Eumenides*. In the Roman period, the Areopagus operated as both the government and chief judiciary of Athens with jurisdiction over cases of kidnapping, assault, and homicide (Lucian, *Bis acc.* 12, 15–17, *Tim.* 46, *Vit. auct.* 7; Pausanias 1.28.5), the regulation of weights and measures, fish sales, marketplace forgery and counterfeiting, the surveillance of contagious diseases, and the introduction of new

12. The philosophers take, ἐπιλαβόμενοι, Paul to or before the Areopagus. ἐπιλάμβανω can mean 'seize, arrest' or, without hostile intent, 'take'. Concerning ἐπιλάμβανω, see Richard Wallace and Wynne Williams, *The Acts of the Apostles: A Companion* (Classical Studies Series; London: Bristol Classical Press, 1993), p. 92.

13. Wallace and Williams, *Acts*, pp. 91–94 esp. 92–93.

14. Luke's narrative is unclear whether Paul appeared before the Areopagus on the hill of the same name or at the Stoa Basileios. The Areopagus council sometimes met at the Stoa during the imperial period; W.E. Wycherly, 'Two Notes on Athenian Topography', *JHS* 75 (1955), pp. 117–21; *idem*, *The Athenian Agora: Literary and Epigraphical Testimonia* (Princeton: American School of Classical Studies at Athens, 1957), III, pp. 126–28 and nn. 117, 138, 407, 427, 511, 530, 543, 557, 636; *idem*, 'St. Paul in Athens', *JTS* 19 (1968), pp. 619–21; Homer A. Thompson and R.E. Wycherly, *The Athenian Agora: The History, Shape, and Uses of an Ancient City Center* (Princeton: American School of Classical Studies at Athens, 1972), XIV, 20, 34, 87, 88 n. 24, 107, 166, 168, 205; Colin J. Hemer, 'Paul at Athens: A Topographical Note', *NTS* 20 (1973–74), pp. 341–50; and Alan L. Boegehold, *et al.*, *The Athenian Agora: The Lawcourts at Athens : Sites, Buildings, Equipment, Procedure, and Testimonia* (Princeton: American School of Classical Studies at Athens, 1995), XXVIII, pp. 44–47, 126–35.

gods.[15] Epigraphic and literary evidence suggests that the Areopagus could impose both exile *and* capital punishment during the Roman period.[16] Paul is brought before the Areopagus because of its role as 'the effective government of Roman Athens and its chief court', including the introduction of new gods (see below).[17] In this light Paul convinces a court that he is not introducing a new god to the Athenian pantheon. Once Paul mentions the resurrection, some members of the Areopagus scoff at him (cf. *Eum.* 647 where Apollo states, 'there is no resurrection'); others wish to defer discussion.[18] But they do not find Paul culpable for anything. If Luke's Greco-Roman readers noted an allusion to *Eumenides*, they may have further reinforced the idea of Paul's innocence in their own minds because a renowned Athenian civic tribunal finds nothing to charge him with.

The Introduction of New Gods
Aeschylus introduces new gods into the Athenian pantheon and the 'conditions' that the new gods expect the Athenians to meet in *Eumenides*. A Greco-Roman reader may have detected a similar introduction of a new god to Athens and that god's 'demands' in Acts. In the *Eumenides*, the Furies become part of the Athenian civic pantheon and expect cult and social stability. In Acts, Paul introduces the 'Unknown God' and expects proper acknowledgment and repentance by the Athenians (17.30–31). In both texts the Areopagus is involved in judging the introduction of the new god(s). A Greco-Roman reader, familiar with the Areopagus' regulation of new gods, may have seen an allusion to *Eumenides* in Acts 17.16–34.[19]

At the end of the play, after Orestes' acquittal and return to his homeland (*Eum.* 754–77), the Furies remain unappeased and threaten to bring destruction to Athens (778–92, 808–22). After a series of moving speeches (774–806, 848–69, 881–91), Athena assuages their anger and convinces them to become part of the Athenian civic cult. The Erinyes will receive hearths or altars and sacred stones anointed with oil (806), the first fruits of the local crops will be offered to them (834), men and women will honor them with a procession (856–57), and the Athenians will honor them with sacrifices (1006–1037). The Furies, assured of a

---

15. Geagan *Athenian Constitution after Sulla*, pp. 32–50; T. D. Barnes, 'An Apostle on Trial', *JTS* 22 (1969), pp. 407–19; Gill, 'Achaia', pp. 447–48; Bruce W. Winter 'On Introducing Gods to Athens: An Alternative Reading of Acts 17.18–20', *TynBul* 47 (1996), pp. 71–90, esp. pp. 80–83. Geagan discusses the epigraphic evidence thoroughly.

16. Exile: B. Keil, *Beiträge zur Geschichte des Areopags* (Berichte über die Verhandlungen der Sächsischen Akademie der Wissenschaft zu Leipzig; Philologische-historische Klasse, 71 Bd, 8; [1919?, 1920?]), pp. 52–53; cited by Barnes, 'An Apostle on Trial', p. 412 n. 5. Capital punishment: J. Delz, 'Lukians Kenntnis der athenischen Antiquitäten' (PhD diss.; Basel, 1950), pp. 108–109, 151ff.; cited by Barnes, 'An Apostle on Trial', p. 412 n. 6. For discussion and older bibliography about the ability of local governments to inflict capital punishment in the Roman provinces, see Barnes, 'An Apostle on Trial', p. 412 and p. 412 nn. 7–8.

17. Barnes, 'An Apostle on Trial', p. 413.

18. At Acts 24.25, the Roman governor Felix similarly dismisses Paul, 'Go for now. When I have time, I will call you'. Talbert understands both 17.32 and 24.25 as the postponement of decisive responses to Paul's proclamation, which in Acts equals unbelief (*Reading Acts*, 165).

19. See Winter 'Introducing Gods', pp. 71–90.

Foreign but Familiar Gods

shrine, cult, and their due honor, promise to bless the citizens of Athens (*Eum.* 916–26, 938–48) but demand just behavior from the Athenians:

> I forbid those deadly accidents
> which cut men down before their time.
>
> ...
>
> I pray man-killing civil strife
> may never roar aloud
> within the city – may its dust
> not drink our citizen's dark blood,
> nor passions for revenge incite
> those wars which kill the state.
> Let men give joy for joy,
> united by their common love,
> united in their enmities –
> for that cures all human ills. (*Eum.* 958–59, 978–87)

The Furies, the new gods, will live in Athens provided they receive their due honors and the Athenians live justly. At the end of the *Eumenides*, the Athenians honor the Erinyes by escorting them in procession to their new shrine, a cave on the slopes of the Areopagus (1003–47). Aeschylus introduces a new cult, the Erinyes, into Athens after the founding of the Areopagus, the governing body that helped regulate the introduction of new gods.

Similarly, Greco-Romans may have understood Paul to be introducing a new god, the Unknown God or the god of the Christians, and associated that introduction of a new god with the Areopagus' official duties. The Athenian philosophers bring Paul before the venerable and ancient Areopagus to discuss his mention of new gods, Jesus and Anastasis.[20] At 17.30, God 'commands', παραγγέλλει, 'all humanity everywhere', τοῖς ἀνθρώποις πάντας πανταχοῦ, 'to repent', μετανοεῖν. Paul's 'new god' demands repentance, i.e. a change in behavior.

Strikingly, Greco-Romans would have been aware of such 'repentance' or change in behavior within their own cultural context. Lucian's *Nigrinus* describes how a young man changes his life from a state of dissolution to moderation and highly ethical behavioral because of his 'conversion' to a philosophical school. This audience would probably have found the demand for repentance in Acts 17.30 as unremarkable, within the context of philosophical discussion (Paul's discussion with Stoics and Epicureans) except in relation to a future judgment by the resurrected Jesus. However, they would have, at least unconsciously, understood 'repentance' in mundane, daily religious life as a substantially different outlook than the usual practices of mundane, daily civic and popular religion.

A Greco-Roman audience may have viewed an allusion to *Eumenides* as ironic. In *Eumenides*, Athena introduces the Furies into the Athenian pantheon as 'new gods', i.e. the Athenians did not before give these gods public worship. In contrast, Paul states that the Athenians already worship the god they believe he is introducing (17.23). Paul's god is not a new god at all but the god the Athenians worship as Ἀγνώστος Θεός, the 'Unknown God'. Paul, and by implication the Christian

---

20. Winter, 'Introducing Gods', pp. 80–81.

movement, is not introducing a new god into the Athenian pantheon. Instead Paul is introducing the true god. The Athenian gods are mere human artistic products made of gold, silver, and stone who reside in temples of human construction and require human care (17.24–25, 29).

Greco-Romans may have seen a second level of irony in an allusion to *Eumenides*. In *Eumenides* the entire *polis* welcomes the Erinyes into the Athenian pantheon. In Acts, the Athenians, excepting Dionysius, Damaris and 'a few others' (17.34), *do not* accept God whom Paul proclaims as they accepted the Erinyes in *Eumenides*.

Accessibility and Analogy: Would Luke's Greco-Roman Audience Have Been Familiar with Aeschylus?

Based on the parallels cited above, I suggest that a Greco-Roman audience may have seen allusions to Aeschylus' *Eumenides* in Acts 17.16–34. A possible argument against my hypothesis is to deny any possibility that this audience had read or was aware of Aeschylus' work because the play was inaccessible to them. On the contrary, classical drama continued to be performed throughout the Mediterranean world at least into the third century CE.[21] Mosaics, wall paintings, papyri and lead 'admission tickets' indicate that classical comedies and tragedies were performed before a wide cross section of society in Ephesus, Oescus, Mytilene, Pompeii, and especially Athens – which remained the center of drama in the ancient Mediterranean world.[22]

John Edwin Sandys' examination of ancient literary scholarship shows that Aeschylus continued to be read and studied throughout antiquity.[23]

1. Euripides was already criticizing Aeschylus' dramatic technique in his own plays.
2. The comic playwright Aristophanes sketched a satirical contest between Euripides and Aeschylus in his *Ranae* (*The Frogs*).
3. Ancient literary critics who commented on Aeschylus include Aristophanes of Byzantium (*c.* 257–*c.* 180 BCE), Aristarchus of Samothrace (220–145 BCE), Didymus (65 BCE–10 CE), the anonymous author of Περὶ Ὕψους (*On the Sublime*, *c.* 30 BCE–early first century), and Dio Chrysostom (40–114 CE).
4. The Christian apologist Clement of Alexandria (*c.* 181–251 or 254? CE) mentions Aeschylus in his discussion of the Eleusinian mysteries (*Strom.* 2.461).

21. C.P. Jones, 'Greek Drama in the Roman Empire', in Ruth Scodel (ed.), *Theater and Society*, pp. 39–52.
22. Jones, 'Greek Drama', pp. 40–43. Excavators have unearthed pieces of stamped lead that appear to have given the bearer right of entry to ancient theatrical performances (Jones, 'Greek Drama', pp. 42–43).
23. From John Edwin Sandys, *A History of Classical Scholarship*. I. *From the Sixth Century B.C. to the End of the Middle Ages* (Cambridge: Cambridge University Press, 1958; repr. New York: Hafner, 1967), pp. 24, 52–4, 65, 128, 132, 142.

Further, Philo (*c.* 20 BCE–40 CE) quotes Aesch. frg. 648: 'And tell me where's the sacred beam that dared the dangerous Euxine Stream? (*Omn. Prob. Lib.* 143)'[24]

Additionally, the travel writer Pausanias, writing about 155 CE, describes the shrine of the Semnai Theai (the Erinyes) on the slopes of the Athenian Areopagus and mentions that Aeschylus was the first to depict the Erinyes with snakes in their hair (1.28.6).

The first- to third-century dates of Dio Chrysostom, Philo, Pausanias, and Clement show that the ancient Mediterranean world knew Aeschylus' works during and after the time Luke wrote Acts. Dio Chrysostom compares and contrasts the tragic style of Euripides and Aeschylus in their treatment of the Philoktetes tale (*Philoc. Arc.* [= *Or.* 52]). Dio's audience was obviously aware of both tragedians and their work; he expected his comments to be understood and appreciated. The educated Jewish writer, Philo, albeit a highly Hellenized writer, was familiar with, quoted, and appeared to expect his audience to catch a reference to Aeschylus. Pausanias was familiar with both Aeschylus' radical new depiction of the Erinyes in his *Eumenides* and the relationship between the Areopagus, the Semnai Theai, and the Erinyes. Clement was familiar with scurrilous gossip about Aeschylus having divulged the secrets of Eleusis. It was fully possible for Luke's Greco-Roman audience to be aware of and perhaps understand literary allusions to Aeschylus' *Eumenides* in the first century CE.

Conclusions

If a Greco-Roman audience did perceive an allusion to Aeschylus' *Eumenides* in Acts 17.16–34, what motivation might have they attributed to Luke for doing so? MacDonald points out that authors use an earlier text because they are friendly to it (writing a commentary, translation, or imitation) or antagonistic to it (parodying or somehow intentionally devaluing an earlier text).[25] Conversely, one can argue that an audience sees an author's use of a source text as a friendly commentary on, translation or imitation of that source text. Also, an audience can see an author as antagonistically parodying or devaluing the source. If Luke's Greco-Roman audience did observe an allusion to *Eumenides*, they may have understood this allusion as both a commendation and condemnation of Greek culture and religion as found in Aeschylus' *Eumenides*.

Luke's Greco-Roman audience would have almost certainly noted that this entire narrative is set in an overwhelmingly Hellenistic context. They may have viewed a contrast between educated Athenian culture (and its classical heritage) and the Christian message.[26] He mentions the statues and altars of the Greek gods

24. Charles Duke Yonge (trans.), *The Works of Philo Judaeus: The Contemporary of Josephus, translated from the Greek* (London: H.G. Bohn, 1854–90). I thank N. Clayton Croy for this reference.
25. MacDonald, *Christianizing Homer*, pp. 6–7, 15 n. 46, 302, citing Gérard Genette, *Palimpsestes: La Littérature au second degré* (Poétique; Paris: Seuil, 1982), pp. 201, 393, 418–19; English trans., Claude Doubinsky and Channa Newman (trans.), *Palimpsests: Literature in the Second Degree* (Stages, 8; Lincoln, NE: University of Nebraska Press, 1997), pp. 180, 343, 367. MacDonald limits himself to the act of direct textual copying or rewriting of one text in a later text.
26. Except for a brief mention in 17.17, Luke does not mention the Judeans in Acts 17.16–34.

that παροξύνω, 'enrage', Paul. Luke has Paul διαλέγομαι (17.16) and συμβάλλω (17.18), 'discuss' or 'dispute', with two major schools of Greek philosophy. Paul appears before the Areopagus, part of Athenian civic government. Paul's speech to the Areopagus possibly alludes to Epimenides, Aratus' *Phaenomena*, and Kleanthes' *Hymn to Zeus* (17.28).[27]

For a Greco-Roman reader, Paul's speech compares the Christian god with the Greek gods: God exists, is already worshipped by the Athenians as Ἄγνωστος Θεός, created humanity and the entire world, rules earth and heaven, calls humanity to repentance, and will judge the world through Jesus whom God raised from the dead. With the exception of the last two points, the Greek gods have all these attributes in common with the Christian God. Greek gods typically did not call their worshippers to repentance. (However, as already mentioned, membership in the philosophical schools required or produced a dramatic change in life.) The Greek gods will not judge humanity through a man raised from the dead (Acts 17.31).

The three possible allusions to Aeschylus' *Eumenides* that Greco-Romans may have seen in Acts 17 further reinforce these comparisons. First, if a Greco-Roman saw an allusion to Aeschylus' use of ἀνάστασις in *Eum.*647, this allusion may have contrasted the importance and reality of resurrection in Luke-Acts to the Greek denial of resurrection found in the *Eumenides*. Second, if Greco-Romans perceived a parallel between the appearance of both Orestes and Paul before the Areopagus, they may have understood Paul and his message as innocent of any threat to social order. Third, this audience may have seen an ironic allusion to the introduction of new gods into Athens and the demands of these gods upon the Athenians at the conclusion of *Eumenides*. This allusion may have suggested to these readers that, within Acts, God cannot be introduced as a 'new' divinity with a new cult. Instead the Christian God is already worshipped as Ἄγνωστος θεός, the 'Unknown God' who demands repentance or a turning away from traditional Athenian religion.[28]

If a Greco-Roman audience did perceive an allusion to Aeschylus' *Eumenides* in Acts 17.16–34, they may have understood the allusion as both a challenge to and an acceptance of the Athenian classical literary heritage. Contrary to this heritage, a Greco-Roman may have seen an argument for Jesus' resurrection and a demand to turn away from the traditional gods of Greece and Rome. A Greco-Roman reader may have as well seen an allusion to *Eumenides* as an indication that the reader's classical heritage could be 'baptized', Aeschylus can be Christianized, and included as part of the Christian perspective.

27. Kirsopp Lake, 'Your Own Poets', *Beginnings*, V, pp. 246–51; Annewies van de Bunt-Van den Hoek, 'Aristobulos, Acts, Theophilus, Clement: Making Use of Aratus' Phainomena: A Peregrination', *Bijdragen* 41 (1980), pp. 290–99, and M.J. Edwards, 'Quoting Aratus: Acts 17, 28', *ZNW* 83 (1992), pp. 266–69.

28. Witherington, *Acts*, pp. 523–32.

Chapter 6

ACTS 19.23–41: VOTIVE OFFERINGS AND ΔΙΟΠΕΤΗΣ OBJECTS

Luke briefly mentions two aspects of Greco-Roman religion in Acts 19.23–41: the manufacture and use of votive offerings (19.24) and the idea that some religious artifacts are διοπετής, 'fallen from the gods' (19.35). In various studies, scholars have briefly discussed the ναοὶ ἀργυροί, 'silver shrines', and the διοπετής, 'the object fallen from the realm of the gods', as historical background or as part of Luke's polemic against gods who ἐν χειροποιήτοις ναοῖς κατοικεῖ, 'live in hand-made temples'.[1]

What associations would Greco-Roman readers have called to mind when reading these two minor details about the Ephesian Artemis in an account in which Paul is all but absent? I suggest that Greco-Roman readers may have seen: (1) an implicit condemnation of votive offerings and the competitive social relations they express, (2) that διοπετής objects are fundamentally impotent, and (3) subtle allusions to earlier passages in Luke's gospel (Lk. 18.9–14 and 10.18). Examining the nature of both votive offerings and διοπετής objects in antiquity will tentatively support these suggestions. I follow with a discussion of the parallels between Lk. 18.9–14 and Acts 19.24 and between Lk. 10.18 and Acts 19.35.

ναοὶ ἀργυροί: The Silver Shrines

Scholars have offered four functions for the ναοὶ ἀργυροί: votive offerings, souvenirs, amulets, or grave goods.[2] In reality such uses probably overlapped.

---

1. E.L. Hicks, 'Demetrius the Silversmith: An Ephesian Study', *The Expositor*, 4th ser., 1 (1890), pp. 401–22; Guy MacLean Rogers, 'Demetrios of Ephesus: Silversmith and Neopoios', *Belletin Türk tarih Kurumu* 50 (1986), pp. 877–83; Lake and Cadbury, *Beginnings*, IV, pp. 245–53; Bruce, *Acts*, pp. 415, 420; Conzelmann, *Acts*, pp. 165–66; and Barrett, *Acts*, II, pp. 422–23. Trebilco provides an excellent discussion of the nature of the Ephesian Artemis cult ('Asia', pp. 316–57); and discusses the silver shrines (pp. 336–38) and the διοπετής object (pp. 351–54). Older literature in Lake and Cadbury (*Beginnings*, IV, pp. 245–52).

2. Votive offering: Bruce, *Acts*, p. 415. Souvenirs: Conzelmann, *Acts*, p. 165. Amulets: Conzelmann, *Acts*, p. 165; and Lionel Casson, *Travel in the Ancient World* (Baltimore: Johns Hopkins University Press, 1994), pp. 34, 286–91, 325–28, esp. 287. Grave goods: Trebilco, 'Asia', p. 338; Trebilco also suggests amulets and souvenirs and cites several sources to interpret the silver shrines as grave goods, but provides no textual evidence from Acts. Haenchen mentions the first three possible functions without favoring any (*Acts*, p. 572). Ellen D. Reeder considers the first three options but seems to lean toward votives ('The Mother of the Gods and a Hellenistic Bronze Matrix', *AJA* 91 [1987], pp. 423–40, esp. 440).

Archaeological excavations confirm primary sources that mention these four uses of miniature statues of the gods (Theokritus, 27.3; Hero, *Spir.* 1.37; Apuleius, *Apol.* 63; Philostratus, *Vit. Apoll.* 5.20; *Acts Pet.* 17).[3] Because 19.23–41 emphasizes the importance of Artemis' temple to the Ephesians themselves, Luke's audience may have understood the ναοὶ ἀργυροί as votive offerings.[4]

The silver shrines were probably small portable niches or headdresses, both consisting of temple-like structures. The niches could contain statues of the goddess, while worshippers could place the headdresses on the goddess' statue. These shrines were left in the temple of the Ephesian Artemis as gifts dedicated to the goddess. What were the implicit cultural meanings that Luke's Greco-Roman audience associated with votive offerings? How would those readers have related these implicit meanings to their theological understanding of Acts? What implications would they have drawn about the use of votive offerings?

Votive offerings

Votive offerings were 'a permanent memorial dedicated of free will to a supernatural being'.[5] They were also the 'logical extension of sacrifice and prayer' in that they expressed thanks for favors received, helped assure 'continuing attention from the gods' or fulfilled a previously promised obligation.[6] Less abstractly, they were various physical objects given to or dedicated to the gods, including clothing placed on the god's statue (Pausanias 3.16.2, 5.16, 6.24.10), physical representations of body parts healed from disease, worker's tools, arms captured in war, small images of the god and so forth.[7]

Based on epigraphic evidence (*I.Eph.* 2212.a.6–7), in which a silversmith is called a ἀργυροκόπου νεωποιοῦ, 'silversmith and temple-warden', both Hicks ('Demetrius the Silversmith') and Rogers ('Demetrios of Ephesus') suggest that Demetrios was a νεωποιός, 'temple warden', one with responsibility for the administrative oversight of the temple and thus, in Acts, Demetrios did not make silver shrines but instead served as temple warden at the temple of Artemis of Ephesus; see discussion in Trebilco, 'Asia', p. 336 n. 203; p. 337 n. 210.

3. See Jan N. Bremmer, 'Aspects of the *Acts of Peter*: Women, Magic, Place and Date', in Jan N. Bremmer (ed.), *The Apocryphal Acts of Peter* (Studies on the Apocryphal Acts of the Apostles, 3; Leuven: Peeters, 1998), pp. 1–20, esp. 7–8; Elizabeth Bartman, *Ancient Sculptural Copies in Miniature* (Columbia Studies in the Classical Tradition, 19; Leiden: Brill, 1992), pp. 43–48; and the literature cited by both Bremmer and Bartman.

4. Because of the immediately preceding episode about the seven sons of Sceva (Acts 19.11–20), Luke's audience may have also understood the ναοὶ ἀργυροι as amulets. The atmosphere of honor, shame and boasting in 19.23–41 suggests that the audience may have primarily, but not solely, understood the silver shrines as votive objects.

5. W. D. Rouse, 'Votive offerings', in James Hastings (ed.), *Encyclopedia of Religion and Ethics* (New York: Scribner's; Edinburgh: T&T Clark, 1922), XII, pp. 641–43 (641).

6. Susan Guettel Cole, 'Greek Cults', in Grant and Kitzinger (eds), *Civilization of the Ancient Mediterranean* (New York: Scribners, 1988), II, pp. 887–908, esp. 890–91.

7. William Henry Denham Rouse, *Greek Votive Offerings* (Cambridge: Cambridge University Press, 1902; repr. Ancient Religion and Mythology; New York: Arno, 1975); F.T. van Straten, 'Gifts for the Gods', in H.S. Versnel (ed.), *Faith, Hope, and Worship*, pp. 65–151; Tullia Linders and Gullög Nordquist (eds), *Gifts to the Gods: Proceedings of the Uppsala Symposium 1985* (Acta Universitatis Upsaliensis; Boreas, Uppsala Studies in Ancient Mediterranean and Near Eastern Civilizations, 15;

What did votives mean in the ancient world? Votive offerings served the same three functions as did sacrifice (above, Chapter 4): 'For we must sacrifice to the gods for three reasons: to honor them, to thank them, or because we need something good' (Theophrastus, *Peri Eus.* frg. 12, ll. 43–44).[8] For example, the woman Meneia honored Athena for her miraculous powers on a fourth-century BCE votive inscription, 'Meneia has dedicated this to Athena, having seen the ἀρετή of the goddess in a vision'.[9] This expression of honor cut two ways: the votive gave pleasure to the god, and visitors to the sanctuary learned of Meneia's laudable reverence. In Herodas, two women visit a sanctuary and see the 'beautiful votive offerings [ἀγαλμάτων]' that others have left (*Mim.* 4.20–21). Not only do the dedicants honor the god, they also honor themselves:

> I, Simo, wife of Zoilos, priestess of Dionysos
> before the city, daughter of Pankratides,
> have presented this image as a proof of the goddess' beauty and my virtue and wealth,
> as an eternal memento for the children and the children's children.[10]

The second function of votives was to offer thanks. In the imperial period, grateful recipients of divine favor frequently used the verb εὐχαριστέω, 'give thanks', in their votive inscriptions: 'We give thanks [εὐχαριστοῦμεν] to Zeus Orneos, the sailors of Heracleia'.[11] Whatever these sailors were grateful for (safe travel? rescue after shipwreck?), they made a tangible physical representation of their gratitude through their votive offering and accompanying inscription to Zeus Orneos.

Finally, regarding Theophrastus' third reason for providing offerings to the gods, worshippers offered votives in the expectation of future benefits from the god:

Uppsala: Academia Upsaliensis, 1987); Robin Hägg, Nanno Marinatos, and Gullög C. Nordquist (ed.), *Early Greek Cult Practice: Proceedings of the Fifth International Symposium at the Swedish Institute at Athens, 26–29 June, 1986* (Skrifter Utgivna av Svenska Institutet i Athen, 4°, 38; Stockholm: Svenska Institutet i Athen, 1988); Folkert van Straten, 'Votives and Votaries in Greek Sanctuaries', in Albert Schachter (ed.) *Le Sanctuaire Grec* (Fondation Hardt, Entretiens 37; Geneva: Fondation Hardt, 1992), pp. 247–90; reprinted in Richard Buxton (ed.), *Oxford Readings in Greek Religion* (Oxford: Oxford University Press, 2000), pp. 191–223; Fritz Graf, 'Sacrifices, Offerings, and Votives: Greece', in Johnston (ed), *Religions of the Ancient World*, pp. 342–43.

    8.   This section follows van Straten, 'Gifts for the Gods', pp. 70–81.
    9.   *IG* II² 4326, trans., van Straten, 'Gifts for the Gods', p. 77. In this context, ἀρετή means 'miraculous power, …concrete miracles performed by the gods', (van Straten, 'Gifts for the Gods', p. 77). Many, if not most, votive offerings have perished. However, the donor's religious expression remains inscribed on the small plaque that usually accompanied votive offerings (van Straten, 'Gifts for the Gods', p. 69).
    10.   Trans. modified from Van Straten, 'Gifts for the Gods', p. 76; the plaque dates from fourth–fifth century BCE. Cited from Helmut Engelmann und Reinhold Merkelbach (ed.), *Die Inschriften von Erythrai und Klazomenai* (Bonn: R. Habelt, 1972–1973), p. 210, inscription 'a'. Van Straten translates l.3 as 'my [Simo's] beauty and my virtue and wealth'.
    11.   J. Robert and L. Robert, *Bulletin Épigraphique* (1976), p. 559, cited by van Straten, 'Gifts for the Gods', p. 72 and 72 n. 34.

...nes and his sons have presented this beautiful votive offering ἄγ[αλμα] to Athena;
may she be well-disposed towards them'.[12]

This man and his sons hoped for future help from Athena because of the quality of their votive offering.

The votive offering honored the god, thanked the god, and requested future benefits from the god. It was, in close connection with prayer and sacrifice, a method that initiated and sustained a relationship between the human individual and god. An event in the recent past often caused the presentation of a votive gift with the presentation of the gift itself intended for the future.[13]

In addition, votive offerings often displayed the ostentatious competitiveness of ancient Greek society.[14] Two women go to an Asklepieion to thank the god for healing one of them. One of them tells the other to display her votive prominently, 'Kokkale, set my votive plaque [πίνακα] to the right of Hygieia' (Herodas, *Mim.* 4.19–20). The women not only honor and express gratitude to the god; they also seek to place the votive in a publicly prominent spot next to the god's statue. After placing the votive, they look around the temple's interior and are both amazed by the other votive offerings to Asklepius, 'What beautiful images!' μᾶ καλῶν... ἀγαλμάτων, (4.20–21). Other worshippers in the same temple had already publicly displayed their reverence *and* their wealth by dedicating expensive votives.

Two additional examples demonstrate this display of reverence and ostentation. An Athenian priestess of Demeter Lysistra dedicated a votive with this accompanying inscription:

> The servant of your holy rites, oh mistress Deo, and of those of your
> daughter, Stephanos' daughter Lysistrata, has presented this show
> piece [the votive, ἄγαλμα] as an ornament of your portal, and she does not spare her
> property but makes abundant gifts to the gods according to her wealth.[15]

The Dionysian priestess Simo explicitly lauded herself, 'I presented this image as a proof of both...my virtue and wealth'. Other worshippers who entered the shrine of the god will read such votive inscriptions and see the dedicant's self-boasting and flamboyant votive.

---

12. Van Straten, trans., 'Gifts for the Gods', p. 73; citing the inscription from A.E. Raubitschek, *Dedications From the Athenian Akropolis, a Catalogue of the Inscriptions of the Sixth and Fifth Centuries, B.C.* (Cambridge, MA: Archaeological Institute of America, 1949), n. 64.

13. Van Straten, 'Gifts for the Gods', p. 80.

14. See the honor–shame models articulated by Jerome K. Neyrey and Bruce Malina: Bruce J. Malina and Jerome H. Neyrey, 'Honor and Shame in Luke-Acts: Pivotal Values of the Mediterranean World', in Jerome H. Neyrey (ed.), *The Social World of Luke-Acts: Models for Interpretation* (Peabody, MA: Hendrickson, 1991), pp. 25–66; Bruce J. Malina, *The New Testament World: Insights from Cultural Anthropology* (Louisville, KY: Westminster/John Knox, 3rd rev. edn, 2001), pp. 27–57.

Van Straten insists that this picture of competitiveness is one-sided and does not represent the genuine piety of the Greeks as a whole. Votives *truly did* express ancient εὐσέβεια, 'reverence', but they could also indicate ostentatious social display as the examples show ('Gifts for the Gods', pp. 76–77).

15. Athens, *c.* 450 BCE; *SEG* 10.321. Van Straten's translation ('Gifts for the Gods', p. 75 and p. 75 n. 52).

The Silver Shrines

What was the physical nature of the ναοὶ ἀργυροί? Diodorus Siculus mentions that the Carthaginians, when besieged by the Syracusan general Agathocles in 310 BCE, sacrificed golden shrines, kept in the Carthaginians' temples, which contained the images of the gods:

> They even sent gold shrines [ἱερῶν] out of their temples for supplication, believing that the anger of the gods would be better appeased if the images were sent as an earnest petition (*Hist.* 20.14.3).

The Carthaginians dedicated aniconic stelai of Baal as cultic figures in their Baal temples. After Roman colonization, families began to include architectural forms on their votive stelai, used to commemorate a family's child sacrifice.[16]

Small shrines were widely used in non-votive contexts in Roman domestic cult, 'In a corner I saw a large cupboard containing a tiny shrine [*aedicule*], in which were silver house-gods [*Lares argentei*], and a marble image of Venus... (Petronius, *Satyr.* 29).[17] Though probably not an offering *per se* to Venus, the shrine served to house the goddess. Quite possibly, the owner of the shrine had purchased it for this use. In Acts 19, Demetrius possibly sells silver shrines to individuals, such as the merchant Trimalchio in Petronius' *Satyricon*, for personal use as votive offerings.

The size and expense of votives varied greatly. Harvard University owns a terracotta statue of Artemis set in a niche that is 0.24 meters (9.36 inches) tall.[18] An excavated bronze knucklebone dedicated to Apollo weighs approximately 200 pounds.[19] A fragment of a small terracotta temple thought to be a votive to Artemis or part of the headdress of a statue of Artemis measures 8 cm long by 19.5 cm wide (3.2 in. by 7.8 in.).[20] Both Rouse and Van Straten mention votives that vary from modest wooden plaques to golden platters and vases.[21] Two people dedicated a gold gorgon, a silver siren, a silver vial, and a bronze lamp stand to Hera in sixth-century BCE Samos worth 212 staters (over a year's pay for a day laborer).[22]

---

16. Gilbert Charles Picard and Colette Picard, *Carthage: A Survey of Punic History and Culture from its Birth to the Final Tragedy* (Great Civilizations Series; London: Sidgwick & Jackson, 1987), pp. 41–48, 17–80, 146–54, 165–71, 224–25, 268–70; David Soren, Aicha ben Abed ben Khader, and Hedi Slim, *Carthage: Uncovering the Mysteries and Splendors of Ancient Tunisia* (New York: Simon and Schuster, 1990), pp. 40, 123–46, 225, 237–41.

17. Translated (slightly modified) by Michael Heseltine, *Petronius' Satyricon* (LCL; Cambridge, MA: Harvard University Press, 1913).

18. John Randolph Coleman, 'A Roman Terracotta Figurine of the Ephesian Artemis in the McDaniel Collection', *Harvard Studies in Classical Philology* 70 (1965), pp. 111–15, esp. p. 111.

19. Parke, *Oracles of Apollo in Asia Minor*, pp. 30–32.

20. Hermann Thiersch, *Artemis Ephesia eine archäologische Untersuchung: I, Katalog der erhaltener Denkmäler*, (*Abhandlungen der Gesellschaft der Wissenschaften zu Göttingen, Philologische-Historische Klasse*, 3rd Folge; Berlin: Weidmannsche Buchhandlung, 1935), p. 52 no. 32, fig. 38.1.

21. Rouse, *Greek Votive Offerings*, throughout; van Straten, 'Gifts for the Gods', throughout; *idem*, 'Votives and Votaries', throughout.

22. David M. Lewis, 'Temple Inventories in Ancient Greece', in Michael Vickers (ed.), *Pots & Pans: A Colloquium on Precious Metals and Ceramics in the Muslim, Chinese, and Graeco-Roman*

Such valuable votives often did not survive. When temple sanctuaries became too crowded with votive offerings, the temple personnel buried the inexpensive offerings and frequently melted precious metal votives together to make one larger offering.[23] During economic hardship or war, the sponsoring city often melted down the precious metal offerings for city coinage. [24] Presumably, the ναοὶ ἀργυροί suffered a similar fate.

Wide varieties of votive relief plaques contained architectural elements. Van Straten pictures 19 plaques whose edges were sculpted to resemble both the interior and exterior views of temples.[25] One example will suffice for my discussion. Xenokrateia dedicated a sanctuary to the river god Kephisos and brought her son there. On her votive plaque, Xenokrateia and her son stand in the midst of a dozen statues of gods and goddesses. The inscription on the plaque reads:

> Xenokrateia has founded the sanctu-
> ary of Kephisos, and has dedicated
> this gift to him and the gods who share his altar for the upbringing (of her son),
> (Xenokrateia) daughter and mother of a Xeniades, from Cholleidai.[26]

Xenokrateia's votive offering was the plaque, which pictured the sanctuary she established, and the accompanying inscription.

Architectural elements were an essential part of Artemis' iconography. Artists usually portrayed Artemis carrying a 'wall crown' or 'temple crown' on her head.[27] Coins portrayed Artemis standing inside her temple.[28] Numerous terra

---

Worlds (Oxford: Board of the Faculty of Oriental Studies, University of Oxford; Oxford University Press, 1986), pp. 71–81; reprinted in David M. Lewis, *Selected Papers in Greek and Near Eastern History* (Cambridge: Cambridge University Press, 1997), pp. 40–50, esp. p. 41.

23. Van Straten, 'Gifts for the Gods', pp. 79–80; *idem*, 'Votives and Votaries'; Lewis, 'Temple Inventories', throughout; Tullia Linders, 'Ritual Display and the Loss of Power', in Pontus Hellström and Brita Alroth (eds), *Religion and Power in the Ancient Greek World: Proceedings of the Uppsala Symposium 1993* (Acta Universitatis Upsaliensis; Boreas, Uppsala Studies in Ancient Mediterranean and Near Eastern Civilizations, 24; Uppsala: Academia Upsaliensis, 1996), pp. 120–24. *IG* II² 1534 states that exact records of votive offerings melted down into one combined larger offering were kept, 'so that the memory of the votive offerings should survive for the offerer'.

24. Trebilco, 'Asia', p. 337; van Straten, 'Gifts for the Gods', pp. 79–80; *idem*, 'Votives and Votaries', pp. 273–74; and Linders, 'Ritual Display and the Loss of Power', pp. 120–24, esp. 121. For these reasons, the contemporary non-existence of ναοὶ ἀργυροί *does not* prove that they are purely Lukan redaction (cf. the harsh, tendentious, and foundationless position of Robert M. Price, *The Widow Traditions in Luke-Acts: A Feminist-Critical Scrutiny* [SBLDS, 155; Atlanta: Scholars Press, 1997], p. 243; cf. Bonnie Thurston's harsh review of Price, *Reviews in Biblical Literature* [online], www.bookreviews.org/pdf/2182_1297.pdf).

25. Van Straten, 'Gifts for the Gods, figs. 8–9, 14–17b, 19a-20, 23?, 26, 28–29, 31, 43?, 45–47, 54?-55? The questionable references are either poorly preserved or the iconography is vague. See also van Straten, 'Votives and Votaries', pp. 265–68.

26. Trans. van Straten, 'Gifts for the Gods', p. 90 and fig. 23.

27. Examples of this headdress in Thiersch, *Artemis Ephesia*, p. 52 n. 32, fig. 38.1; and Robert Fleischer, *Artemis von Ephesos und verwandte Kultstatuen aus Anatolien und Syrien* (EPRO, 35; Leiden: Brill, 1973), figs. 6, 10, 12, 14–17. Trebilco seems to understand Thiersch's example as a freestanding model of a temple ('Asia', p. 336 and 336 n. 225; citing W. Oberleitner, *Funde aus Ephesos und Samothrake* [Kunsthistorisches Museum, Wien, Katalog der Antikensammlung 2;

cotta statues and reliefs show Artemis sitting inside a niche or lintel and column structure that appears to represent a temple.[29] Ellen D. Reeder published a bronze matrix, or casting mold, that depicted Artemis surrounded by architectural elements similar to the columns and pediments of a temple.[30] A bilingual inscription from Tarentum in Italy proves that, at least in Italy, small shrines were dedicated to Artemis as votives: 'To Artemis, he gave a shrine [*aidicolam*/ναίσκον] as a vow' (*IGRR* 1.467).

The above evidence suggests that Luke's Greco-Roman audience would have understood a reference to a common phenomenon: worshippers dedicated small shrines as votive offerings to Artemis. However, most of these shrines were probably not small freestanding models, but were instead either niches that housed the goddess' statue or headdresses traditionally associated with the goddess' artistic representation.

A Greco-Roman Audience and the Votive Offerings in Acts 19.23–41

How might have a Greco-Roman audience understand the silver shrines offered as votives to Artemis? If such an audience read Acts 19.23–41 after reading the Gospel of Luke, they may have detected a harsh Lukan criticism of ostentatiously displaying one's public religiosity for public approval. In depicting Judean worship (Lk. 18.9–14), Luke sets the self-aggrandizing religious practices of (his polemically constructed, ahistorical) Pharisees in opposition to a social outcast, a tax collector. A Pharisee presents himself in the Jerusalem Temple, as if he were (from the Greco-Roman perspective) his own votive offering to God. He expresses gratitude (one function of a votive offering) that he is not like the rest of humanity who are ἄρπαγες, 'thieves', ἄδικοι, 'the unjust', μοιχοί, 'adulterers', nor is he like ὁ τελώνης, 'the tax collector' (Lk. 18.11). Also, just as Simo the priestess of Dionysius, Lysistrata the Athenian priestess of Demeter, and the two women in Herodas displayed their superlative piety and personal attributes for all to see by dedicating votive offerings (see above), the Pharisee displays his personal catalog of virtuous religiosity (another function of a votive offering) in his prayer: 'I fast twice per week', and 'I tithe from all of my income'. Judean religious practices required fasting only once annually on the Day of Atonement (Lev. 16.31) and the giving of a tithe only on what people themselves produced (Deut. 14.22–29).

Vienna: Kunsthistorisches Museum, 1978], p. 56 n. 20). However, both Thiersch and Oberleitner (who cites Thiersch) consider the artifact a *polosfragment*, i.e., a headdress fragment.

28. Fleischer, *Artemis von Ephesus*, pp. 294–95, fig. 125b; and Richard E. Oster, 'Numismatic Windows into the Social World of Early Christianity: A Methodological Inquiry', *JBL* 101 (1982), pp. 195–223, esp. pp. 215–17 and pl. VII.

29. Coleman, ' Roman Terracotta Figurine', pp. 111–15; Fleischer, *Artemis von Ephesus*, 27–34. Coleman notes that the figurine and niche were manufactured separately, fastened together, and then fired as a whole ('Roman Terracotta Figurine', p. 112).

30. Reeder, 'Mother of the Gods', figs. 1, 3. Reeder specifically connects this object to Acts 19.24 ('Mother of the Gods', p. 440).

The Pharisee publicly proclaims his 'over-fulfillment' of these obligations.[31] In contrast, in vv. 13–14, Luke's Jesus mentions the humility of the tax collector who appeals for mercy from God; he does not offer himself as an ostentatious votive.

In Acts 19.23–41 Luke does not refer to generic offerings or to shrines in general but to expensive *silver* shrines. Because of this, a Greco-Roman reader may have not only understood Luke to condemn idolatry as such but also the ostentation often associated with it. On this basis such a reader might have concluded that ostentatious religiosity is strongly disassociated from true worship.

Διοπετής: *The Object Fallen from the Realm of the Gods*

Exegetes consistently and briefly note the meaning and use of διοπετής in antiquity without developing Luke's brief mention of the object.[32] After reviewing some of the ancient references to διοπετής objects, I will draw parallels between Luke's mention (Acts 19.35) of an aniconic, i.e., non-figurative, object used in the cult of Artemis and the enigmatic saying of Jesus in Luke 10.18. From these parallels I suggest that Greco-Roman readers may have drawn contrasting parallels between Satan in Luke 10.18, the demons in Acts 19.1–20, and the διοπετής object in 19.35.

Διοπετής *Objects in the Ancient World*

Throughout antiquity, both the Greeks and the Romans considered various objects διοπετής, literally 'fallen from Zeus' or 'descended from Zeus'. According to the available texts, such objects were meteorites, unusual rocks (also probably meteorites), or ancient pieces of wood. The Greeks considered the wooden image of Athena, known as the Palladium, as a διοπετής object:

> Having prayed to Zeus that some sort of sign appear to him, he saw, during the day, the Palladium, fallen [διιπετές] from the realm of the gods, lying in front of his tent… Zeus threw…the Palladium into the Ilian region. Ilus built a temple for it and honored it. (Ps.-Apollodorus, *Bibl.* 3.12.3)[33]
>
> But the holiest thing…is Athena's image [ἄγαλμα] which is now in the acropolis… They say about it that it has fallen from the realm of the gods [πεσεῖν ἐκ τοῦ οὐρανοῦ]. (Pausanias 1.26.6)
>
> But the statue of Athena, called the Palladium and believed to be fallen [διοπετές] from the realm of the gods, some think was found there unbroken, fallen on the encircling wall (Appian, *Mith.* 53.213)

31. The Pharisee's location in the Temple is unclear. The wording seems to imply that he is praying audibly and publicly for display (Fitzmyer, *Luke*, II, p. 1186; and Joel B. Green, *The Gospel of Luke* [NICNT; Grand Rapids: Eerdmanns, 1997], p. 646).

32. Haenchen, *Acts*, p. 575 and p. 575 n. 5; Conzelmann, *Acts*, p. 166 and p. 166 n. 39; Bruce, *Acts*, p. 420; Johnson, *Acts*, p. 350 and Trebilco, 'Asia', pp. 351–53. Trebilco provides an excellent historical commentary about διοπετής objects in antiquity.

33. James George Frazer discusses the Palladium in both Greek and Roman contexts in detail including its nature as a διοπετής object (*Apollodorus, The Library*, trans. James George Frazer [LCL; Cambridge, MA: Harvard University Press, 1921], p. 38 n. 2).

The historians Appian and Herodian recorded the Phrygian origins of the image of the Roman goddess *Magna Mater*, a large black meteorite.[34]

> This same image ἄγαλμα is said to be 'from the realm of the gods [διοπετές]'. No one knows what it is made of nor the craftsman. Some have the opinion that it was not made by the touch of human hands. The account is that it was brought down 'from the realm of the gods [ἐξ οὐρανοῦ] in ancient times into some part of Phrygia (the name of the place is Pessinous, and gets its name from the statue's fall from the 'realm of the gods' [ἐξ οὐρανοῦ] and was first seen there (Herodian 1.11.1).

> Because terrifying signs from Jupiter appeared in Rome, the *decemviri* who consulted the Sybilline oracles said that something would come from the realm of the gods [ἐξ οὐρανοῦ] to Pessinus in Phrygia (where the Phrygians worship the mother of the gods) convinced that this should be claimed and that it was necessary to bring it to Rome. After a short time, it was announced that the object had fallen [πεσεῖν] and the image of the god was brought to Rome. And now they celebrate the day on which the mother of the gods arrived (Appian, *Hann.* 56).

The διοπετής also figured in Greek mythology:

> Near where the the lightning bolt was hurled into Semele's bridal room, a log fell [πέσοι] from the realm of the gods [ἐξ οὐρανοῦ]. They say that Polydorus decorated this log with bronze, calling it Dionysius Kadmus (Pausanias 9.12.4).

The διοπετής persisted as a Greco-Roman concept into late antiquity. The third-century BCE historian Herodian noted the existence of a διοπετής stone in the Roman city of Emessa:

> There was an image [ἄγαλμα], not a handmade statue bearing the image of the god, such as the Greeks and Romans erect; but instead there was an enormous stone, round at the base, ending in a point, cone shaped, and black in color. They treat it with reverence as if it was fallen [διοπετῆ] from the gods. (Herodian 5.3.5)

Were διοπετής objects associated with Artemis? Euripides' treatment of the complex literary and mythological cycle about the house of Atreus includes two references to an 'image' [ἄγαλμα] of 'Zeus' daughter' or Artemis, that 'fell from the realm of the gods' [οὐρανοῦ πεσεῖν ἄπο]:

> You told me to come to the Taurian land,
> where your sister, Artemis, has altars,
> to take the image of the goddess [ἄγαλμα θεᾶς], which they say
> fell from the realm of the gods [οὐρανοῦ πεσεῖν ἄπο] into this temple.
> * * *
> Lifting [his sister, Iphigenia] to his left shoulder,
> he waded into the sea and jumped on the ladder,
> and set his sister on the well-built ship,
> along with the object fallen from the realm of the gods [οὐρανοῦ πέσημα],
>   the image [ἄγαλμα]
> of the daughter of Zeus. (*Iph. taur.* 85–88, 1381–85)[35]

---

34. After consulting the Sybilline oracles, the Senate formally summoned *Magna Mater* to Rome in 205 BCE. The image arrived in 204 and was housed in a temple consecrated to *Magna Mater* in 191 (Livy 24.10–14).

35. Because of a lacuna in the mss., critical editions and translations differ in their line numbering.

Though set in the far distant land of Tauris (modern day Crimea), Euripides'
play associates Artemis with a cultic object that is διοπετής. Apart from Luke's
comment in Acts, there are no other ancient literary sources that associate Artemis
and διοπετής objects. Charles Seltman presents circumstantial numismatic and
archaeological evidence to suggest that a small elongated stone (now in a museum
in Wales) was the Ephesian Artemis' διοπετής that Luke mentioned in Acts
19.35.[36] Most likely Luke was referring to a real cult object in Ephesus that was
part of a long tradition of Greco-Roman cult objects. These naturally occurring
objects were aniconic 'images' of a god and often considered διοπετής, 'fallen
from the realm of the gods' precisely because they were not of human manufacture and often of extraterrestrial origin.

Luke's Use of the ΔΙΟΠΕΤΗΣ
How would a Greco-Roman have understood Luke's passing reference to the
Ephesian διοπετής in 19.35? Such a reader may have possibly related Acts 19.35
to the traditional Judean polemic against idolatry (out of many examples: Isa.
40.18–20; 44.9–20; Wis. 13.10–14.1). The city of Ephesus was νεωκόρος, 'temple
keeper' or 'guardian' of both Artemis' temple and the διοπετής (19.35). Therefore, though seemingly 'fallen from Zeus', the διοπετής is an object tended to
by human hands and housed in a temple of human construction (Acts 7.48–50;
17.24–25; 19.26); it is an idol.[37]
    More probably, a Greco-Roman reader, unfamiliar with the Hebrew Scriptures,
may have noted a subtle reference back to Luke's Gospel. I speculatively suggest
that such a reader may have seen an allusion to a Jesus saying in Lk. 10.8, 'He
said to them, "I saw Satan like lightning [ὡς ἀστραπήν] falling from heaven [ἐκ
τοῦ οὐρανοῦ πεσόντα]" '.[38] This enigmatic and almost fragmentary logion has

For consistency, I follow J. Diggle (ed.), *Euripidis Fabulae* (OCT; Oxford: Oxford University Press,
1981). See his apparatus for details.
    36. Charles Seltman, 'The Wardrobe of Artemis', *Numismatic Chronicle* Series 6, 12 (1952), pp.
33–51, esp. 49–51; *idem, The Twelve Olympians and Their Guests* (rev. and enlarged ed.; London:
Max Parrish, 1956), pp. 128–29, 131.
    37. Lake and Cadbury, *Beginnings*, IV, p. 250; Johnson, *Acts*, p. 350; Trebilco, 'Asia', pp. 353–53;
Witherington, *Acts*, p. 598. Cf. Haenchen, 'That this διοπετές [*sic*] was an answer by the chancellor to
Paul's polemic against the gods made with hands…is a conjecture which by-passes the Lucan meaning
of the scene' (*Acts*, p. 575, n. 5).
    38. Cf. Scott Schauf, *Theology as History, History as Theology: Paul in Ephesus in Acts 19*
(BZNW, 133; Berlin: Walter de Gruyter, 2005), p. 255 n. 442. He argues against that my linkage of
Acts 19.35 and Lk. 10.8 (in my original dissertation) is a 'tremendous stretch' that 'ignores the vastly
different context in which the two locutions occur'. Instead he understands the use of διοπετής in
19.35 as Luke's 'round-about defense of Paul'. The *grammeteus* argues that the διοπετής is 'fallen
from the realm of the gods', and therefore not made by human hands, thus implying that Paul did not
blaspheme in his teaching about 'gods that come about through human hands' (19.26).
    I willingly concede Schauf's point about Luke's defense of Paul but Schauf does not address in
detail the similarities that I see between Lk. 10.8 and Acts 19.35. Also, he unintentionally overstates
my confidence in my conclusions. As stated in Chapter 1, my conclusions about Acts 19.23–41 are a
'sounding' or of very a tentative, hypothetical nature. Finally, is it not possible for multiple interpretations of a given text to be simultaneously valid and cohere with authorial intention? Even if we

spurred widely ranging interpretations.[39] Whatever Luke's use of this passage in his gospel, there may be parallels and distant echoes of it in Acts 19.35 (Table 6).

Table 6. *Parallels Between Luke 10.18 and Acts 19.35*

Lk. 10.18	Acts 19.35
Reliance upon Judean apocalyptic traditions Satan 'fell from heaven' [ἐκ τοῦ οὐρανοῦ πεσόντα]	Reliance upon Greco-Roman myth Artemis' image [ἄγαλμα] was 'fallen from Zeus' or 'fallen from the realm of the gods' [διοπετής]
Reliance upon Judean traditions in which Satan falls 'like lightning' [ὡς ἀστραπήν]	Background Greco-Roman mythological traditions associating an ἄγαλμα, 'image', made of wood with a lightning bolt (Pausanias 9.12.4)
Logion occurs immediately after successful exorcisms (Luke 10.1–17)	Mention of the διοπετής occurs in Ephesus after both successful and unsuccessful exorcisms in the same city (Acts 19.12–16)
Logion is set in missionary context	διοπετής set in missionary context

If Greco-Roman readers understood Luke to allude to his Gospel, they would perhaps understand Luke as paralleling Satan and Artemis in their ability to intervene in the world. In Lk. 18.10, Satan himself falls from heaven. In Acts 19.35, Artemis' image and *not Artemis herself* falls from Zeus' realm.[40]

The exorcism narratives in Luke-Acts, portray Satan as a living, threatening entity who opposes both God and God's followers and seeks to dominate them (e.g., Jesus' temptation, Lk. 4.1–13, or Simon Bar Jesus, Acts 13.6–12). Conversely, Artemis is just a 'handmade god' or a mere meteorite. Satan poses a very

consider understanding Luke's authorial intention, is it not possible to reconstruct multiple interpretations for an ancient audience?

39. Friedrich Spitta, 'Der Satan als Blitz', *ZNW* 9 (1908), pp. 160–63; Ulrich B. Müller, 'Vision und Botschaft: Erwagungen zur prophetischen Struktur der Verkündigung Jesu', *ZThK* 74 (1977), pp. 416–48; Samuel Vollenweider, 'Ich sah den Satan wie einen Blitz vom Himmel fallen (Lk 10.18)', *ZNW* 79 (1988), pp. 187–203; Garrett, *Demise of the Devil*, pp. 46–54; David Crump, 'Jesus, the Victorious Scribal-Intercessor in Luke's Gospel', *NTS* 388 (1992), pp. 51–65; Julian Victor Hills, 'Luke 10.18–Who Saw Satan Fall?', *JSNT* 46 (1992), pp. 25–40; Twelftree, *Jesus the Exorcist*, pp. 125–27 and Joel Marcus, 'Jesus' Baptismal Vision (Satan Falling From Heaven)', *NTS* 41 (1995), pp. 512–21. Twelftree provides additional bibliography.

40. Greco-Roman readers may have also associated Satan's fall with the fall of the διοπετής because πίπτω was often used as the passive of βάλλω (Wilhelm Michaelis, 'πίπτω', *TDNT* VI (1968), pp.161–66, esp. p. 161 and p. 163 n.9). If this argument is valid, a Greco-Roman audience may have understood both Satan's and Artemis' fall from the divine realm as an active expulsion by either 'the living god' or Zeus. Since Zeus is a 'god made by human hands', Greco-Romans may have also considered both expulsions as the work of 'the living god'.

Joachim Jeremias argued that the participle πεσόντα in Lk. 10.18 is a Semitic quasi-passive that should be translated, 'be cast out' (*New Testament Theology: The Proclamation of Jesus* [New York: Scribners, 1971], p. 95; accepted by both Aune [*Prophecy in Early Christianity*, p. 163 and p. 391 n. 81] and Garrett [*Demise of the Devil*, pp. 50–51]). However, a Greco-Roman, unfamiliar with Hebrew or Aramaic, would have construed the grammar of Lk. 10.18 in light of their own linguistic background.

real threat to the Christian community; Artemis does not; only her misguided followers do.

The immediate literary contexts of both Luke 10.18 and Acts 19.23–41 involve both missionary outreach and the performance or attempted performance of exorcisms. Jesus sends 70 (or 72?) disciples on an advance mission for his ministry (Lk. 10.1–16). They return reporting that they had power over demons (10.17); Jesus' responds that he saw Satan, 'falling like lighting from heaven' (1.18). In some fashion Jesus has witnessed Satan's defeat.[41] In Acts 19.11–20, the 'seven sons of Sceva' attempt to exorcise evil spirits but instead are attacked, wounded, and flee naked. As Garrett has pointed out, the seven would-be exorcists do not have Jesus' authority and are therefore spectacularly unsuccessful.[42] Paul, however, is fully able to exorcise demons precisely because he has the authority of Jesus. Satan's forces are active and dangerous during Paul's mission, but those, like Paul, who have Jesus' authority can defeat the demonic.

Acts 19.21–22 serves as a transitional unit between the seven sons of Sceva (19.11–20) and the near riot in Ephesus (19.23–41).[43] By separating these two episodes, this brief transition contrasts the aborted exorcism and indication of demonic power in 19.11–20 with the impotence of the 'handmade god' Artemis in 19.23–41. A Greco-Roman reader (or any reader) would probably have noticed that Luke consistently depicts 'magical' practices as demonic and defeated by God's power through the early Christians.[44] For Luke and these readers, the demons of 19.11–20 are real personal forces that contend with the Christians and must be exorcised.

In contrast, Demetrius and the citizens of Ephesus intervene to defend Artemis' honor. God toppled Satan from heaven; Artemis' image merely fell. The revered διοπετής is a mere meteorite, fallen to earth from the sky, and created by the living God who 'created the universe and the earth and the sea and everything in them' (14.15).

Conclusions

In Acts 19.23–41, Luke makes two brief comments about the cult of the Ephesian Artemis: locally manufactured ναοὶ ἀργυροί, 'silver shrines', are used in her cult; and Ephesus is the guardian of her διοπετής, her 'image fallen from the realm of the gods'. Luke's Greco-Roman audience may have understood these brief references as allusions to a broad range of highly familiar cultural phenomena: the use of votive offerings ostentatiously displayed in worshipping the gods (or God), and

41. There is extensive disagreement on the chronology of Satan's fall in this passage (discussion and references in Garrett, *Demise of the Devil*, pp. 46–60). Is Jesus, in Luke's conception, predicting Jesus' fall? Or is he stating that Satan has already been defeated? For my purposes, the exact chronology of Satan's fall is unimportant.

42. Garrett, *Demise of the Devil*, pp. 89–99 esp. pp. 91–94.

43. Johnson, *Acts*, p. 346; Talbert, *Reading Acts*, p. 177; Witherington, *Acts*, p. 588.

44. Garrett, *Demise of the Devil*, throughout.

the worship of aniconic images considered διοπετής, 'fallen from the realm of the gods'.

If Luke's Greco-Roman readers perceived cultural allusions to votive offerings and διοπετής objects, they may have concluded that true worship does not involve public display of one's superlative religiosity. Secondly, if they perceived intertextual allusions to Lk. 10.18 and 18.9–14, they may have also concluded that though Satan and his minions are a real and dangerous force, the Greco-Roman gods are impotent and unable to intervene in human affairs because they are human creations. Greco-Roman readers probably developed a theological and conceptual universe when reading Luke-Acts. If so, they may have concluded from within this universe that the Christian community has only two enemies: human ego-centrism and demonic forces. The ναοὶ ἀργυροι are but the empty and ostentatious accouterments of an impotent and human-created deity, while διοπετής objects are but natural created objects fallen from the sky. Therefore, the Christian community can benignly ignore the Greco-Roman gods as a threat.

Chapter 7

ACTS 28.1–11: ΕΧΙΔΝΑ, ΔΙΚΗ, AND THE ΔΙΟΣΚΟΥΡΟΙ

In Acts 28.1–11, Paul is shipwrecked on Malta, survives a snakebite, performs healings and departs for Rome on a ship whose figurehead is the Διόσκουροι, 'the Twins' (Castor and Pollux). There are at least three elements in this text that would resonate in the minds of a Greco-Roman audience: ἔχιδνα, 'snake', Δίκη, 'justice', and the Διόσκουροι. This audience would read Acts 28.1–11 in light of existing mythological and cultic traditions about snakes, the concept of personified abstractions, and the Dioskuroi as 'savior gods' and possibly conclude: (1) Paul is divinely declared innocent, (2) the 'living God' (θεὸς ζῶν) ultimately controls Paul's safety and mission, and (3) Paul's message i.e., the Lukan Paul's message, is reliable and free from duplicity or subversion.[1]

Snakes in Greek Myth and Religion

Ophidian imagery was widely used in Greek art, mythology, and cult.[2] According to Erich Küster, the earliest snake imagery in ancient Greek cultures is in late

---

1. Relevant studies of this passage include Franz Joseph Dölger, '"Dioskuroi". Das Reiseschiff des Apostels Paulus und seine Schutzgötter', *Antike und Christentum* 6 (1950), pp. 276–85; S.H. Kanda, 'The Form and Function of the Petrine and Pauline Miracle Stories in the Acts of the Apostles' (PhD dissertation, Claremont, 1974), pp. 288–303; Gary B. Miles and Garry Trompf, 'Luke and Antiphon: The Theology of Acts 27–28 in the Light of Beliefs about Divine Retribution, Pollution, and Shipwreck', *HTR* 69 (1976), pp. 259–67; David Ladouceur, 'Hellenistic Preconceptions of Shipwreck and Pollution as a Concept for Acts 27–28', *HTR* 73 (1980), pp. 435–49; Susan Marie Praeder, 'Acts 27.1–28.16: Sea Voyages in Ancient Literature and the Theology of Luke-Acts', *CBQ* 46 (1984) 'Acts 27.1–28.16', pp. 683–706; G.W. Trompf, 'On Why Luke Declined to Recount the Death of Paul: Acts 27–28 and Beyond', in *Luke-Acts: New Perspectives from the Society of Biblical Literature Seminar* (ed. Charles H. Talbert; New York: Crossroad, 1984), pp. 225–39, at pp. 226, 232–33, and 236 nn. 7–8; Jürgen Wehnert, 'Zu einem neuen These zur den Shiffbruch der Apostels Paulus auf den Wege nach Rom (Apg. 27–28)', *ZThK* 87 (1990), pp. 67–99, esp. p. 94; Lou H. Silberman, 'Paul's Viper: Acts 28.3–6', *Forum* 8 (1992), pp. 247–253; C.H. Talbert and J.H. Hayes, 'A Theology of Sea Storms in Luke-Acts', *SBLSP* 34 (1995), pp. 321–36; Schreiber, *Paulus als Wundertäter*, pp. 122–37; Spencer, *Acts*, pp. 234–36; *idem*, 'Paul's Odyssey in Acts: Status Struggles and Island Adventures', *BTB* 28 (1998), pp. 150–59; Talbert, *Reading Acts*, pp. 215–25. Schreiber furnishes a discussion of the immediate literary context of Acts 28.3–9, a thorough form-and redaction-critical study, vocabulary and stylistic analyses, and important comparative materials. Spencer's conclusions parallel mine but we disagree strongly on details (see below; 'Paul's Odyssey', pp. 157, 158).

2. The basic work remains Erich Küster, *Die Schlange in der griechischen Kunst und Religion* (RVV, 13.2; Giessen, Germany: Alfred Töpelmann, 1913); also, H. Gossen-Steier, 'Schlange', PW II/5 (1921), cols 494–557.

neolithic art from Eleusis, Crete and Cyprus.[3] One continues to find snake imagery in Greek art through the Mycenean, geometric, archaic, classical, Hellenistic and Roman periods.[4] Mitropolou has cataloged the wide use of snake imagery and symbolism in Classical and post-classical banquet scene reliefs and as representations of Greek deities and heroes on stelae, altars, columns, sculptures, coin images and vase paintings.[5]

The Greeks associated snakes with a wide variety of their heroes, myths, gods, and cults. Most commonly they regarded snakes as chthonic beings but also regarded snakes in diverse and often contradictory ways.[6] Snakes were the embodiment of the 'souls' of the murdered, guardians of graves and shrines (Herodotus 8.41), associated with the hero cult, considered 'earth spirits', the totem of several gods (Zeus Meilichios, Zeus Ktesios, Zeus Trophonios, Amphiaraos, Zeus Hades, Hera, Artemis, Hecate, Athena and her aegis, Nike, Hygieia, Ares, Dionysos, Hermes, Asclepius), and associated with prophesying and manticism, healing cults (Asclepius and Hygeia), fertility, and 'water spirits'.[7] Both the Greeks and the Romans had positive images of snakes as associated with domestic cult. The Romans closely associated the family *Genius* and ophidian imagery in their *lararia*, domestic shrines.[8]

Snakes and Justice

During the classical era, the Greeks closely associated snakes, divine justice for murder victims, and the Erinyes. As mentioned above (chapter 5), Aeschylus was considered the first to depict the Erinyes with ophidiform hair, in the opening scenes of his *Eumenides*. Similar imagery appears in Euripides (*Iph. taur.* 286) and much later in Virgil where snakes are referred to as *Dirae* who are wreathed with 'coiled serpents' (*serpentum spiris; Aen.* 12.845–48, also 6.570, 7.445–55). Shortly before Luke's time, one Greek poet, presumably the Augustan-era poet Statyllius Flaccus, associated survival from shipwreck, fated death and snakebite:

> The shipwrecked sailor had fled from the storm and fury of the destructive
>   sea. Lying on the Libyan sands,
> not far from the beach, deep in his final sleep,
>   naked, exhausted from the dreadful wreck,
> a venomous snake killed him. Why did he vainly struggle with the waves,
>   fleeing the fate [μοῖραν] that came due on land? (*Anth. Pal.* 7.290).[9]

   3. Küster, *Die Schlange*, pp. 21–27.

   4. Küster, *Die Schlange*, pp. 27–55; Elpis Mitropoulou, *Horses' Heads and Snake* [sic] *in Banquet Reliefs and Their Meaning* (Athens: Pyli Editions, 1976); and *idem, Deities and Heroes in the Form of Snakes*, (2nd edn; Athens: Pyli Editions, 1977).

   5. Mitropolou, *Horses' Heads*, pp. 83–145; *idem, Deities and Heroes*, throughout.

   6. Küster, *Die Schlange*, pp. 157–58.

   7. Küster, *Die Schlange*, pp. 62–157.

   8. Martin P. Nilsson discusses the origins of Greek snake cult in domestic worship (*Greek Popular Religion* (1940); repr. *Greek Folk Religion*; Torchbook Editions, 78; The Cloister Library; New York: Harper, 1961), pp. 67–72. David G. Orr discusses the close relationship of snake imagery to Roman domestic shrines ('Roman Domestic Religion: The Evidence of the Household Shrines', *ANRW* II/16, part 2 (1978), pp. 1557–91; esp. pp. 1570–75 and pl. II, fig. 4; pls. IV, VI, VIII fig. 17; and pl. IX.

   9. On this poem, see the commentary by A.S.F. Gow and D.L. Page (eds), *The Greek Anthology:*

Though the sailor is not depicted as a murderer or the victim of revenge, he receives his 'apportioned fate' [μοῖραν ὀφειλομένην], from a venomous snake.

This association of snakes and just or fated death persisted into at least the third to fourth century of the late Empire. The second century naturalist Aelian described a snake that only killed the evil or irreverent:

> The asp [ἀσπίδα], *thermouthis*, the name given to it by the Egyptians, they say is sacred... Further, they say it is not to cause the destruction or harm of people. But they are exaggerating when they say that it spares the virtuous [τῶν ἀγαθῶν], but kills the irreverent [τοὺς δὲ ἀσεβοῦντας ἀποκτιννύναι]. If this is true, then above all things Justice [ἡ Δίκη] should honor this asp [ἀσπίδα] for taking vengeance on her behalf [τιμωροῦσαν] and for its penetrating sight. Others add that Isis sends the snake against the worst offenders (*Nat. an.* 10.31).

Heliodorus describes the death of the Egyptian thief and low-life Thermouthis [!] who dies by snakebite because of his evil character:

> Thermouthis lay down to sleep, but the sleep he slept was the final sleep, the brazen sleep of death, for he was bitten by a viper [εἵλκυσεν ἀσπίδος δήγματι]. Perhaps it was destiny's [μοιρῶν] will that his life should end in a way so befitting his character (*Aeth.* 2.20).[10]

Ancient Greek art also associated snakes, the Erinyes and vengeance for homicide.[11] Mitropoulou cataloged fourteen examples of art works that associate snakes with the Erinyes, i.e., snakes are associated with the mythological and literary persona of vengeance personified.[12] A.J.N.W. Prag has published art works (primarily Greek vase paintings) that display elements of the Oresteia cycle.[13] He lists several vases (and six pictures) that display either snakes or Erinyes carrying snakes avenging the dead.[14] A fifth-century BCE vase painting shows an Erinyes

---

The Garland of Philip and Some Contemporary Epigrams (Cambridge: Cambridge University Press, 1968), I, p. 423; II, p. 452.

10. J.R. Morgan (trans.), *CAGN*.

11. Jane Ellen Harrison, 'Delphika', *JHS* 19 (1899), pp. 205–51 esp. pp. 205–25; *eadem, Prolegomena to the Study of Greek Religion* (Cambridge: Cambridge University Press, 1903), pp. 212–56, esp. pp. 232–39, and figs. 53–56. The Erinyes: Harrison, *Prolegomena*, pp. 212–56; Ernst Wüst, 'Erinyes', PWSup, 8 (1956), pp. 82–166; B.C. Dietrich, *Death, Fate and the Gods* (London: Athlone, University of London, 1965), pp. 91–156; Haigamich Sarian and Peter Delev, 'Erinyes', *LIMC*, III, part 1, pp. 826–43; Herbert Jennings Rose and B.C. Dietrich, 'Erinyes', *OCD*, p. 556; and Sarah Iles Johnston, *Restless Dead: Encounters between the Living and the Dead in Ancient Greece* (Berkeley: University of California Press, 1999), pp. 127–60, 250–88.

12. Mitropolou, *Deities and Heroes*, pp. 46–48. Mitropolou helpfully catalogs obscurely published and non-extant works, and provides bibliography through to 1976.

13. A.J.N.W. Prag, *The Oresteia: Iconography and Narrative Tradition* (Chicago: Bolchazy-Carducci, 1985). Additional plates in Haigamich Sarian and Peter Delev, 'Erinyes', *LIMC*, III, part 2, pp. 595–606.

14. Prag, *The Oresteia*, pp. 44–48, 57, figs. 28–33; also H.B. Walters, *History of Ancient Pottery: Greek Etruscan, and Roman* (New York: Scribners, 1905), II, pl. 52. According to Prag, the iconography of vase painting associated snakes, vengeance and victims of homicide in the sixth century BCE. Under the influence of Aeschylean and Euripidean tragedy, this iconography changed from snakes by themselves to women carrying snakes, the Erinyes, about 458 BCE.

carrying a snake with the word ἔσθ[ε]τον or ἔσθ [ι]τον, 'Eat!' written next to the Erinyes' mouth.[15] The snake is to attack and devour the person who is the target of the Erinyes' vengeance. A fifth-century vase painting depicts a snake rising up from the corpse of a murder victim and threatening the fleeing murderer with its gaping jaws.[16]

The Parallel in Luke

For a Greco-Roman audience there may have been parallels between their cultural association of snakes, justice and vengeance for murder. Luke depicts the Maltese islanders making this very association when the snake bites or grasps Paul:

> When the natives saw the wild animal hanging from his hand, they were saying to one another, 'Certainly this man is a murderer, who being saved from the sea, Justice [ἡ Δίκη] will not permit to live!' (Acts 28.4)

Luke's imagery in Acts 28.4 is directly parallel to the literature and vase painting that at least a portion of his audience was familiar with. A snake grasps Paul by the hand (Acts 28.4). The Maltese, who witness the event, immediately call Paul a murderer (φονεύς) and assume that the snake is the agent of Justice (Δίκη), who will not permit Paul to live (Acts 28.4).

Δίκη: Justice Personified

Both the Greeks and the Romans created 'personified abstractions', which were deified abstract concepts such as peace, health, or victory.[17] These 'deified' or

---

15. Prag, *The Oresteia*, p. 117, n. 41.

16. Harrison, *Prolegomena*, p. 237, fig. 56. Cf. Friedrich Hauser's discussion of this vase ('Eine Tyrrhenische Amphora der Sammlung Bourguinon', *Jahrbuch des deutschen archaologischen Instituts* 8 [1893], pp. 93–103 and table 1).

17. On personified abstractions in Greek religion, see L. Deubner, 'Personifikation abstrakter Begriffe', *ALGRM*, III/2 cols 2068–169; L. Peterson, *Zur Geschichte der Personifikation in griechischer Dichtung und Bildener Kunst* (Würzburg: Konrad Triltsch, 1939); William Chase Greene, 'Personifications', *OCD* (1st edn), pp. 669–71 (this article was deleted from the subsequent editions); T.B.L. Webster, 'Language and Thought in Early Greece', *Memoirs and Proceedings of the Manchester Literary and Philosophical Society* 94 (1952–53), pp. 17–38; *idem*, 'Personification as a Greek Mode of Thought', *Journal of the Wartburg and Courtald Institute* 17 (1954), pp. 10–21; Harvey Alan Shapiro, 'Personification of Abstract Concepts in Greek Art and Literature to the End of the Fifth Century B.C.', (PhD dissertation, Princeton University, 1977), esp. pp. 42–48; *idem, Personifications in Greek Art: The Representation of Abstract Concepts 600–400 B.C.* (Crescens, 1; Zurich: Akanthus 1993), esp. pp. 12–27; Burkert, *Greek Religion*, pp. 184–86; Parker, *Athenian Religion*, pp. 227–37; and Emma Stafford, *Worshipping Virtues: Personification and the Divine in Ancient Greece* (London: Duckworth; Swansea, Wales: The Classical Press of Wales, 2004), pp. 1–44. Thorough bibliographies in Shapiro, Parker and Stafford.

On personified abstractions in Roman religion: Harold L. Axtell, *The Deification of Abstract Ideas in Roman Literature and Inscriptions* (Chicago: University of Chicago Press, 1907), throughout; Deubner, 'Personifikation abstrakter Begriffe;' Greene, 'Personifications;' and J. Rufus Fears, 'The Cult of Virtues and Roman Imperial Ideology', *ANRW* II/17, part 2 (1981), pp. 828–948. Fears provides thorough bibliography.

Shapiro posits ten different types of personified abstractions: physical conditions, social goods,

"personified" abstract concepts elicited all the hallmarks of ancient religiosity, 'The moment a "personification" receives a cult, and prayers and sacrifices, hopes and fears are connected with her, she becomes as concrete a divinity as any other deity'.[18]

One of these abstractions was Δίκη, 'Justice', (Latin, *Iustitia*).[19] Δίκη appears in Greek myth at least as early as the seventh century BCE in Hesiod's *Theogony* as the daughter of Zeus and Themis (886, 901). She also appears in his *Opera et Dies* where she informs Zeus of the injustices committed by humanity (220–73). In the pre-Socratic philosopher Heraklitus, Δίκη has the Erinyes as her helpers.[20] She sits next to Zeus in Sophocles', *Oed. Col.* 1381–82, and in a lost play of Aeschylus where she also keeps a record of human 'sins'.[21] In the portraits of Δίκη by Aratus (*Phaen.* 96–136), Virgil (*Ecl.* 4.6, *G.* 2.473–74), and Ovid (*Metam.* 1.149–50), she left the earth at the start of the Bronze Age. Δίκη was usually depicted as a woman carrying a sword and sometimes as a winged denizen of Hades.[22] In the third century CE *Orphic Hymns* (no. 62), she sits besides Zeus. Though unknown in extant ancient Greek literature, in Greek art Δίκη is frequently seen beating Ἀδικία, 'Injustice', with her staff.[23] Over time Δίκη developed from the goddess who oversaw justice, and she began to assume the dark aspect of the Erinyes. As van der Horst notes, 'the original distinction [between Δίκη and the Erinyes] became more and more blurred as Δίκη progressively changed from an accuser or plaintiff into *a mighty and relentless deity who wrathfully wielded the weapons of revenge*'.[24]

Greek literature also associated Δίκη with the sea. The Augustan-era poet Antipater of Thessalonica made this connection:

ethical and moral qualities, metaphysical ideas, geographical features, natural phenomena, products of the earth, kinds of individuals, collective groups, and social enjoyments ('Personification of Abstract Concepts', p. 23; citing E. Pottier, 'Les représentations allégoriques dans les peintues de vases grecs', *Monuments Grecs*, pp. 15–18 [1889–90] and Walters, *History of Ancient Pottery*, II, pp. 77–92; see also Shapiro, *Personifications in Greek Art*, p.26 and p. 26 n. 47).

18. Karl Lehmann, review of Per G. Hamber, *Studies in Roman Imperial Art*, in *Art Bulletin* 29 (1947), p. 138. Cited with approval by Shapiro, *Personifications in Greek Art*, p. 12.

19. Otto Waser, 'Dike', PW 5 (1903), pp. 574–78; Hugh Lloyd-Jones, *The Justice of Zeus* (Sather Classical Lectures, 41; Berkeley: University of California Press, 1971), *passim*; Burkert, *Greek Religion*, pp. 130, 185, 230; H. Alan Shapiro, 'Dike', *LIMC*, III, part 1, pp. 388–91; and III, part 2, pp. 280–81, pls. 3–16; P.W. van der Horst, 'Dike', *DDD*, pp. 476–80.

20. Diels, *Die Fragmente der Vorsokratiker* 22 B 94.

21. Hans Joachim Mette (ed.), *Die Fragmente der Tragödien des Aischylos* (Berlin: Akademie-Verlag, 1959) frg. 530, 9a, 10–11.21. Walters cites examples of vase paintings depicting Δίκη (*History of Ancient Pottery*, p. 89).

22. Shapiro, 'Dike', p. 388.

23. Pausanias saw an example on the Chest of Kypselos (5.18.2) where Δίκη was depicted as choking Ἀδικία. Pausanias' discussion of this chest is one of our primary sources for understanding the development of personified abstractions in Greek antiquity; discussion and bibliography in Shapiro, *Personifications in Greek Art*, pp. 22–23, 39–43, and 39 pl. 6. Examples from vase painting in Shapiro, 'Dike', p. 280, pl. 3.

24. van der Horst, 'Dike', *DDD* (2nd edn), p. 477, my emphasis.

When the ship had been smashed to pieces in the water, two men
   struggled with each other fighting for a single piece of the wreckage.
Antagoras struck Peisistratos. This was not unpardonable,
   because it was a matter of life and death, but it concerned Justice [Δίκη].
One swam on, but a shark caught the other. The Avenger-of-all-evil
   knows no rest in the depths of the sea (*Anth. Pal.* 9.269).[25]

A Greco-Roman audience would probably have seen direct parallels between Luke's narrative and Greek literary, mythological, and artistic traditions. To paraphrase van der Horst, Luke depicts Δίκη as a relentless deity who wrathfully wields the weapons of revenge. Paul is shipwrecked, but survives. Despite Paul's survival, Δίκη pursues him on shore and attacks him in the form of an avenging snake.

The Dioskuroi

The Dioskuroi were twin brothers, Kastor and Polydeukes (Latin, *Pollux*), the sons of Zeus and Leda.[26] They became known as 'savior gods' to those in distress: soldiers in war, women in various forms of distress, travelers in foreign lands, victims of illness, and most especially sailors and other travelers in danger on the sea.[27] The epiphany of the Dioskuroi saves those individuals who put their faith in the Dioskuroi.[28] The ancient *Homeric Hymn, To the Dioskuroi*, illustrates the Dioskuroi's role as savior gods for sailors by their epiphany:

[Leda] bore [these] children as saviors [σωτῆρας] of the people on earth
[and] of swift ships, when winter storms rush
along the merciless sea. Then the sailors
pray, calling upon the sons of great Zeus
with white lambs going to the stern
deck. But when the great winds and waves of the sea
swamp her, they suddenly appear,
darting through the air with shrill whistling wings,
instantly they calm the harsh wind storms,

25. My translation (esp. ll. 2, 4, and 6) is informed by the translation and commentary of Gow and Page, *Greek Anthology*, I, pp. 80–81; and II, p. 106.

26. Primary sources for the Dioskuroi mythology in Pierre Grimal, *The Dictionary of Classical Mythology* (London: Blackwell, corrected edn, 1986), p. 482. Secondary discussion: Erich Bethe, 'Dioskuren', PW, V/1 (1903), pp. 1087–1903, esp. 1096–97; W. Klaus, 'Dioskuren', *RAC* 3 (1975), pp. 1122–58; Burkert, *Greek Religion*, pp. 212–13 and Robert Christopher Townley Park, 'Dioskuri', *OCD* (3rd edn), p. 484. Ancient iconography: Antoine Hermary, 'Dioskouroi', *LIMC*, III, part 1, pp. 567–93; Christian Auge and Pascal Linant de Bellefonds, 'Dioskouroi (in Peripheria Orientali)', *LIMC*, III, part 1.593–97; Richard Damel de Pena, 'Dioskouroi/Tinas Clinian', *LIMC*, III, part 1, pp. 597–608; and Françoise Gury, 'Dioskouroi/Castores', *LIMC*, III, part 1, pp. 608–34; and the plates in *LIMC*, III, part 2, pp. 456–503. John S. Kloppenborg, writing in a substantially different context, provides additional primary and secondary sources for the Dioskuroi, 'ΦΙΛΑΔΕΛΦΙΑ, ΘΕΟΔΙΔΑΚΤΟΣ, and the Dioscuroi: Rhetorical Engagement in 1 Thessalonians 4.9–12', *NTS* 39 (1993), pp. 265–89, esp. pp. 283–89, nn. 71–96; and Ken Dowden, 'Dioskouroi', *DDD* (2nd edn), pp. 490–94.

27. See the excellent summary in Bethe, 'Dioskuren', pp. 1094–97. Other primary sources include *Orphic Hymn* 38, Aristophanes *Pax* 276–86, *schol.* Aristophanes *Pax* 277–78, and Diodorus 4.43.1–2.

28. Park, 'Dioscuri', p. 484.

they level the waves of the white foaming high seas.
These are welcome signs to the sailors' labor. When they see them
they rejoice and rest from their miserable labor. (33.6–17)[29]

Euripides (*Orest.* 1635–37), Theokritos (*Hymn to the Dioskuroi* 14–22), and Diodorus Siculus (*Hist.* 4.43.1–2) make similar comments.

Since the Dioskuroi were protectors and rescuers of sea travelers, their use as a figurehead in Luke's narrative is logical.[30] A lamp in the shape of a ship seems to bear the sign of the Dioskuroi.[31] A ship's name is the name of its figurehead; if a deity is depicted, that deity becomes the special 'patron' of the ship (e.g. Petronius, *Satyr.* 105.4; Statius, *Theb.* 8.269–70).

The Romans closely associated the Dioskuroi with the imperial family.[32] Scott discovered several references to Castor and Pollux (the Roman form of the Dioskuroi) in Latin literature: Statius, *Silv.* 1.1.55; Martial, *Spect.* 9.3; Ovid, *Fast.* 1.705–708, *Tr.* 2.167–68, *Pont.* 2.2.81–84., [Ovid?] *Consolatio ad Liviam* 283–84, 409–10; Tacitus, *Ann.* 2.8.4. According to Scott, Tiberius was delighted to be associated or identified with the demi-gods who expressed fraternal affection.[33] Under Domitian, Roman poets were 'accustomed' to comparing the emperor to the demi-gods of Greco-Roman mythology: Bacchus, Heracles, and the Dioskuroi.[34] Statius even compared Cyllarus, the horse of the twins Castor and Pollux, to Domitian's horse (*Silv.* 1.1.55). Coins minted during Caligula's reign depicted Caligula's older brothers using iconography characteristic of the Dioskuroi.[35] An inscription in Ephesus reads: 'newborn Dioskuroi, sons of Drusus Caesar'.[36]

The iconography of the Dioskuroi also became closely associated with the imperial family and imperial cult. The shield, spear, armor, and horse employed

29. My translation is informed by Daryl Hine, *The Homeric Hymns and The Battle of the Frogs and the Mice* (New York: Atheneum, 1972), p. 84; Apostolos N. Athanassakis, *The Homeric Hymns: Translation, Introduction, and Notes* (Baltimore: The Johns Hopkins University Press, 1976), pp. 69–70; and Lee T. Pearcy, *The Shorter Homeric Hymns* (Bryn Mawr, PA: Bryn Mawr Greek Commentaries, 1989), pp. 45–46.

30. Dölger thoroughly analyzes the nature of these figureheads, 'Dioskuroi', throughout.

31. Dölger, 'Dioskuroi', pp. 278–80, and p. 279, pl. 8. The lamp was published by H.B. Walters, *Catalogue of the Greek and Roman Lamps in the British Museum* (London: British Museum, 1914), p. 390, pl. X.

32. Kenneth Scott, 'Drusus, Nicknamed Castor', *CP* 25 (1930), pp. 155–61; *idem*, 'The Dioscuri and the Imperial Cult', *CP* 25 (1930), pp. 379–80; *idem, Imperial Cult under the Flavians*, pp. 114, 141, 143; Ladouceur, 'Hellenistic Preconceptions', pp. 446–47; Kloppenborg, 'ΦΙΛΑΔΕΛΦΙΑ', pp. 285–86; Brite Poulsen and Jesper Karlsen, 'A Relief from Croceae: Dioscuri in Roman Laconia', *Acta Hyperborea: Danish Studies in Classical Archaeology* 3 (1991), pp. 235–48; Brite Poulsen, 'The Dioscuri and Ruler Ideology', *SO* 66 (1991), pp. 235–48.

33. Scott, 'Drusus, Nicknamed Castor', p. 158.

34. Scott, *Imperial Cult Under the Flavians*, p. 141.

35. Harold Mattingly, *Coins of the Roman Empire in the British Museum* (London: British Museum, 1923–50), I, p. cxlvi; p. 154 no. 44, p. 157 no. 70, p. 158 no. 71, pls. 29.1, 30.2.

36. Josef Keil, 'Vorläufiger Bericht über die Ausgrabungen in Ephesos', *Jahreshefte des Österreichischen archäologischen Instituts, Beiblatt* 24 (1929), pp. 1–67, esp. pp. 62–66.

by Castor and Pollux became symbols of the dominance of Roman imperial power.[37]

The cult of the Dioskuroi, or some aspect of it, was widely dispersed throughout the Mediterranean. Among many other places, the cult existed in Rome (under the guise of Castor and Pollux), Thessalonica, Ephesus, and Cyprus.[38]

A Greco-Roman Audience, Snakes, Justice, and the Dioskuroi[39]

In Acts 28.1–11, a Greco-Roman audience would possibly notice multiple levels of reference to Greco-Roman motifs. In Acts 28.1–6, they would parallel ancient pre-existing Greek, and later Roman, imagery that transforms snakes into agents of vengeance for murder victims to the Maltese misapprehension that Paul was a murderer. In 28.4 Greco-Roman readers would notice the personification of this vengeance as Δίκη, 'Justice', in light of the ancient Greek religious tradition of personified and deified justice.[40] In 28.11, this readership may have also noted the related images of sea travel, the Dioskuroi as guardians of sea travelers, ship figureheads and names, and the imperial cult (as represented by soldiers escorting Paul to see the emperor).[41]

Greco-Romans may have interpreted these motifs in three ways. First, these motifs declare Paul innocent. In 28.1–6, Δίκη, justice personified, justifies Paul as innocent. The implacable, pitiless nature of Δίκη is irrelevant in this narrative; Paul *is* innocent. In Greco-Roman terms, the Maltese islanders have made an understandable mistake. Avenging Justice has caught up with a murderer who has been saved from shipwreck merely to suffer his preordained fate at the hands

---

37. Gury, 'Dioskouroi/Castores', p. 631; see plates in *LIMC*, III, part 2, pp. 489–503. Gury lists some thirty examples of ancient art associating Castor and Pollux, their arms and horse, and Roman imperial power.

38. Rome: Scott, 'Drusus, Nicknamed Castor', 155–61; *idem*, 'Dioscuri and the Imperial Cult', pp. 379–80; Ephesus: Keil, 'Vorläufiger Bericht;' Thessalonika: Kloppenborg, 'ΦΙΛΑΔΕΛΦΙΑ', p. 286 nn. 84–88; Cyprus: *IGRR* 3.977.

39. Throughout this section my conclusions generally follow Ladouceur, 'Hellenistic Preconceptions', pp. 444–48; Trompf, 'On Why Luke', in Talbert (ed.), *Luke-Acts*, pp. 225–39 at pp. 226, 232–33, and 236 nn. 7–8; Talbert and Hayes, 'Theology of Sea Storms', pp. 326–27, 335–36; Wehnert, 'Zu einem neuen These'; Spencer, *Acts*, p. 236; *idem*, 'Paul's Odyssey', pp. 157, 158; Talbert, *Reading Acts*, pp. 221–25. However, I offer additional primary evidence (vase painting, the Oresteia cycle, Greek myth, personified abstractions), develop these conclusions in detail, and push in new directions. A detailed analysis of the entire sea storm and shipwreck episode (Acts 27–28) is beyond my scope.

40. Wehnert briefly discusses the snake as the embodiment of Δίκη, 'Zu einem neuen These', p. 94. Schreiber so emphasizes form- and redaction-critical questions that despite his acceptance of Dike's presence in Acts 28.4 as the goddess of justice, he understands it to be merely a 'contrasting interpretive model' which is subsidiary to the theme of divine accompaniment and protection for Paul (*Paulus als Wundertäter*, pp. 127–132 and 127 n. 509).

41. Kee, citing *CIG* 14.60, states that the πρῶτος of Malta was the resident imperial authority who was a benefactor and had responsibilities as a magistrate and as the chief priest of the imperial cult, *To Every Nation*, p. 293. Would informed Greco-Roman readers have understood Luke to have made a very subtle allusion to the imperial cult by mentioning the πρῶτος (28.7) and then the Διόσκουροι (28.11)?

of Justice in the form of a snake (= Erinyes?). Paul's survival of the snakebite effectively confirms his innocence in Greco-Roman terms.[42] This Greco-Roman concept of innocence is not just associated with literary texts of the elite, but also with epitaphs, theatrical performances, and artworks visible to non-elites. Paul and his message are innocent before *all* levels of Greco-Roman society including 'barbarian' Maltese islanders.

The second way in which a Greco-Roman audience may have interpreted the traditional Greco-Roman imagery of Acts 28.1–11 is by understanding that it is the θεὸς ζῶν, the 'living God' of the Judeans and the Christians, is solely responsible for Paul's safety. The Dioskuroi are but paintings or wooden figures on the ship's bow. They are not living and are incapable of action. At 19.26,

---

42. Several exegetes trace the motif of divine justice and snakes to Judean sources (Silbermann, 'Paul's Viper;' Eugene Boring, Klaus Berger, and Carsten Colpe, *Hellenistic Commentary to the New Testament* [Nashville: Abingdon, 1995], pp. 333–34; Wehnert, *Paulus als Wundertäter*, p. 126; and Talbert, *Reading Acts*, pp. 221–22). However, one example, *b. Ber.* 33a, is not about divine justice as delivered by divinely impelled snakes but about the deadly effects of sin. The other rabbinic example, *Mek. R. Ishmael* 3.78.12, 'illustrates that the Torah...must be respected even when it seems to thwart justice' (Boring, Berger, and Colpe, *Hellenistic Commentary*, p. 334).

Silbermann, citing the NEB translation of the Hebrew, suggests that Jer. 8.17 lies behind these traditions: 'I am about to send poisonous snakes among you which no one can charm. They shall bite you. An oracle of the LORD'. Against Silbermann, Luke (and his Christian Greco-Roman audience) would have read the LXX, 'Therefore, I am sending out deadly snakes among you whom no one is able to attack and they will bite you'. Also, this passage does *not* suggest that resisting the snakebite proves one's innocence.

Wehnert cites Amos 5.19 and 9.3 as parallels from the Hebrew Scriptures. 5.19 is irrelevant while 9.3 pictures a snake biting those unjust Judeans who have fled to the bottom of the sea. This *is* a direct parallel in that it combines the images of snakebite, unjust individuals and the sea. In contrast, Acts 28.1–6 narrates survival from snakebite and shipwreck, not escape by sea. Additionally, Acts 28.1–6 specifically names the Greek god Δίκη as the causal agent. Amos does not use 'non-Judean' gods nor does he personify justice.

Johnson implausibly connects Acts 28.1–6 with Jesus' resurrection and Mk. 16.18 (*Acts*, p. 466). Though Luke may reflect early Christian concepts about snakes and snake handling, he is surely *not directly dependent upon* Mk. 16.18 in Acts 28.1–6. As narrated by Luke, Paul's encounter with the snake is entirely unintentional; nor is there anything in the text that suggests resurrection imagery. Regarding the relationship of these traditions of snakes and snake handling in Mk. 16.18 to Acts 28.1–6, see James Kelhoffer, *Miracle and Mission: The Authentication of Missionaries and their Message in the Longer Ending of Mark* (WUNT, 112; Tübingen: Mohr-Siebeck, 1999), pp. 402–403, 410.

Spencer links Acts 28.1–6 to Lk. 10.17–19 (*Reading Acts*, p. 235): 'The seventy-two joyfully returned to him, saying, "Lord, the demons subjected themselves to us in your name". He said to them, "I saw Satan falling like lightning from heaven. I have given you the authority to walk on snakes, scorpions, and every power of the enemy. Nothing will injure you".' There is nothing in the Malta episode to indicate any symbolism for evil or the demonic. Nor is it the nature of Satan, according to New Testament authors, to declare a character innocent. The snake *is not* associated with Satan but with the *very non-Satanic* virture of justice. Spencer has recently reiterated his view understanding Acts 28.1–6 as Paul's conquest of 'diabolical forces', i.e., the poisonous viper, which in turn displays Paul's dramatically elevated honor ('Paul's Odyssey in Acts', pp. 150–50, esp. 157). In honor–shame terms, one can indeed argue that Paul's honor increases. However, this is because Δίκη, Justice personified and not some 'diabolical force', proclaims Paul's *absolute innocence*. Attempts to describe Luke's portrayal of Paul purely in terms of θεῖος ἀνήρ, a 'divine man', miss precisely this the point (Haenchen, *Acts*, pp. 715–16; Kanda, 'Form and Function', pp. 288–303; Conzelmann, *Acts*, p. 223).

Demetrios, the Ephesian silversmith attributes to Paul the statement, 'there are no gods made by human hands'. Near the end of Acts, this readership encounters again the utter impotence of yet another set of handmade deities, the Greco-Roman marine 'savior gods', the Dioskuroi, who are merely but a ship's figurehead.[43] The entire sea storm and shipwreck sequence in Acts 27.1–28.4 emphasizes God's deliverance of Paul. As Paul sets out, again by sea, in 28.11, readers may have noticed that the Dioskuroi, 'useless mythological brothers', offered their protection to a ship that safely overwintered in Alexandria while Paul was saved by the living God.[44]

For a Greco-Roman reader, the declaration of Paul's innocence may have served two functions: it reinforces the reliability of the central character and his message and sets the stage for Paul's appearance in Rome at the end of Acts. Paul does not die or suffer any ill effects after snakebite; therefore he is innocent in terms of the Greco-Roman religious system, i.e., Δίκη, or justice personified, implied Paul's innocence. If Paul is innocent, the logical consequence, for the reader, is that his message is not culpable of charlatanism (cf. the charlatan prophets and philosophers in Lucian's *The Death of Peregrinus* and *Alexander the False Prophet*).

Since Paul and his message are reliable, the reader would assume that Paul's appearance before the emperor would reliably present the Christian message. At the end of Acts (28.31), Paul is detained in Rome, 'proclaiming the kingdom of God and teaching about the Lord Jesus Christ boldly and publicly without interference'. Not only is the message reliable but it is also being proclaimed in Rome, at the heart of the ancient Roman Empire. The messenger and the message are both reliable; therefore, there should be no possible grounds for indictment. In Acts 28.1–6, God has proclaimed Paul and his message reliable and innocent of wrongdoing by using traditional Greco-Roman motifs. Therefore, the emperor should, on the very grounds of Greco-Roman religion, find Paul, and by implication, the early church, innocent and reliable.

A Greco-Roman reader would probably not have noted any fierce polemic against or denigration of the Greco-Roman gods or religiosity in Acts 28.1–11. For this reader there are two remarkable details: (1) as shown above, Greco-Roman religion finds no fault with Paul and is adopted and 'transvalued' for Christian use;

---

43. David Ravens understands the Dioskouroi, who are twin brothers, as Luke's symbol for Jewish [*sic*] and Gentile Christians and Luke's theology of outreach to these same two groups (*Luke and the Restoration of Israel* [JSNTSup, 119; Sheffield: Sheffield Academic Press, 1995], p. 246). Whatever the merits of his monograph, he has derived this interpretation without support from the text itself. Luke does not refer to 'Judean' Christianity in the immediate context and Judeans do not appear again in the narrative until Paul's arrival in Rome in 28.17–28.

44. Spencer, *Acts*, p. 236; Talbert, *Reading Acts*, p. 224. The phrase 'useless mythological brothers' is Spencer's. For the theology of Acts 27, see Miles and Trompf, 'Luke and Antiphon', pp. 264–67; Ladouceur, 'Hellenistic Preconceptions', throughout; Praeder, 'Acts 27.1–28.16', throughout; Trompf, 'Why Luke Declined', in Talbert (ed.), *Luke-Acts*, pp. 225–39 at 226, 232–33, 236, nn. 7–8; Wehnert, 'Zu einem neuen These', pp. 67–99; Talbert and Hayes, 'A Theology of Sea Storms', throughout; Spencer, *Acts*, pp. 229–34; and Talbert *Reading Acts*, pp. 215–21.

(2) the Greco-Roman concept of Δίκη correlates with the emphasis on justice already seen in Luke's gospel.

In Acts 28.1–11, Luke's audience probably would not have understood Luke to be condemning all Greco-Roman religiosity because it emphasizes Paul's innocence in Luke's narrative. Since this audience may have seen Paul as reliable, they would then also see Luke 'baptizing' some components of Greco-Roman religion because these components judge Paul innocent. Possibly Luke's Greco-Roman readership would have understood their own Greco-Roman religiosity as acceptable, and 'adoptable', when its claims were parallel to or Christian claims. A careful reader would have noted Luke's acceptance and use of the concepts of creator and unknown gods in Acts 14.15–17 and 17.22–31. Similarly in Acts 28.1–6, a careful Greco-Roman reader would notice that Luke again 'baptizes' an element of Greco-Roman religiosity, i.e. the concept of divine justice.

Seeing (or hearing) Δίκη in 28.4, Luke's reader may have mentally returned to a theme announced in Lk. 4.18–19:

> The spirit of the Lord is upon me, therefore he has anointed me to proclaim good news to the poor, he has sent me to announce release to the captives and sight to the blind, to set free the oppressed, to proclaim the acceptable year of the Lord.

In Acts 28, the emphasis changes from concerns for the hungry and poor (e.g., Lk. 16.19–31; 18.18–25) to a concern for the just treatment of one individual, Paul. Paul is a captive (αἰχμάλωτος) who is seeking release, (ἄφεσις) a theme found in Luke's probable programmatic declaration in Lk. 4.18–19. In Acts 28.1–11, he has placed his protagonist in the midst of the Greco-Roman world. Therefore, the ancient reader may have seen the 'release for the captives' themes developed by the use of a Greco-Roman religious concept, an 'abstract personification', justice personified as Δίκη. In the movement from the gospel (Luke's first volume) to Acts (Luke's second volume), Greco-Romans may have perceived a movement from Judean concepts (the world of Galilee and Judea) to Greco-Roman concepts (the larger Greco-Roman Mediterranean world). Previously in Acts, Greco-Romans may have observed a Lukan polemic against various aspects of Greco-Roman religion. However, in Acts 28.1–11 Greco-Romans may have noticed a willing and free adoption and use of their traditional religious concepts when these concepts agree with and promote the themes of Acts.

Luke's Greco-Roman audience may have drawn four conclusions from the images of Δίκη (justice personified), the snake as the agent of justice, and the Dioskouroi: (1) Paul is innocent even from the perspective of Greco-Roman religion; (2) ultimately Paul's safety has always been in the hands of the 'living God' (θεὸς ζῶν); (3) Paul's message is reliable; (4) the emperor (as alluded to by the Dioskouroi) is irrelevant; and (5) Greco-Roman religious concepts can be used by the Christian community. At the narrative level, these images help precipitate the closure of Luke's work for his audience. At the theological level, they elevate Paul, demean handmade gods, embrace the noble concept of 'justice' common to the religiosity of both Luke and his Greco-Roman audience, and assert that Greco-Roman culture is capable of incorporation into the Christian message and community.

Chapter 8

CONCLUSIONS

Summary

At the beginning of this study I asked the following questions:

1. In overt references to Greco-Roman religious phenomena in Acts, are there previously unexplored issues?
2. Did a Greco-Roman audience perceive references and allusions to Greco-Roman religions or religious phenomena in Acts that are overlooked by modern readers?
3. What cultural knowledge did Luke's ancient Greco-Roman readers bring to these references and allusions to Greco-Roman religion that informed their reading of Acts?
4. How would a Greco-Roman audience have understood Luke's theology in light of these possible references and allusions to Greco-Roman religion?
5. Does understanding the perceptions of a Greco-Roman audience help us to better understand Lukan theology?
6. When reading Acts, would Greco-Romans have seen an implicit contrast between Greco-Roman religion and early Christianity?

I summarize my answers and tentative suggestions below.

Previously Unexplored Issues
I have examined several largely unexplored appearances of Greco-Roman religion in Acts: Luke's mention of a Greco-Roman sacrificial ritual (Acts 14.18–20; Chapter 4), of votive offerings and διοπετῆς objects (19.23–41; Chapter 6), and of Δίκη and the Dioskuroi (28.1–6, 11; Chapter 7). I have performed an in-depth analysis of each of these deities and rituals and suggested that a Greco-Roman reader may have seen a parody of Greco-Roman sacrificial ritual (14.13–18), an intertextual condemnation of votive offerings and the ostentatious displays associated with them (14.24), an intertextual mockery of the impotence of Artemis' διοπετῆς object (14.35), and a promotion of Paul's innocence and divine protection in the terms of a snake as the servant of Δίκη, Justice personified (28.1–6), and a dismissal of the Dioskuroi as idols.

Allusions to Greco-Roman Religion in Acts
In Chapters 2 to 6 of this study, I have suggested that Greco-Romans may have seen the following allusions to various aspects of Greco-Roman in Acts: klero-mantic oracles (Acts 1.15–26) and inspiration oracles (16.16–18), ruler cult (12.20–23), and Greek myth in Aeschylus' *Eumenides* (17.16–33). I sought to demonstrate each of these allusions by examining the specific Greco-Roman divinity or religious practice within its ancient context, comparing this infor-mation to Luke's text, and noting the parallels that may have been suggestive to a Greco-Roman audience. My examination of the ancient context of the Greco-Roman religious phenomena in Acts also suggests the cultural and religious competencies that ancient readers may have brought to Luke's text. If these arguments are tenable, they suggest that Greco-Romans may have seen Greco-Roman religion as a subsidiary theme in Acts.

Implications for Understanding Lukan Theology
This study of how Greco-Romans may have read Greco-Roman religion in Acts suggests how Greco-Romans may have understood Lukan theology. In turn this has implications for our own understanding of Lukan theology.

Luke, Prophetic Oracles, and Divination. Greco-Roman readers/auditors of Acts would have possibly made associations between early Christian kleromancy, the fulfillment of Scripture (Acts 1.16–18, 20; cf. Pss. 69.25; 109.8), and Greco-Roman concepts about *Fortuna*, Τυχή, and λαγχάνω, 'fate', 'fortune' and 'receiving one's fate' (*Anth. Pal.* 9.158). Greco-Romans may have interpreted Luke as accepting the use of kleromancy among the early Christian community, but only as a thing of the past (1.4–26).

Many scholars have noted Luke's emphasis on prophecy and its fulfillment within the newly established Christian community.[1] In addition, a Greco-Roman reader may have understood Luke as implicitly addressing Greco-Roman proph-ecy, oracles, and divination. By literary and popular reputation, if not in historical actuality, Greco-Roman oracles were often ambiguous and required craft and wit for their proper interpretation. For a Greco-Roman, Luke seems to state that Chris-tian prophecy is by nature unambiguously clear. All Christian prophetic oracles in Acts are fulfilled or will be fulfilled in a clear and unambiguous manner.[2] In this Greco-Roman reading, one should accept whatever truths Greco-Roman oracles proclaim, but reject any idea of oracular ambiguity (16.16–18). Because a Greco-Roman may have concluded that it is necessary to reject oracular ambiguity, by

---

1.   See David Tiede, *Prophecy and History in Luke-Acts* (Philadelphia: Fortress Press, 1980); Darryl L. Bock, *Proclamation from Prophecy and Pattern: Lucan Old Testament Christology* (JSNTSup, 12; Sheffield: JSOT Press, 1987); York, *The Last Shall Be First*, pp. 176–84; Squires, *The Plan of God in Luke-Acts*, pp. 121–94; Rebecca I. Denova, *The Things Accomplished Among Us: Prophetic Tradition in the Structural Pattern of Luke-Acts* (JSNTSup, 141; Sheffield: Sheffield Academic Press, 1997).

2.   Tiede contrasts Luke's emphasis upon the *clarity* of the *divine message* and the *ambiguity* of the *human reception* of that message (*Prophecy and History*, pp. 31–32).

nature an essential component of Greco-Roman oracles, this reader may have also effectively rejected Greco-Roman oracles.

Greco-Romans and the Chronology of Luke's History. Greco-Romans may have viewed the presence of kleromancy in Acts 1.15–26 as one chronological division in Luke's conception of history.[3] First there was the time of Israel (the narratives of the Hebrew Scriptures), then the time of Jesus (Luke's Gospel; Acts 1.1–11), then the time of the isolated and expectant community (Acts 1.15–26), and finally the time of the Spirit (Acts 2.1–28.31). The interim period in Jerusalem (Acts 1.15–26) is notable for the absence of Jesus, a mention of the fulfillment of scripture, double entendres on the words λαγχάνω and κλῆρος, and the kleromantic appointment of Matthias to replace Judas. Before Pentecost, kleromancy is an acceptable means of understanding the divine will. After Pentecost, the church understands the divine will by direct inspiration of the Holy Spirit and through the scriptures.[4]

Greco-Romans, Retribution and Roman Authority. In Acts 12.20–23, Greco-Romans would probably have understood Luke as depicting ruler cult, and Roman imperial cult, as both oppressive and worthy of the harshest penalties of divine retribution and wrath. On the basis of 12.23, they may have viewed Luke as being harshly critical of all who presume to take or accept the δόξα properly given to God. Because of a Greco-Roman audience's location within the Roman Empire, they may have applied this perception to the Roman imperial cult. In the larger context of Acts 12, this audience may have understood Luke to say that: (1) such presumption asserts itself in oppression (the actions of Agrippa I against James and Peter); (2) God punishes such presumption and oppression with divine retribution[5] and (3) in contrast, the Christian community is powerless and totally dependent upon God for security and retribution on its behalf. From Luke's description of Agrippa's ruler cult ritual, a Greco-Roman reader may have concluded that Jesus embodies the proper attitude towards divine δόξα.

---

3. Scholars have proposed various salvation historical models for Luke-Acts. Hans Conzelmann initiated recent discussion by dividing Lukan time into the time of Israel, the time of Jesus, and the time of the church (*The Theology of St. Luke* [Philadelphia: Fortress Press, 1980]). Mark Allan Powell provides a succinct summary of recent discussion (*What Are They Saying About Luke?* [New York: Paulist Press, 1989], pp. 8–10, 42–45, 83–85). I am not interested in developing a comprehensive understanding of Lukan salvation history but am only seeking to develop one specific component of a Greco-Roman's perception of that history.

4. Forbes argues that 'Luke and Paul excluded all forms of inductive divination absolutely' (*Prophecy and Inspired Speech*, p. 302). On the previous page, he correctly acknowledges the occurrence of Matthias' kleromantic selection before Pentecost, but does not discuss the issue further (*Prophecy and Inspired Speech*, p. 301).

It is also possible that the time of direct inspiration has also ended for Luke. By the end of Acts, Luke has all but abandoned the use of inspired speech, instead portraying Paul's missionary preaching and argumentation. Perhaps Luke understands Paul's speaking as divinely inspired and a replacement for mantic speech or he now emphasizes a time of reliance upon scripture and divinely mandated leaders such as Paul. This issue exceeds the narrow focus of this monograph.

5. Allen, *The Death of Herod*, throughout.

Greco-Roman readers may have also connected 12.20–23 to a wider Lukan theology of retribution.[6] The Magnificat foreshadows divine retribution (Lk. 1.51–55), while the deaths of Judas (Acts 1.18–19) and Ananias and Sapphira (Acts 4.32–5.11) provide examples of it.

If Greco-Romans read an implicit and harsh condemnation of ruler (or imperial) cult in 12.20–23, they may have juxtaposed this condemnation over against Luke's generally friendly attitude towards both local civic and Roman imperial officials.[7] Helen K. Bond has recently shown that 'Luke's community' would have seen Pontius Pilate as weak and inept who, despite asserting Jesus' innocence, hands Jesus over to 'Jewish mob pressure'.[8] In light of Luke-Acts, a Greco-Roman may have well considered Roman authority as exercised through the emperor, governors, client kings and lesser officials as generally benevolent. However, when one of these representatives usurps God's δόξα, God's retribution is both inevitable and justified.

Greco-Romans and Ritual in Acts. From a reading of Acts, a Greco-Roman audience may have drawn fundamental conclusions about the nature of ritual behavior in their cultural world. After reading Acts 12, a Greco-Roman reader may have implicitly contrasted ruler or imperial cult ritual with early Christian practices. On the one hand, Greco-Romans experienced Hellenistic ruler cult (and its descendant Roman imperial cult) as ritually expressing human divinization and a hierarchy of human power.[9] On the other hand, early Christian communal ritual, as seen in Acts 12, expressed unity and common dependence of believers upon God. Also, this putative Greco-Roman reader may have observed an implicit contrast between Jesus' 'divine filiation' in his baptism (Lk. 3.21–22), transfiguration (Lk. 9.28–36) and ascension (Lk. 24.50–51, Acts 1.9–11) over and against Herod Agrippa I's 'divine filiation' in Acts 12.20–23. This contrast portrays Agrippa's acceptance of divinity as the worst sort of *hybris*, while portraying Jesus as worthy of his divine filiation. Additionally, Greco-Romans may have noted parallels between Greco-Roman myth and ruler cult ritual to the divine filiation rituals of Jesus and Herod.

A Greco-Roman audience may have also implicitly contrasted Agrippa's ruler cult ritual in Acts 12.20–23 with the rituals of the early Jerusalem community in the larger context of Acts 12. Agrippa was the center of a divinizing ritual that

6. Allen, *The Death of Herod*, esp. pp. 200–202. Also, Marla J. Selvidge, 'Acts of the Apostles: A Violent Aetiological Legend', *SBLSP* 25 (1986), pp. 330–40; repr. *Women, Violence, and the Bible* (Studies in Women and Religion, 37; Lewiston, NY: Edwin Mellen, 1996), pp. 95–109.

7. Paul Walaskay, *'And so we came to Rome': The Political Perspective of St. Luke* (SNTSMS, 49; Cambridge: Cambridge University Press, 1983); and Philip Esler, *Community and Gospel in Luke-Acts: The Social and Political Motivations of Lucan Theology* (SNTSMS, 57; Cambridge: Cambridge University Press, 1987).

Cf. Richard J. Cassidy and Philip J. Sharper, eds, *Political Issues in Luke-Acts* (Maryknoll, NY: Orbis Books, 1983); and Richard J. Cassidy, *Society and Politics in the Acts of the Apostles* (Maryknoll, NY: Orbis Books, 1987). These two works advance the thesis that Luke was anti-imperial.

8. Helen K. Bond, *Pontius Pilate in History and Interpretation* (SNTSMS, 100; Cambridge: Cambridge University Press, 1998), pp. 138–62, esp. pp. 150–62.

9. Price, *Rituals and Power*, throughout.

also expressed his presumptive divine power. The Jerusalem community celebrated Passover and expressed their powerlessness and dependence upon God by praying for divine assistance. Greco-Roman readers would probably have observed that this Christian ritual did not express human power. Those Greco-Romans familiar with the Hebrew Scriptures may have realized that Passover in part expresses the rule and authority of God over and above any human authority.

Greco-Romans may have noticed dark comedic parody and ironic reversal in the Greco-Roman sacrificial ritual in Acts 14.8–18. If they did see such parody and reversal, they may have concluded that it was necessary to reject Greco-Roman animal sacrifice rituals as a means of expressing devotion to the divine.

Lastly, Greco-Romans may have concluded that there is no place for ostentatious display and competitive religiosity in Christian rituals when reading Acts 19.23–41 in light of their earlier reading of Lk. 18.9–14. On the basis of this earlier text, they may have understood votive offerings to be ostentatious, self-glorifying, competitive, and unworthy components of true worship (19.23–28).

Idolatry. In both Acts 19.23–41 and 28.11, Greco-Romans may have seen a subtly humorous Lukan polemic against idolatry, i.e., the worship of natural objects or humanly-crafted images that are set in hand-made temples. They may have read the riot concerning Ephesian Artemis and her διοπετῆς image (19.23–41) in the wider context of struggles against magic and demons in Ephesus (19.1–20). In the Seven Sons of Sceva episode (19.11–20), the demons have personality and power; the Ephesians must guard and tend the διοπετῆς. The demons are personal entities and require the power of God through exorcism for their defeat. By contrast, the διοπετῆς is merely a natural phenomenon, a rock or a meteorite. Therefore, a Greco-Roman audience may have rejected διοπετῆς objects (19.35) because they are empty human conceptualizations of god and utterly powerless and impotent. Though the Ephesians protect it, the διοπετῆς has no power to affect Christians.

Similarly, the Dioskuroi, the patron gods of mariners, are but mere wooden figureheads for a ship that has to seek shelter during the winter (28.11), because the Διόσκυροι are mere pieces of wood unable to save the passengers. By contrast, Greco-Romans would have seen Paul, his companions, guards, and the ship's crew being saved from death at sea by the living God (27.13–44).

Greco-Romans Reading Culture and Theology in Acts. If Greco-Romans read Acts in light of their own cultural competencies, they may have interpreted Luke as adopting and adapting traditions from Greco-Roman literature, myth, and religion. Such readers may have seen a condemnation of ruler cult by reading the death of Herod Agrippa I in light of Greco-Roman bodily assumption and apotheosis myths (12.20–23). By possibly perceiving an allusion to Aeschylus' *Eumenides* in Acts 17.23–34, Greco-Romans may have contrasted the importance of the resurrection in Lukan Christianity to its absence in Greek religion. A possible second consequence of Greco-Romans reading Acts 17.23–34 in light of Aeschylus' *Eumenides* is that they may have viewed Paul as innocent of disrupting the established and traditional religious order. Lastly, Greco-Romans may have seen Luke as transmuting elements of Greco-Roman mythology – snakes as agents of divine justice, personified abstractions, and the savior gods, the Διόσκυροι – into Christian statements about Paul's innocence (28.1–11).

The Resurrection. It is a scholarly commonplace that Lukan theology greatly emphasizes the resurrection.[10] However, apart from philosophical religion, scholars have generally ignored how a Greco-Roman audience would have interpreted references to Greco-Roman religion in Acts 17.16–34.[11] My analysis suggests that Greco-Romans may have understood an allusion to Athenian civic-foundation mythology, as seen in Aeschylus' *Eumenides*, and contrasted the grimness of traditional Greek religion, to Luke's Christian understanding of the resurrection.

Greco-Romans Reading Luke's 'Openness' to Greco-Roman Religion. In the texts I have analyzed, a Greco-Roman reader may have seen Luke as maintaining an openness to practitioners of Greco-Roman religion. In light of Acts 1.15–26, readers may have considered kleromancy a thing of the past. However, they probably would not understand a specific condemnation of those who practice kleromancy because the text expresses no condemnation. Therefore Luke's Greco-Roman readers would welcome those who practice kleromantic divination into the Christian community. However, by understanding kleromancy as relegated to the past, Greco-Roman readers may have suggested that other Greco-Romans interested in Christianity abandon kleromancy as a means of discerning the divine will. Instead they should rely upon the scriptures and the inspiration of the Holy Spirit.

In the episodes at Lystra (14.8–18), Athens (17.16–34), Ephesus (19.23–41) and Malta (28.1–10), a Greco-Roman reader may have seen an openness to Greco-Roman religionists because these texts describe healings and preaching directed towards the practitioners of various forms of Greco-Roman religion. This reader may have also noted that despite this openness, there are difficulties in converting Greco-Romans into the Christian community. Out of these four episodes, only Paul's appearance before the Athenian Areopagus narrates the conversion of Greco-Roman religionists to Christianity.

Presumably Greco-Romans would have (unconsciously?) viewed Luke's openness to practitioners of Greco-Roman religion as nuanced by an emphasis upon social class and education since the adherents of Greco-Roman religion who maintain consistent friendliness towards Paul and his coworkers are either members of the elite classes or heads of households.[12] Paul exorcises the Philippian slave girl

---

10. A classic statement of Luke's emphasis on the resurrection is Everett F. Harrison, 'The Resurrection of Jesus Christ in the Book of Acts and in Early Christian Literature', in John Reumann (ed.), *Understanding the Sacred Text: Essays in Honor of Morton S. Enslin on the Hebrew Bible and Christian Beginnings* (Valley Forge, PA: Judson Press, 1972), pp. 217–33.

11. Neyrey contrasts Epicureanism, Stoicism, and Lukan theology on the issue of the resurrection ('Acts 17', pp. 118–34, esp. pp. 121–22).

12. Cf. Reimer who asserts that Lydia the dealer of purple cloth (Acts 16:13–15, 40) was a lower-class woman (*Women in the Acts of the Apostles*, pp. 71–150). Despite this Lydia *was* the head of a household (as Reimer herself asserts, pp. 109–13) and she was a 'godfearer', a group Luke evaluates positively throughout Acts (see the bibliography in Fitzmyer, *Acts*, p. 450).

(16.16–18), but Luke nowhere mentions her conversion. As L. Michael White has shown, only the heads of the households can convert: Once the head of the household converts, everyone else follows.[13] The woman with a pythonic spirit is a slave and not the head of a household. Also, among the few non-God-fearing Greeks converted to Christianity is Dionysisus, a member of the Areopagus, and the woman Damaris (17.34). By implication, both were possibly philosophers, and Damaris may have had a relationship to or membership of the Areopagus.[14] The Lystran commoners first deify Paul and then turn against him (14.8–18), while the Maltese islanders first consider Paul a murderer and then a god (28.1–6). Despite this, Paul heals the Maltese of various diseases after Publius, a man of high social standing, shows hospitality to him and his companions by providing them with food and lodging. Greco-Romans would probably have observed that the Ephesian elites in 19.23–41 appear substantially more favorable than the craftsmen. Though the elites, the asiarchs, never convert, they are friends of Paul's and prevent him from going before the threatening crowd. Another member of the elite, the γραμματεύς or 'town clerk', quells the uprising the craftsmen initiate.

Lukan Social Location. Vernon K. Robbins has recently used the work of Thomas F. Carney and John H. Elliott to describe Luke's social location by analyzing nine 'arenas of the social system': previous events, natural environment and resources, population structure, technology, socialization and personality, culture, foreign affairs, belief systems and ideologies, and the political-military-legal system.[15] Religion is visibly absent in the analysis of Carney and somewhat less so in that of Elliott and Robbins.[16]

---

13. Michael White, 'Visualizing the "Real" World of Acts 16: Toward Construction of a Social Index', in White and Yarbrough (eds), *The Social World of the First Christians: Essays in Honor of Wayne A. Meeks* (Minneapolis: Fortress Press, 1995), pp. 258–59; 259 n. 75.

14. Richter Reimer, *Women in the Acts of the Apostles*, pp. 246–48; 257 nn. 79–86.

15. Robbins, 'The Social Location of the Implied Author of Luke-Acts', pp. 305–32; Thomas F. Carney, *The Shape of the Past: Models and Antiquity* (Lawrence, KS: Coronado Press, 1975), p. 246; and John H. Elliott, 'Social-Scientific Criticism of the New Testament: More on Methods and Models', *Semeia* 35 (1986), pp. 1–34.

16. Carney specifically mentions religion only twice. He first states that, 'Magico-religious beliefs flourished… [and] subscription to such beliefs welded the communities of antiquity together…[while] the elites subscribed to such religions less fully than did the commons' (*Shape of the Past*, p. 250). A page later he contrasts the values of ancient authoritarian societies with 'the Hebrew [*sic*] and Christian religions' and their emphasis on moral responsibility and concern for the poor and social outcasts (*Shape of the Past*, p. 251). Missing in these observations and Carney's model as a whole is the reality of elite 'personal piety' (among many: Domitian's personal devotion to Minerva, Apuleius' devotion to Isis) and the embeddedness of religion within social institutions.

Elliott recognizes the degree to which 'religion was…embedded within all sectors of the [social] system [of ancient Palestine] as a whole' (Elliot, 'Social Science Criticism of the New Testament', p. 16) and implicitly builds this recognition into his proposed cross-cultural model. However, the very degree of implicit recognition of religion in his model may hinder *explicit comparative analysis* of Judean, early Christian, and Greco-Roman religious systems and their social roles.

Robbins briefly describes Judean-Christian interactions in Luke's world and concludes, '[Luke] wishes to show that God has 'cleansed' a widely divergent and mixed group of peoples within a movement inaugurated by Jesus of Nazareth…[that] challenges the purity system of Judaism at its center'

My study of Luke's use of Greco-Roman religion suggests that analyses of the ancient Mediterranean social arenas and Lukan social location should include Luke's depiction of the interaction between early Christianity and its Greco-Roman religions. My study suggests that Luke, or 'the implied author' of Luke-Acts, is familiar with and has a working knowledge of many elements of Greco-Roman religion: oracular procedures (1.15–26), Greco-Roman concepts of fate and chance (1.15–26), inspired manticism (16.16–18), the imperial cult and its rituals (12.20–23), Greco-Roman sacrificial procedures and terminology (14.8–18), Greek mythology and its literary expression (17.16–34), votive offerings (19.23–28), the cultic use of aniconic objects (19.35), the cults of personified abstractions (28.4), mythological traditions regarding divine justice (28.4) and the cults of Zeus, Hermes, Artemis, and the Dioskuroi (14.11–13, 19.23–41, 28.11).[17]

What does this further suggest about Luke's social location and the social location of his audience? Despite his overall theological program, Luke appears to take a genuine interest in the details of Greco-Roman religion (cultic images, myths, divination procedures) for their own sake. He seems to have had specific knowledge of cultic practices in Athens and Ephesus. We can infer that Luke probably had researched sources such as Strabo or writers similar to Pausanias to learn about the subtle details of local cultic ritual. If this is true, Luke also expected his audience to also have sufficient knowledge to comprehend his narrative.

Luke expected his audience (the 'implied reader') to understand the references to Greco-Roman religion in his narrative. Based on the nature of the references, what was the nature of his audience's social location? Luke may have expected at least some of his audience to 'catch' allusions to Greco-Roman myth and perhaps to classical Attic drama; therefore, at least a portion of his audience may have possessed a 'middling' level of literary knowledge and education.[18] If Theophilus,

---

(Robbins, 'Social Location of the Implied Author', p. 328). His analysis does not consider early Christianity's interaction with Greco-Roman religion.

17. To these, we may add a Lukan popular knowledge about Greek philosophical religion (Epicureanism, Stoicism, 17:18), the cult of the Unknown God(s) (17:23), magic (8:4–25, 13:4–12, 19:17–20) and demons (19:13–16); issues not addressed in this study.

18. Both classical and Hellenistic authors made similar assumptions about their audiences. They assumed that the educated portions of their audiences would understand subtle allusions and 'insider' jokes and references to literature, philosophy, and religion. Aristophanes' allusions to technical poetic devices were 'hardly...decoded by the mass of the spectators, whereas they would easily be grasped by that cultural elite to which he meant to refer', (Giuseppe Mastromarco, *The Public of Herondas* [London Studies in Classical Philology, 11; Amsterdam: J.C. Gieben, 1984] pp. 65–97, quoting 79; also, S. Halliwell, 'Aristophanes' Apprenticeship', *CIQ* 30 (1980), pp. 33–45; further bibliography in Mastromarco, *Public of Herondas*, p. 79 n. 26; and Halliwell, 'Aristophanes' Apprenticeship', throughout). Similarly, the Hellenistic epigrammatist Herodas wrote his mimes to operate at multiple levels. In his sixth mime, he makes a ribald reference to an ancient Greek sex toy, the βαυβών, burlesques Orphic myth and ritual, and refers to his own poetics (Jacob Stern, 'Herodas Mimiamb 6', *GRBS* 20 [1979] pp. 247–53; Mastromarco, *Public of Herodas*, pp. 72–73).

In addition to my suggested allusions to Aeschylus (Chapter 5, above), there are also possible allusions to Euripides' *Bacchae* in Acts 12.6–17 and 26.14 (Wilhelm Nestle, 'Anklange an Euripides in der Apostelgeschichte', in *idem, Griechische Studien, Untersuchung zur Religion, Dichtung und*

the addressee and dedicatee of Luke-Acts, had a basic education in the 'standard' texts of classical literature, he may have been able or expected to catch Luke's allusions to *Eumenides* and other ancient literature.[19]

Implications for Studying Acts. Judith Lieu, among others, has discounted the importance of Greco-Roman religion in Acts: 'We would hardly know [about the cities Paul visits in Greece] that we are in a Greek city and competing deities are noticeable by their absence'.[20] My analysis suggests precisely the opposite. At least from the perspective of the ancient Greco-Roman authorial audience, Luke specifically engages with various elements of Greco-Roman religion. Therefore, no matter the exegetical method utilized, we must acknowledge this engagement in our exegetical investigations of Acts and realize that Luke used these elements of Greco-Roman religion within the structure of his narrative on *his* terms as an author and *not* on our terms as modern interpreters.

Areas for Further Research

My study suggests several possible new lines of investigation into Luke-Acts:

1. Would Greco-Romans have observed additional passages in Acts that they may have understood to be references or allusions to Greco-Roman religion? For example, would Greco-Romans have understood Acts 14.19–20 (Paul's stoning, apparent death, and escape to safety) as a φαρμακός ritual? What is the possible significance of Cornelius' pros-kynesis to Peter in Acts 10? How would Greco-Romans have read the healing efficacy of Peter's shadow (Acts 5.15) or Paul's handkerchiefs (19.12)?[21] Would Greco-Romans have compared Acts 1.15–26 (or any

Philosophie der Griechen [repr. Aalen: Scientia Verlag, 1968], pp. 226–39; Portefaix, *Sisters Rejoice*, pp. 169–71); Stephen R. Wiest, 'A Propaedeutic from the *Bacchae* of Euripides for Interpreting Luke's Stephen-Section (Acts 6:1–8:4)' (paper presented at the annual meeting of the Midwest Region of the SBL, Chicago, Feb. 14, 2000); *idem*, 'Stephen and the Angel: A Typological Reading of the Story of Stephen in the Acts of the Apostles' (PhD dissertation; Marquette University; Milwaukee, 2001); and Homer's *Odyssey* (Dennis Ronald MacDonald, 'Luke's Eutychus and Homer's Elpenor: Acts 20.7–12 and *Odyssey* 10–12', *Journal of Higher Criticism* 1 [1994] pp. 5–24; and *idem*, *Does the New Testament Imitate Homer*. The existence of such allusions would strengthen the premise that both Luke and his audience had a moderately advanced literary education.

19. Robbins, 'Social Location of the Implied Author', pp. 320–23. Cf. Alexander, *The Preface to Luke's Gospel*, pp. 187–200.

20. Judith M. Lieu, *Neither Jew Nor Greek?: Constructing Early Christianity* (Studies of the New Testament in its World; London: T&T Clark, 2004), p. 72. Lieu mentions Acts 14, 17, and 19 but ignores 28:1–6, 11 and does not apprehend the presence of Greco-Roman religious motifs in 12.20–23 and 16.16–18.

21. See Werner Bieder, 'Der Petrusschatten, Apg. 5, 15', *TZ* 16 (1960), pp. 407–9; Peter W. van der Horst, 'Peter's Shadow: The Religio-Historical Background of Acts v.15', *NTS* 23 (1976–77), pp. 204–12; and T.J. Leary, 'The "Aprons" of St. Paul – Acts 19:12', *JTS* 41 (1990), pp. 527–29. Bieder takes a theological approach, van der Horst lists ten parallels from Greco-Roman texts without developing them (pp. 207–10), and Leary only discusses the translation of σιμικίνθιον. None of these authors fully investigates the *Greco-Roman* backgrounds of these healing miracles.

other mention of prophecy and scripture or 'holy writings') to the *Oracula Sibyllina*?

2. How would Greco-Romans have compared a seeming polemic against ruler cult in Acts 12.20–23 with Luke's positive treatment of the centurion Cornelius (Acts 10), who by virtue of his office participated in the Roman imperial cult?[22]

3. Would Greco-Romans have seen Luke as open to charges of ἀσέβεια or *maiestas* disruptive of the *mos maiorum*?[23]

4. Would Greco-Romans have noticed an implied contrast between the temple in Jerusalem and Greco-Roman temples?

5. How do the references to Greco-Roman religion and their narrative context structure and advance Luke's narrative? Are some of these references, following Pervo, purely entertaining?[24]

6. Does Luke hide or gloss over troubling aspects of Greco-Roman religion in his narrative? For example, as stated above, Cornelius the centurion would have probably had a role in the imperial cult. Does Luke ignore or conceal this fact or is he simply unaware of it? Instead, he emphasizes Cornelius' benefactions on behalf of the Judean community (10.2, 4).

7. How do Luke's descriptions of Greco-Roman religion contrast with other ancient writers? Are his descriptions parallel to ancient novels, Pausanias' discussions of antiquities and ancestral religion, Lucian's satires, the blanket condemnations of ancient Judean literature, the elitist condescension of Cicero, or other ancient writers and genres?

8. Is it possible to outline and develop a synthetic Lukan theology of religion including Second Temple Judean practices and beliefs, early Christianity, and the pluriform varieties of Greco-Roman religions?

Closing Remarks

As I showed in Chapter 1, there are a number of unexplored aspects of Greco-Roman religion in Acts. I have attempted to address some of these issues by making tentative but detailed investigations into the Greco-Roman religious world that lies behind the text of Acts. Additionally, I have interpreted specific elements of this religious world as 'cultural competencies' possessed by Greco-Roman readers of Acts. Understanding the references and possible allusions to

22. Levinskaya, *Diaspora Setting*, pp. 121–26, esp. 121. Joseph B. Tyson has noted that Luke almost consistently presents centurions favorably: Lk. 7; 23.47; Acts 21.32; 22.25–29; 23.17, 23; 24.23; 27.1, 6, 31, 43 with Acts 27.11 as the only exception (*Images of Judaism in Luke-Acts* [Columbia, SC: University of South Carolina Press, 1992], pp. 37–38).

23. See R.A. Baumann, 'Tertullian and the Crime of *Sacrilegium*', *JRH* 4 (1966–67), pp. 175–83; *idem*, *The Crimen Maiestatis in the Roman Republic and Augustan Principate* (Johannesburg: Witwatersrand University Press, 1967) and *idem*, *Impietas in Principem: A Study of Treason against Roman Emperors with Special Reference to the First Century A.D.* (Münchener Beiträge zur Papyforschung und Antiken Rechtgeschicte, 67; Munich: C.H. Beck, 1974).

24. Richard I. Pervo, *Profit with Delight: The Literary Genre of the Acts of the Apostles* (Philadelphia: Fortress, 1987), esp. pp. 12–85.

Greco-Roman religion in Acts will better enable us to comprehend Luke, his writings, his religious and socio-cultural world, his audience and the cultural competencies they brought to the text, the origins and early history of our own Christian tradition, and to apply Luke's Acts in our contemporary setting. In a post 9/11 world of near apocalyptic religious rivalries and wars, we can not afford to do any less.

BIBLIOGRAPHY

Collections of Inscriptions

Engelmann, Helmut and Reinhold Merkelbach (eds), *Die Inschriften von Erythrai und Klazomenai* (Bonn: R. Habelt, 1972–73.)

Kaibel, Georg (ed.), *Epigrammata Graecae ex lapidibus conlecta* (Berlin: G. Reimer, 1878).

Raubitschek, A.E, *Dedications From the Athenian Akropolis: A Catalogue of the Inscriptions of the Sixth and Fifth Centuries, B.C.* (Cambridge, MA: Archaeological Institute of America, 1949).

Rehm, Albert and Richard Harder (eds), *Didyma II: Die Inschriften* (Berlin: Mann, 1958).

Critical Editions and Translations

Aeschylus, *Die Fragmente der Tragödien des Aischylos*, Hans Joachim Mette (ed.); (Berlin: Akademie-Verlag, 1959).

—'Aeschylus, The Eumenides [The Kindly Ones] 458 BC', (2003, online), http://www.mala.bc.ca/~johnstoi/aeschylus/aeschylus_eumenides.htm.

—*Aeschylus' Eumenides* (ed. Alan H. Sommerstein; Cambridge Greek and Latin Classics; Cambridge: Cambridge University Press, 1989).

Apollodorus, *Apollodorus, The Library* (ed. and trans. James George Frazer; LCL; Cambridge, MA: Harvard University Press, 1921).

Artemidorus, *The Interpretation of Dreams, Oneirocritca*; (trans. Robert J. White; Noyes Classical Studies, Park Ridge, NJ: Noyes, 1975).

Cicero, *De Senectute, De Amicitia, De Divinatione* (trans.William Armistead Falconer; LCL; Cambridge, MA: Harvard University Press, 1923).

—*De Re Publica, De Legibus* (trans. Clinton Walter Keyes; LCL; Cambridge, MA: Harvard University Press, 1928).

Diels, Hermann (ed. and trans.); *Die Fragmente der Vorsokratiker* (Berlin: Weidmann, 1951, 6th edn by Walther Kranz).

Erotianus Grammaticus, *Erotiani Vocum Hippocraticarum Collectio cum Fragmentis*, (ed. Ernst Nachmanson; Collectio Scriptorum Veterum Upsaliensis; Göteburg: Eranos, 1918).

Euripides, *Euripidis Fabulae* (ed. J. Diggle; OCT; 3 vols; Oxford: Oxford University Press, 1981).

Gow, A.S.F. and D.L. Page (eds and trans.), *The Greek Anthology: The Garland of Philip and Some Contemporary Epigrams* (2 vols; Cambridge: Cambridge University Press, 1968).

Heliodorus, *An Ethiopian Story* (trans. J.R. Morgan), in B.P. Reardon (ed.), *Collected Ancient Greek Novels* (Berkeley: University of California Press, 1989).

Heraclitus, *The Art and Thought of Heraclitus: An Edition of the Fragments with Translation and Commentary* (ed. and trans. C.H. Kahn; Cambridge: Cambridge University Press, 1979).

Herodas, *Mimiambi* (ed. I.C. Cunningham; Oxford: Oxford University Press, Clarendon, 1971).

Herodian, *Herodian* (trans. C.R. Whittaker; LCL; 2 vols; Cambridge, MA: Harvard University Press, 1969).

Homer, *The Iliad* (trans. Robert Fagles; New York: Viking Penguin, 1990).

—*The Odyssey* (trans. A. T. Murray, rev. and ed. George E. Dimock; LCL; 2 vols; Cambridge, MA: Harvard University Press, 1995).

The Homeric Hymns (ed. T.W. Allen, W.R. Halliday and E.E. Sikes; Oxford: Clarendon Press, Oxford University Press, 2nd edn, 1936.)

The Homeric Hymns: Translation, Introduction, and Notes (ed. and trans. Apostolos N. Athanassakis; Baltimore: The Johns Hopkins University Press, 1976).

The Homeric Hymns and The Battle of the Frogs and the Mice (trans. Daryl Hine; New York: Atheneum, 1972).

Jacoby, Felix (ed.), *Die Fragmente der griechischen Historiker* (3 vols; Berlin: Weidmann, 1929).

Livy, *History of Rome* (trans. B.O. Foster *et al.*; LCL; 14 vols; Cambridge, MA: Harvard University Press, 1961 [1935]).

Longus, *Daphnis and Chloe* (trans. Christopher Gill), in *Collected Ancient Greek Novels* (ed. B.P. Reardon; Berkeley: University of California Press, 1989).

Miller, Karl (ed.), *Fragmenta Historicorum Graecarum* (Paris: Didot, 1872; repr. Frankfurt: Minerva, 1975).

Müller, Karl, *Fragmenta Historica Graecorum* (Paris: Didot, 1872; repr. Frankfurt: Minerva, 1975.

Novum Testamentum Graecae (ed. Kurt Aland *et al.*; 27th rev. edn; Stuttgart: Deutsche Bibelgesellschaft, 1993).

Ogden, Daniel *Magic, Witchcraft, and Ghosts in the Greek and Roman Worlds: A Sourcebook* (Oxford: Oxford University Press, 2002).

Page, Denys L., *Further Greek Epigrams Epigrams before A.D. 50 from the Greek Anthology and other sources, not included in Hellenistic Epigrams or The Garland of Philip* (ed., rev. and prepared for publication by R.D. Dawe and J. Diggle; Cambridge: Cambridge University Press, 1981).

Pausanias, *Pausanias's Description of Greece* (ed. James George Frazer; 6 vols; London: Macmillan, 1897?; repr.; New York: Biblo and Tannen, 1965).

—*Pausanias Description of Greece* (trans. W.H.S. Jones; LCL; 5 vols; London: Heinemann; Cambridge, MA: Harvard University Press, 1918).

Petronius, *Petronius' Satyricon* (ed. Michael Heseltine; LCL; London: Heinemann; Cambridge, MA: Harvard University Press, 1913).

Pindar, *The Odes of Pindar: Including the Principal Fragments* (trans. John Sandys; 2nd rev. edn; LCL; Cambridge, MA: Harvard University Press, 1919).

—*The Odes of Pindar* (trans. C.M. Bowra; Penguin Classics; Harmondsworth, England: Penguin Books, 1969).

—*Pindar* (trans. William Race; LCL; Cambridge, MA: Harvard University Press, 1997).

Plutarch *Plutarch's Moralia* (trans. W.C. Helmbold; LCL; Cambridge, MA: Harvard University Press, 1939).

—*Plutarch: Selected Essays and Dialogues* (trans. Donald Russell; World's Classics. Oxford: Oxford University Press, 1993).

Polyaenus, *Stratagems of War* (ed. and trans. Peter Krentz and Everett L. Wheeler; 2 vols; Chicago: Ares, 1994).

Reardon, B.P. (ed.), *Collected Ancient Greek Novels* (Berkeley: University of California Press, 1989).

Rice, David G. and John E. Stambaugh (eds), *Sources for the Study of Greek Religion* (SBLSBS, 14; Missoula, MT: Scholars Press, 1979).

Septuagainta (ed. Alfred Rahlfs; reduced edn; 2 vols in 1; Stuttgart: Deutsche Bibelgesellschaft, 1979).

Sophocles, *Sophoclis Fabulae* (ed. Hugh Lloyd-Jones and Nigel G. Wilson; OCT; Oxford: Oxford University Press, 1990).

—*Sophocles* (ed. and trans. Lloyd-Jones; LCL; 3 vols; Cambridge, MA: Harvard University Press, 1994–96).

Suetonius, *Lives of the Caesars* (trans. J.C. Rolfe; LCL; 2 vols; New York: Putnam, 1920).

Suidas, *Suidae Lexicon* (ed. Ada Adler; Leipzig: Teubner, 1928–38)

Tacitus, *Annals* (trans. Clifford Herschel Moore and John Jackson; LCL; 4 vols; Cambridge, MA: Harvard University Press, 1931).

Yonge, Charles Duke (trans.), *The Works of Philo Judaeus: The Contemporary of Josephus, translated from the Greek* (London: H.G. Bohn, 1854–90).

Secondary Literature

Abrahamsen, Valerie A., *Women and Worship at Philippi: Diana/Artemis and Other Cults in the Early Christian Era* (Portland, ME: Astarte Shell, 1995).

Africa, Thomas, 'Worms and the Death of Kings: A Cautionary Note on Disease and History', *Classical Antiquity* 1 (1982) pp. 1–17.

Alcock, Susan E., *Graecia Capta: The Landscapes of Roman Greece* (Cambridge: Cambridge University Press, 1993).

Alexander, Bobby C., 'An Afterword on Ritual in Biblical Studies', *Semeia* 67 (1994), pp. 209–26.

Alexander, Loveday, 'Luke's Prefaces in the Context of Greek Preface-Writing', *NovT* 28 (1986), pp. 48–74.

—*The Preface to Luke's Gospel: Literary Convention and Social Context in Luke 1.1–4 and Acts 1.1* (SNTSMS, 78; Cambridge: Cambridge University Press, 1993).

Alföldi, Andreas, 'Insignien und Tracht der Römischen Kaiser', *Mitteilungen der römischen Abteilung des Deutschen Archäologischen Institutes (Römische Abteilung)* 50 (1935), pp. 1–158; repr., *Die monarchische Repräsentation im römischen Kaiserreiche* (Darmstadt: Wissenschaftliche Buchgesellschaft, 1980) pp. 121–276.

—'Die Ausgestaltung des Monarchischen Zeremoniells am Römischen Kaiserhofe', *Mitteilungen der römischen Abteilung des Deutschen Archäologischen Institutes* 49 (1934), pp. 3–118; repr., *Die monarchische Repräsentation im römischen Kaiserreiche* (Darmstadt: Wissenschaftliche Buchgesellschaft, 1980), pp. 3–118.

Allen, O. Wesley, *The Death of Herod: The Narrative and Theological Function of Retribution in Luke-Acts* (SBLDS, 158; Atlanta: Scholars Press and The Society of Biblical Literature, 1997).

Amandry, Pierre, 'Convention religieuse conclue entre Delphes et Skiathos', *BCH* 63 (1939), pp. 183–219.

—*La mantique Apollinienne à Delphes: Essai sur le fonctionnement de l'Oracle* (Paris: Bocard, 1950).

Anderson, J.G.C., 'Festivals of Mên Askaênos in the Roman Colonia at Antioch of Pisidia', *JRS* 3 (1913), pp. 267–300.

Asad, Talal, *Genealogies of Religion: Discipline and Reasons of Power in Christianity and Islam* (Baltimore: John Hopkins University Press, 1993).

Augé, Christian and Pascal Linant de Bellefonds, 'Dioskouroi (in Peripheria Orientali)', *LIMC* (Zurich: Artemis, 1986), III/1, pp. 593–97; III/2 pp. 477–81, pls. 1–22.

Aune, David E., *Prophecy in Early Christianity and the Ancient Mediterranean World* (Grand Rapids: Eerdmans, 1983).

Axtell, Harold L., *The Deification of Abstract Ideas in Roman Literature and Inscriptions* (Chicago: University of Chicago Press, 1907).

Balch, David L., 'The Areopagus Speech: An Appeal to the Stoic Historian Posidonius against Later Stoics and the Epicureans', in Balch (ed.), *Greeks, Romans, and Christians*, pp. 52–79.

Balch, David L. (ed.), *Greeks, Romans, and Christians: Essays in Honor of Abraham L. Malherbe* (Minneapolis: Fortress Press, 1990).

Baldick, Chris, *The Concise Oxford Dictionary of Literary Terms* (Oxford: Oxford University Press, 1990).

Barber, Elizabeth Wayland, *Women's Work: The First 20,000 Years: Women, Cloth, and Society in Early Times* (New York: Norton, 1994).

Barnes, T.D., 'An Apostle on Trial', *JTS* 22 (1969), pp. 407–19.

Barrett, C.K., *The Acts of the Apostles* (2 vols; ICC; Edinburgh: T&T Clark, 1994–98).

Bartman, Elizabeth, *Ancient Sculptural Copies in Miniature* (Columbia Studies in the Classical Tradition, 19; Leiden: Brill, 1992).

Baumann, Richard A., 'Tertullian and the Crime of Sacrilegium', *JRH* 4 (1966–67), pp. 175–83.

—*The Crimen Maiestatis in the Roman Republic and Augustan Principate* (Johannesburg: Witwatersrand University Press, 1967).

—*Impietas in Principem: A Study of Treason against Roman Emperors with Special Reference to the First Century A.D.* (Münchener Beiträge zur Papyforschung und Antiken Recht- geschicte, 67; Munich: C.H. Beck, 1974).

Baus, Karl, *Der Kranz in Antike und Christentum: Eine religionsgeschichtliche Untersuchung mit besonder Berüsichtigugen Tertullians* (Theophaneia, 2; Bonn: Hanstein, 1940).

Beard, Mary, 'Priesthood in the Roman Republic', in Beard and North (eds), *Pagan Priests*, pp. 17–48.

Beard, Mary and John North (eds), *Pagan Priests: Religion and Power in the Ancient World* (Ithaca, NY: Cornell University Press, 1990).

Beard, Mary, John North and Simon Price, *Religions of Rome. I. A History* (Cambridge: Cambridge University Press, 1998).

Beardslee, William A. 'The Casting of Lots at Qumran and in the Book of Acts', *NovT* 4 (1960–61), pp. 245–62.

Behm, Johannes, 'θύω', *TDNT* III (1965), pp. 180–90.

Bell, Catherine, *Ritual: Perspectives and Dimensions* (New York and Oxford: Oxford University Press, 1997).

—*Ritual Theory, Ritual Practice* (New York and Oxford: Oxford University Press, 1992).

Bethe, Erich, 'Dioskuren', PW, V/1 (1903), pp. 1087–1903.

Betz, Hans Dieter, *Galatians: A Commentary on Paul's Letter to the Churches in Galatia* (Hermeneia; Philadelphia: Fortress Press, 1979)

—*2 Corinthians 8 and 9: A Commentary on Two Administrative Letters of the Apostle Paul* (Hermeneia; Philadelphia: Fortress Press, 1985)

Betz, Otto, 'φωνης', *TDNT* IX (1974), pp. 278–99.

Bieder, Werner, 'Der Petrusschatten, Apg. 5, 15', *TZ* 16 (1960), pp. 407–9.

Björck, Gudmund, 'Heidnische und Christlich Orakel mit Fertigen Antworten', *SO* 119 (1939), pp. 86–98.

Blech, Michael, *Studien zum Kranz bei den Griechen* (Religionsgeschichtliche Versuche und Vorarbeiten, 38; Berlin : Walter de Gruyter, 1982).

Bock, Darryl L., *Proclamation from Prophecy and Pattern: Lucan Old Testament Christology* (JSNTSup, 12; Sheffield: JSOT Press, 1987).

Bodnar, Edward William, SJ, *Cyriacus of Ancona and Athens* (Collection Latomus, 43; Brussels: Latomus, Revue D'Études Latines, 1960).

Boegehold, Alan L., *et al.*, *The Athenian Agora. XXVIII. The Lawcourts at Athens: Sites, Build- ings, Equipment, Procedure, and Testimonia* (Princeton: American School of Classical Studies at Athens, 1995).

de Boer, Jelle Zeilinga and John R. Hale, 'Was She Really Stoned? The Oracle of Delphi', *Archaeology Odyssey* 5.6, (Nov/Dec, 2002), pp. 46–53, 58.

Bokser, Baruch M., 'Unleavened Bread and Passover, Feasts of', *ABD* VI, pp. 755–65.

Bond, Helen K., *Pontius Pilate in History and Interpretation* (SNTSMS, 100; Cambridge: Cambridge University Press, 1998).

Bonner, Robert J. and Gertrude Smith, *The Administration of Justice from Homer to Aristotle* (2 vols; Chicago: University of Chicago Press, 1930).

Boring, Eugene M., *The Continuing Voice of Jesus: Christian Prophecy and the Gospel Tradition* (Louisville, KY: Westminster/John Knox Press, 1991)

—'Early Christian Prophecy', *ABD* V, pp. 495–502.

Boring, Eugene, Klaus Berger, and Carsten Colpe (eds), *Hellenistic Commentary to the New Testament* (Nashville: Abingdon Press, 1995).

Bourdillon, M.F.C., 'Introduction', in Bourdillon and Fortes (eds), *Sacrifice*, pp. 1–28.

Bourdillon, M.F.C. and Meyer Fortes (eds), *Sacrifice* (London: Academic Press, Royal Anthropological Institute of Great Britain and Ireland, 1980).

Bowersock, G.W., *Fiction as History: Nero to Julian* (Sather Classical Lectures, 58; Berkeley: University of California Press, 1994).

Bremmer, Jan N., 'Aspects of the *Acts of Peter:* Women, Magic, Place and Date', in *idem* (ed.), *The Apocryphal Acts of Peter* (Studies on the Acts of the Apostles, 3; Leuven: Peeters, 1998), pp. 1–20.

Brent, Allen, *The Imperial Cult and the Development of Church Order: Concepts and Images of Authority in Paganism and Early Christianity before the Age of Cyprian* (Vigiliae Christianae Supplements, 45; Leiden: Brill, 1999).

Breytenbach, Cilliers, 'Zeus und der Lebendige Gott: Anmerkungen zu Apostlegeschichte 14.11–17', *NTS* 39 (1993), pp. 396–413.

Broughton, T. Robert S., 'New Evidence on Temple Estates in Asia Minor', in P.R. Coleman-Norton (ed.), *Studies in Roman Economic and Social History in Honor of Allan Chester Johnson* (Princeton: Princeton University Press, 1951), pp. 235–60.

Bruce, F.F., *The Book of Acts* (rev. edn; NICNT; Grand Rapids: Eerdmans, 1988).

—*The Acts of the Apostles: The Greek Text with Introduction and Commentary* (3rd rev. and enlarged edn; Grand Rapids: Eerdmanns, 1990).

Brug, John F., 'Acts 1:26—Lottery or Election?', *Wisconsin Lutheran Quarterly* 95 (1998), pp. 212–114.

Bultmann, Rudolf, *History of the Synoptic Tradition* (rev. edn; New York: Harper & Row, 1963).

Bunt-Van den Hoek, Annewies van de, 'Aristobulos, Acts, Theophilus, Clement: Making Use of Aratus' Phainomena: A Peregrination', *Bijdragen* 41 (1980), pp. 290–99.

Burford, Alison, *Craftsmen in Greek and Roman Society* (Aspects of Greek and Roman Life; Ithaca, NY: Cornell University Press, 1972).

Burkert, Walter, *Homo Necans: The Anthropology of Ancient Greek Sacrificial Ritual and Myth* (Berkeley: University of California Press, 1983).

—*Greek Religion in the Archaic and Classical Periods* (Cambridge, MA: Harvard University Press, 1985).

—*Ancient Mystery Cults* (Carl Newell Jackson Lectures; Cambridge, MA: Harvard University Press, 1987).

Caird, G.B., *Principalities and Powers: A Study in Pauline Theology* (Queen's University Chancellor's Lectures; Oxford: Clarendon, 1954).

Calder, W.M., 'Colonia Caesareia Antiocheia', *JRS* 2 (1912), pp. 79–120.

Carney, Thomas F., *The Shape of the Past: Models and Antiquity* (Lawrence, KS: Coronado Press, 1975).

Cassidy, Richard J., *Society and Politics in the Acts of the Apostles* (Maryknoll, NY: Orbis Books, 1987).

Cassidy Richard J. and Philip J. Sharper (eds), *Political Issues in Luke-Acts* (Maryknoll, NY: Orbis Books, 1983).

Casson, Lionel, *Travel in the Ancient World* (Toronto: Hakkert, 1974; repr., Baltimore: The Johns Hopkins University Press, 1994).

Cate, Houwink ten, *The Luwian Population Groups of Lycia and Cilicia Aspera During the Hellenistic Period* (Documenta et Monumenta Orientis Antiqui, 10 ; Leiden: Brill, 1961).

Chance, John K., 'The Anthropology of Honor and Shame: Culture, Values, and Practice', *Semeia* 68 (1996), pp. 139–63.

Cichorius, Conrad, *Römische Studien: Historisches, Epigraphisches, Literargeschichtliches aus vier Jahrhundertes Roms* (Leipzig: Teubner, 1922).

Claus, Manfred, *Kaiser und Gott: Herrscherkult im römischen Reich* (Stuttgart: Teubner, 1999).

Clinton, Kevin E., *The Sacred Officials of the Eleusinian Mysteries* (American Philosophical Society Proceedings, n.s., 64.3; Philadelphia: American Philosophical Association, 1974).

—'Sacrifice at the Eleusinian Mysteries', in Hägg, Marinatos and Nordquist, (eds), *Early Greek Cult Practice*, pp. 69–80.

—*Myth and Cult: The Iconography of the Eleusinian Mysteries* (Skrifter Utgivna av Svenska Institutet i Athen; Stockholm: Svenska Institute i Athen, 1992).

Cole, Susan Guettel, 'Greek Cults', in Michael Grant and Rachel Kitzinger (eds), *Civilization of the Ancient Mediterranean: Greece and Rome* (New York: Scribners, 1988), II, pp. 887–908.

—'Procession and Celebration at the Dionysia', in Scodel (ed.), *Theater and Society*, pp. 25–38.

Coleman, John Randolph, 'A Roman Terracotta Figurine of the Ephesian Artemis in the McDaniel Collection', *Harvard Studies in Classical Philology* 70 (1965), pp. 111–15.

Collart, Paul, 'Le sanctuaire des dieux égyptiens à Philippes', *BCH* 53 (1929), pp. 69–100.

—'Inscriptions de Philippes', *BCH* 56 (1932), pp. 193–231.

—'Inscriptions de Philippes', *BCH* 57 (1933), pp. 313–79.

—'Philippes', *DACL* 14 (1939), pp. 712–42.

—*Philippes: Ville de Macèdoine depuis ses origines jusqu' à le fin de l'èpoque romaine* (2 vols; Paris: E. de Boccard, 1937).

Collart, Paul and Pierre Ducrey, *Philippes I: Les reliefs rupestres* (Bulletin de Correspondance Hellénique Supplément, 2 ; Athens: Ècole Française d'Athènes, 1975).

Collins, Nina L., Review of Daniel R. Schwartz, *Agrippa I: Last King of Judea*, *NovT* 34 (1992), pp. 90–101.

Conacher, D.J., *Aeschylus' Oresteia: A Literary Commentary* (Toronto: University of Toronto, 1987).

Connor, W.R., 'Tribes, Festivals and Processions', *JHS* 107 (1987), pp. 40–50.

Conte, Gian Biagio, *The Rhetoric of Imitation: Genre and Poetic Memory in Virgil and Other Poets* (Cornell Studies in Classical Philology, 44; Ithaca, NY: Cornell University Press, 1986).

Conzelmann, Hans, *The Theology of St. Luke* (Philadelphia: Fortress Press, 1980).

—*Acts* (Hermeneia; Philadelphia: Fortress Press, 1987).

Croy, N. Clayton, 'Hellenistic Philosophies and the Preaching of the Resurrection (Acts 17.18, 32)', *NovT* 39 (1997), pp. 21–39.

Crump, David, *Jesus the Intercessor: Prayer and Christology in Luke-Acts* (WUNT 2/49; Tübingen: Mohr-Siebeck, 1992).

—'Jesus, the Victorious Scribal-Intercessor in Luke's Gospel', *NTS* 388 (1992), pp. 51–65.

Cuddon, J.A., *A Dictionary of Literary Terms* (Oxford: Blackwell, 3rd rev. edn, 1991).

Culler, Jonathan, *Structuralist Poetics: Structuralism, Linguistics, and the Study of Literature* (Ithaca, NY: Cornell University Press, 1975).

—*The Pursuit of Signs: Semiotics, Literature, Deconstruction* (Ithaca, NY: Cornell University Press, 1981).

Danker, Frederick W., *Luke* (Proclamation Commentaries; Philadelphia: Fortress Press, 2nd edn, 1987).

Darr, John, 'Glorified in the Presence of Kings: A Literary Critical Study of Herod the Tetrarch in Luke-Acts' (PhD dissertation, Vanderbilt University, 1987).

—*Herod the Fox: Audience Criticism and Lukan Characterization* (JSNTSup, 163; Sheffield: Sheffield Academic Press, 1998).

De Morgan, J. (ed.), *Délégation en Perse*, VII (Recherches Archélologiques, Deuxième série; Paris: Ministère de l'Instruction publique et des Beaux-Arts, 1905).

De Pena, Richard Damel, 'Dioskouroi/Tinas Clinian', *LIMC* (Zurich: Artemis, 1986), III, part 1, pp. 597–608; III, part 2, pp. 456–503, pls. 2–85.

Delz, J., 'Lukians Kenntnis der athenischen Antiquitäten' (PhD dissertation, Basel, 1950).

Denaux, A. 'The Theme of Divine Visits and Human (In)Hospitality in Luke-Acts: Its Old Testament and Graeco-Roman Antecedents', in J. Verheyden (ed.), *The Unity of Luke-Acts* (BETL, 142; Leuven: Leuven University Press and Peeters, 1999), pp. 255–80.

Denova, Rebecca I., *The Things Accomplished Among Us: Prophetic Tradition in the Structural Pattern of Luke-Acts* (JSNTSup, 141; Sheffield: Sheffield Academic Press, 1997).

Derow, Peter Sidney. 'Philhellenism', *OCD* (3rd edn, 1996), pp. 1159–60.

Destro, Adriana and Mauro Pesce, 'Exorcism, Magic, and Public Activities of the Preachers', in *The Anthropology of Christian Origins*, provisional English translation of *Antropologia delle origini cristiane* (Bari, Italy: Laterza, 2nd edn, 1997), n.p. E-mail document in author's possession.

Detienne, Marcel, *et al. The Cuisine of Sacrifice Among the Greeks* (trans. Paula Wissing; Chicago: University of Chicago Press, 1989).

Deubner, Ludwig, 'Personifikation abstrakter Begriffe', in Wilhelm Roscher (ed.), *Ausführliches Lexicon der griechischen und romischen Mythologie* (Leipzig: Teubner, 1884–86), III, part 2, cols 2068–169.

—'Die Bedeutung des Kranzes im klassischen Altertum', *ARW* 30 (1933), pp. 70–104.

Dickie, Mathew W., *Magic, Witchcraft, and Ghosts in the Greek and Roman World* (London: Routledge, 2001).

Dietrich, B.C., *Death, Fate and the Gods* (London: Athlone Press, University of London, 1965).

—'The Instrument of Sacrifice', in Hägg, Marinatos, and Nordquist (eds), *Early Greek Cult Practice*, pp. 35–40.

Dillery, John, 'Chresmologus and *Manteis:* Independent Diviners and the Problems of Authority', in Johnston and Struck (eds), *Mantikê*, pp. 167–32.

Di Salvator, Massimo, 'Il sorteggio fra politica e religion. Un caso tessalico', in Federica Cordano and Cristiano Grottanelli (eds), *Sorteggio pubblico e cleromanzia dall'antichità* (Milan: ET, 2001) pp. 119–30.

Dölger, Franz Josef, 'ΘΕΟΥ ΦΩΝΗ', *Antike und Christentum* 5 (1933), pp. 219–23.

Dölger, Franz Josef, ' "Dioskuroi". Das Reiseschiff des Apostels Paulus und seine Schutzgötter', *Antike und Christentum* 6 (1950), pp. 276–85.

Dowden, Ken, 'Dioskouroi', *DDD* (Leiden: Brill, 2nd edn, 1998), pp. 476–80.

—*Religion and the Romans* (Classical World Series; Bristol: Bristol Classical Press, 1992).

Durand, Jean-Louis, 'Greek Animals: Toward a Topology of Edible Bodies', in Marcel Detienne and Jean-Pierre Vernant (eds) *The Cuisine of Sacrifice among the Greeks* (Chicago: University of Chicago Press, 1989).

Dyer, R.R., 'The Evidence for Apolline Purification Rituals at Delphi and Athens', *JHS* 89 (1969), pp. 38–57.

Edwards, M.J., 'Quoting Aratus: Acts 17,28', *ZNW* 83 (1992), pp. 266–69.

Eitrem, Samson, 'De paulo et Barnaba deorum numer habitus (Acta XIV)', ConBNT 3 (1930), pp. 9–12.

Elliott, John H., 'Social-Scientific Criticism of the New Testament: More on Methods and Models', *Semeia* 35 (1986), pp. 1–34.

—'Temple versus Household in Luke-Acts: A Contrast in Social Institutions', in Neyrey (ed.), *The Social World of Luke-Acts*, pp. 211–40.

—'Jesus Wasn't a Christian. Historical, Social, and Theological Implications of the Disparaging Label Christianos and Other Nomenclature', unpublished paper presented to the annual meeting of the Context Group; Portland, Oregon, 13–16 March 1997.

Epp, Eldon Jay, 'The Oxyrhynchus New Testament Papyri: "Not Without Honor Except in Their Hometown?"' *JBL* 123 (2004) pp. 5–55.

Esler, Philip, *Community and Gospel in Luke-Acts: The Social and Political Motivations of Lucan Theology* (SNTSMS, 57; Cambridge: Cambridge University Press, 1987).

Faraone, Christopher, 'Necromancy Goes Underground: The Disguise of Corpse and Skull Divination in the Paris Magical Papyri PGMIV 1928–2144)' in Johnston and Struck (eds) *Mantikê*, pp. 255–82.

Fauth, Wolfgang, 'Pythia', PW, XXIV/2 (1963), pp. 515–47.

Fears, J. Rufus, 'The Cult of Virtues and Roman Imperial Ideology', *ANRW*, II/17, part 2 (1981), pp. 828–948.

Ferguson, Everett, *Backgrounds of Early Christianity* (Grand Rapids: Eerdmanns, 3rd edn, 2003).

Fiore, Benjamin 'NT Rhetoric and Rhetorical Criticism', *ABD* V, pp. 715–19.

Fitzmyer, Joseph A., SJ, *The Gospel According to Luke* (2 vols; AB, 28–28A; Garden City, NY: Doubleday, 1981–85).

—*Luke the Theologian: Aspects of his Teaching* (New York: Paulist Press, 1989).

—*The Acts of the Apostles: A New Translation with Introduction and Commentary* (AB, 31; New York: Doubleday, 1998).

Flacelière, Robert, *Greek Oracles* (London: Paul Elek, 2nd edn, 1976).

Fleischer, Robert, *Artemis von Ephesos und verwandte Kultstatuen aus Anatolien und Syrien* (EPRO, 35; Leiden: Brill, 1973).

Flückinger-Guggenheim, Daniela, *Göttliche Gäste: Die Einkehr von Göttern und Heroen in der griechischen Mythologie* (European University Studies, Series 3; History and Allied Studies, 237; Bern: Peter Lang, 1984).

Foerster, Werner, 'Πύθων', *TDNT* VI (1968), pp. 917–20.

Fontenrose, Joseph, 'Philemon, Lot, and Lycaon', *University of California Publications in Classical Philology* 13 (1945), pp. 93–120.

—*The Delphic Oracle: Its Responses and Operations with a Catalogue of Responses* (Berkeley: University of California Press, 1978).

—*Didyma: Apollo's Oracle, Cult and Companions* (Berkeley: University of California Press, 1988).

Forbes, Christopher, *Prophecy and Inspired Speech in Early Christianity and its Hellenistic Environment* (WUNT, 75; Tübingen: Mohr-Siebeck, 1995).

Fortes, Meyer, Preface to *Sacrifice* (ed. M.F.C. Bourdillon and Meyer Fortes; London: Academic Press, Royal Anthropological Institute of Great Britain and Ireland, 1980), pp. v–xix.

Foucart, P., 'Décret Athénien de L'Anée Trouvé a Éleusis', *BCH* 13 (1889), pp. 433–67.

Frankenberry, Nancy and Hans Penner, 'Geertz's Long-Lasting Moods, Motivations, and Metaphysical Conceptions', *JR* 79 (1999): pp. 617–40.

Fraser, P.M., 'The Kings of Commagene and the Greek World', in Sencer Sahin, Elmar Schwertheim, and Jörg Wagner (eds), *Studien zur Religion und Kultur Kleinasiens: Festschrift für Friedrich Karl Dörner zum 65. Geburstag am 28. Februar 1976* (EPRO, 66; Leiden: Brill, 1966), I, pp. 359–74.

Friesen, Steven J., *Twice Neokoros: Ephesus, Asia, and the Cult of the Flavian Imperial Family* (Leiden: Brill, 1993).

Funk, Robert, 'The Enigma of the Famine Visit', *JBL* 75 (1956), pp. 130–36.

Garland, Robert, *Introducing New Gods: The Politics of Athenian Religion* (Baltimore: The Johns Hopkins University Press, 1992).

—*Religion and the Greeks* (Classical World Series; London: Bristol Classical Press, an imprint of Gerald Duckworth, 1995).

Garrett, Susan R., *The Demise of the Devil: Magic and the Demonic in Luke's Writings* (Minneapolis: Fortress Press, 1989).

—'Exodus from Bondage: Luke 9:31 and Acts 12:1–24', *CBQ* 52 (1990), pp. 656–80.

Gärtner, Bertil, *The Areopagus Speech and Natural Revelation* (ASNU, 21; Uppsala: Almqvist & Wiksells, 1955).

Gasque, W. Ward, *A History of the Interpretation of the Acts of the Apostles* (Grand Rapids: Eerdmanns, 1975; repr., Peabody, MA: Hendrickson, 1989).

Gaventa, Beverly Roberts, *Acts* (Abingdon New Testament Commentaries; Nashville: Abingdon, 2003).

Geagan, D.J., *The Athenian Constitution after Sulla* (Hesperia Supplement, 12; Princeton: American School at Athens, 1967).

—'Ordo Areopagitarum Atheniensium', in Donald William Bradeen and Malcom Francis McGregor (eds), *ΦΟΡΟΣ: Tribute to Benjamin Dean Meritt* (Locust Valley, NY: J.J. Augustin, 1974), pp. 51–56.

Geertz, Clifford, 'Religion as a Cultural System', in Clifford Geertz, *The Interpretation of Cultures* (San Francisco: Basic Books, a Division of HarperCollins, 1973), pp. 87–125.

Genette, Gérard. *Palimpsestes: La Littérature au second degré.* (Poétique; Paris: Seuil, 1982). English translation: Claude Doubinsky and Channa Newman (trans.), *Palimpsests: Literature in the Second Degree* (Stages, 8; Lincoln, NE: University of Nebraska Press, 1997).

Gill, David W.J., 'Acts and Roman Religion, A Religion in a Local Setting', in David W.J. Gill and Conrad Gempf (eds), *The Book of Acts in Its Graeco-Roman Setting*, vol. II in the 5-volume set, *The Book of Acts in Its First Century Setting* (ed. Bruce W. Winter; Grand Rapids: Eerdmanns, 1994; Carlisle: Paternoster Press, 1994), pp. 79–102.

—'Achaia', in, *The Book of Acts in its Graeco-Roman Setting*, Bruce W. Winter (ed.); vol. II in David W.J. Gill and Conrad Gempf (eds), *The Book of Acts in Its First Century Setting* (Grand Rapids: Eerdmans; Carlisle: Paternoster Press, 1994), pp. 447–48.

Goldhill, S., 'The Great Dionysia and Civic Ideology', *JHS* 107 (1987), pp. 58–76.

Gooding, D.W., *True to the Faith* (London: Hodder & Stoughton, 1990).

Gordon, Richard, 'From Republic to Principate: Priesthood, Religion and Ideology', in Beard and North (eds), *Pagan Priests*, pp. 177–198.

—'The Veil of Power: Emperors, Sacrificers and Benefactors', in Beard and North (eds), *Pagan Priests*, pp. 199–232.

—'Religion in the Roman Empire: the Civic Compromise and its Limits', in Beard and North (eds), *Pagan Priests*, pp. 233–56.

—'Divination and Prophecy: Rome', in Johnston (ed.) *Religions of the Ancient World*, pp. 387–89.

Gorman Jr, Frank H., 'Ritual Studies and Biblical Studies: Assessment of the Past, Prospects for the Future', *Semeia* 67 (1994), pp. 13–36.

Gossen-Steier, H., 'Schlange', *PW* II/2 (1921), pp. 494–557.

Gradel, Ittai, *Emperor Worship and Roman Religion* (Oxford Classical Monographs; Oxford: Clarendon Press, 2002).

Graf, Fritz, 'What is New About Greek Sacrifice'? in H.F.J. Horstmanshoff, *et al.* (eds), *Kykeon: Studies in Honour of H.S. Versnel* (RGRW, 142; Leiden: Brill, 2002), pp. 113–26.

—'Zeus', *OCD* (3rd edn, 1996), p. 1636–38.

—'Rolling the Dice for an Answer', in Johnston and Struck (eds) *Mantikê*, pp. 51–98.

—'Sacrifice (Further Considerations)', *ER* XII (2nd edn), pp. 8008–10.

Grant, Robert M., *Gods and the One God* (LEC, 1; Philadelphia: Westminster Press, 1986).

Green, Joel B., *The Gospel of Luke* (NICNT; Grand Rapids: Eerdmanns, 1997).

—'Persevering Together in Prayer: The Significance of Prayer in the Acts of the Apostles', in Richard N. Longenecker (ed.), *Into God's Presence: Prayer in the New Testament* (McMaster New Testament Studies; Grand Rapids:Eerdmans, 2001), pp. 183–202.

Greene, William Chase, 'Personifications', *OCD* (1st edn), pp. 669–71.

Grimal, Pierre, *The Dictionary of Classical Mythology* (corrected edn; London: Blackwell, 1986).

Grimes, Ronald L., *Symbol and Conquest: Public Ritual and Drama in Santa Fe* (Ithaca, NY: Cornell University Press, 1976).

—*Research in Ritual Studies: A Programmatic Essay and Bibliography* (ATLA Bibliography Series 14; Metuchen, NJ: American Theological Library Association and Scarecrow, 1985).

—*Ritual Criticism: Case Studies in Its Practice, Essays on Its Theory* (Studies in Comparative Religion; Columbia, SC: University of South Carolina Press, 1990)

—*Beginnings in Ritual Studies* (Studies in Comparative Religion; Columbia, SC: University of South Carolina Press, 1995).

Grottanelli, Cristiano, 'Sorte unica pro casibus pluribus enotata: Literary Text and Lot Inscriptions as Sources for Ancient Kleromancy', in Johnston and Struck (eds) *Mantikê*, pp. 129–46.

Gruen, Erich S. *The Hellenistic World and the Coming of Rome* (Berkeley: University of California Press, 1984).

—*Studies in Greek Culture and Roman Policy* (Cincinnati Classical Studies, New Series, 7; Leiden: Brill, 1996).

Gury, Françoise, 'Dioskouroi/Castores', *LIMC* (Zurich: Artemis, 1986), III/1, pp. 608–34; vol. 3, part 2, pp. 489–503, pls. 1–162.

Gutzwiller, Kathryn J., *Poetic Garlands: Hellenistic Epigrams in Context* (Hellenistic Culture and Society, 28; Berkeley: University of California Press, 1998).

Habicht, Christian, *Gottmenschentum und griechische Städte* (Munich: C.H. Beck'sche, 2nd edn, 1970).

Haenchen, Ernst, 'Das 'Wir' in der Apostelgeschichte und das Itinerar', *ZThK* 58 (1961), pp. 329–66.

—*The Acts of the Apostles: A Commentary* (Philadelphia: Westminster Press, 1971).

Hägg, Robin, Nanno Marinatos and Gullög C. Nordquist (eds), *Early Greek Cult Practice: Proceedings of the Fifth International Symposium at the Swedish Institute at Athens, 26–29 June, 1986* (Skrifter Utgivna av Svenska Institutet i Athen, 4°, 38; Stockholm: Svenska Institutet i Athen, 1988).

Halliday, W.R., *Greek Divination: A Study of its Methods and Principles* (London: Macmillan, 1913; repr., Chicago: Argnonaut, 1967).

Halliwell, S., 'Aristophanes' Apprenticeship', *ClQ* 30 (1980), pp. 33–45.

Hanson, Richard S., *Tyrian Influence in the Upper Galilee* (Meiron Excavation Project, 2; Cambridge, MA: American Schools of Oriental Research, 1980).

Harrill, J. Albert, 'The Dramatic Function of the Running Slave Rhoda (Acts 12.12–16): A Piece of Greco-Roman Comedy', *NTS* 46 (2000), pp. 150–57.

Harris, H.A., *Greek Athletics and the Jews* (Cardiff: University of Wales Press, 1976).

Harris, O.G., 'Prayer in Luke-Acts: A Study in the Theology of Luke' (PhD dissertation, Vanderbilt University, 1966).

Harris, William, ' "Brass" and Hellenistic Technology', *BARev* 8 (Jan–Feb 1982), pp. 38–41.

Harrison, Everett F., 'The Resurrection of Jesus Christ in the Book of Acts and in Early Christian Literature', in John Reumann (ed.), *Understanding the Sacred Text: Essays in Honor of Morton S. Enslin on the Hebrew Bible and Christian Beginnings* (Valley Forge, PA: Judson, 1972), pp. 217–33.

Harrison, Jane Ellen, 'Delphika', *JHS* 19 (1899), pp. 205–51.

—*Prolegomena to the Study of Greek Religion* (Cambridge: Cambridge University Press, 1903).

Hauser, Friedrich, 'Eine Tyrrhenische Amphora der Sammlung Bourguinon', *Jahrbuch des deutschen archaologischen Instituts* 8 (1893), pp. 93–103.

Hays, Richard B., *Echoes of Scripture in the Letters of Paul* (New Haven: Yale University Press, 1989).

Heinevetter, F., *Würfel-und-Buchstaben Orakel in Griechenland und Kleinasien* (PhD dissertation, Breslau, 1912).

Hemer, Colin J., 'Paul at Athens: A Topographical Note', *NTS* 20 (1973–74), pp. 341–50.

—*The Book of Acts in the Setting of Hellenistic History* (WUNT, 49; Tübingen: Mohr-Siebeck, 1989).

Hengel, Martin, *Judaism and Hellenism: Studies in Their Encounter in Palestine During the Early Hellenistic Period* (2 vols in 1; Philadelphia: Fortress Press, 1981).

—*The 'Hellenization' of Judea in the First Century After Christ* (Philadelphia: Trinity Press International, 1989).

Henninger, Joseph, 'Sacrifice', *ER*, XII, pp. 544–57.

Hepding, H., 'Die Arbeiten zu Pergamon 1908–1909. II: Die Inschriften', *MDAI (Athenische Abteilung)*, 35 (1910), pp. 454–57.

Hermary, Antoine, 'Dioskouroi', *LIMC* (Zurich: Artemis, 1986), I/1, pp. 567–93; I/2, pp. 456–77, pls. 2–257.

Herzfeld, Michael, 'Honor and Shame: Some Problems in the Comparative Analysis of Moral Systems', *Man* 15 (1980), pp. 339–51.

Hicks, E.L., 'Demetrius the Silversmith: An Ephesian Study', *The Expositor*, 4th ser., 1 (1890), pp. 401–22.

Hills, Julian Victor, 'Luke 10:18—Who Saw Satan Fall?' *JSNT* 46 (1992), pp. 25–40.

Hodot, P., 'Décret de Kymè en l'honneur du prytane Kleanax', *The J. Paul Getty Museum Journal* 10 (1982), pp. 165–80.

Höfer, O., 'Pythia, Pythios, Python', *ALGRM*, III/2, cols 3370–412.

Hogan, James C., *A Commentary on the Complete Greek Tragedies: Aeschylus* (Chicago: University of Chicago Press, 1984).

Hollander, John, *The Figure of Echo: A Mode of Allusion in Milton and After* (Berkeley: University of California Press, 1981).

Holmboe, Henrik, *Concordance to Aeschylus' Supplices* (Århus: Akademisk Boghandel, 1971).

—*Concordance to Aeschylus' Prometheus Vitens* (Århus: Akademisk Boghandel, 1971).

—*Concordance to Aeschylus' Persiae* (Århus: Akademisk Boghandel, 1971).

—*Concordance to Aeschylus' Septem Contra Thebas* (Århus: Akademisk Boghandel, 1971).

—*Concordance to Aeschylus' Agamemnon* (Århus: Akademisk Boghandel, 1972).

—*Concordance to Aeschylus' Choephoroi* (Århus: Akademisk Boghandel, 1973).

—*Concordance to Aeschylus' Eumenides* (Århus: Akademisk Boghandel, 1973).

Horst, Peter W. van der, 'Peter's Shadow: The Religio-Hisotrical Background of Acts v.15', *NTS* 23 (1976–77), pp. 204–12.

—'The Altar of the "Unknown God" in Athens (Acts 17:23), and the Cults of "Unknown Gods" in the Graeco-Roman World', *ANRW* II/18, part 2 (1989), pp. 1426–56. Repr., *Hellenism-Judaism-Christianity: Essays on Their Interaction* (CBET, 8; Kampen: Kok Pharos, 1994), pp. 165–202.

—'Dike', *DDD* (2nd edn; 1998), pp. 476–80.

Hughes, Dennis D., *Human Sacrifice in Ancient Greece* (London and New York, 1991).

Humphreys, S.C., *The Family, Women, and Death: Comparative Studies* (London: Routledge & Kegan Paul, 1983).

Iser, Wolfgang, *The Implied Reader: Patterns in Communication in Prose Fiction from Bunyan to Beckett* (Baltimore: The Johns Hopkins University Press, 1974).

—*The Act of Reading: A Theory of Aesthetic Response* (Baltimore: The Johns Hopkins University Press, 1978).

Jacquier, E., *Les Actes des Apôtres* (EBib; Paris: Victor Lecoffre, 1926).

Jameson, Michael, 'Sacrifice and Ritual: Greece', in Grant and Kitzinger (eds), *Civilization of the Ancient Mediterranean* (New York: Scribners, 1988), II, pp. 959–80.

—'Sacrifice and Animal Husbandry in Classical Greece', in C.R. Whittaker (ed.), *Pastoral Economics in Classical Antiquity* (Proceedings of the Cambridge Philological Society, 14; Cambridge: Cambridge Philological Society, 1988), pp. 87–119.

—'Sacrifice and Human Husbandry' in Whittaker (ed.), *Pastoral Economics in Classical Antiquity* (Proceedings of the Cambridge Philological Society, 15; Cambridge: Cambridge Philological Society, 1988), pp. 87–119.

Jauss, Hans R., 'Literary History as a Challenge to Literary Theory', *New Literary History* 2 (1970), pp. 7–38.

—'Literary History as a Challenge to Literary Theory', in *idem, Toward an Aesthetic of Reception*, (trans. Timothy Bahti; Theory and History of Literature, 2; Minneapolis: University of Minnesota Press, 1982), pp. 3–45.

Jeremias, Joachim, *New Testament Theology: The Proclamation of Jesus* (New York: Scribners, 1971).

Johnson, Luke Timothy, *The Gospel According to Luke* (SP, 3; A Michael Glazier Book. Collegeville, MN: Liturgical Press, 1991).

—*The Acts of the Apostles,* (SP, 5; A Michael Glazier Book; Collegeville: Liturgical Press, 1992).

Johnston, Sarah Iles, Restless Dead: Encounters between the Living and the Dead in Ancient Greece (Berkeley: University of California Press, 1999).

—'Lost in the Shuffle: Roman Sortition and Its Discontents', *Archiv für Religionsgeschichte* 5 (2003), pp. 46–56.

—Introduction to 'Divination and Prophecy: Greece', in Sarah Iles Johnston (ed.), *Religions of the Ancient World: A Guide* (Harvard University Press Reference Library; Cambridge, MA: Belknap Press of Harvard University Press, 2004) pp. 370–71.

—*Religions of the Ancient World: A Guide* (Harvard University Press Reference Library; Cambridge, MA: Belknap Press of Harvard University Press, 2004).

—'Delphi and the Dead', in Johnston and Struck (eds) *Mantikê*, pp. 283–306.

Johnston, Sarah Iles and Peter T. Struck (eds), *Mantikê: Studies in Ancient Divination* (RGRW; Leiden: Brill Academic, 2005).

Jones, A.H.M., *The Cities of the Eastern Roman Provinces* (2 vols; Oxford: Oxford University Press, 2nd edn, 1971).

Jones, C.P., 'Greek Drama in the Roman Empire', in Scodel (ed.), *Theater and Society*, pp. 39–52.

Kadletz, Edward, 'The Sacrifice of Eumaios the Pig Herder', *GRBS* 25 (1984), pp. 99–105.

Kaibel, Georg (ed.), *Epigrammata Graecae ex lapidibus conlecta* (Berlin: G. Reimer, 1878).

Kanda, S.H., 'The Form and Function of the Petrine and Pauline Miracle Stories in the Acts of the Apostles' (PhD dissertation, Claremont University, 1974).

Kearns, Emily, 'Religion, Greek', *OCD* (3rd edn, 1996), pp. 1300–1301.

Kearsley, R.A., 'Acts 14.13: The Temple Just Outside the City', *NewDocs*, VI, pp. 209–10, §32.

Kee, Howard Clark, *To Every Nation under Heaven: The Acts of the Apostles* (The New Testament in Context; Harrisburg, PA: Trinity Press International, 1997).

Keil, B., *Beiträge zur Geschichte des Areopags* (Berichte über die Verhandlungen der Sächsischen Akademie der Wissenschaft zu Leipzig, Philologische-historische Klasse, 71, Band 8; Leipzig: Sächsischen Akademie der Wissenschaft zu Leipzig, 1920).

Keil, Josef, 'Vorläufiger Bericht über die Ausgrabungen in Ephesos', *Jahreshefte des Österreichischen archäologischen Instituts, Beiblatt* 24 (1929), pp. 1–67.

Kelhoffer, James, *Miracle and Mission: The Authentication of Missionaries and Their Message in the Longer Ending of Mark* (WUNT, 2/112; Tübingen: Mohr-Siebeck, 2000).

Kirk, G.S. 'Some Methodological Pitfalls in the Study of Ancient Greek Sacrifice (in Particular)', in Rudhardt and Reverdinm (eds), *Le Sacrifice*, pp. 41–80.

Klauck, H.J., 'With Paul in Paphos and Lystra: Magic and Paganism in the Acts of the Apostles', *Neot* 28 (1994), pp. 93–107.

—*Magic and Paganism in Early Christianity: The World of the Acts of the Apostles* (Edinburgh: T&T Clark, 2000).

—Des Kaisers schöne Stimme. Herrscherkritik in Apg 12,20–23', in H.J. Klauck, *Religion und Gesellschaft im frühen Christentum* (WUNT, 152; Tübingen: Mohr-Siebeck, 2003).

Klaus, W., 'Dioskuren', *RAC*, III (1975), pp. 1122–58.

Klauser, Theodor, 'Akklamation', *RAC*, I (1950), 216–33.

Klein, William W., 'Noisy Gong or Acoustic Vase: a Note on 1 Corinthians 13:1', *NTS* 32 (1986), pp. 86–89.

Kloppenborg, John S., ΦΙΛΑΔΕΛΦΙΑ, ΘΕΟΔΙΔΑΚΤΟΣ, and the Dioscuroi: Rhetorical Engagement in 1 Thessalonians 4.9–12', *NTS* 39 (1993), pp. 265–89.

Knowling, R. J., *The Acts of the Apostles*. II in W. Robertson Nicoll (ed.), *The Expositor's Greek Testament* (New York: Dodd, Mead, 1910).

Koester, Helmut (ed.), *Ephesos: Metropolis of Asia* (Peabody, MA: Hendrikson, 1995).

Koets, P.J., *Δεισιδαιμονία: A Contribution to the Knowledge of the Religious Terminology in Greek* (Purmerend, The Netherlands: J. Muusses, 1929).

Kokkinos, Nikos, *The Herodian Dynasty: Origins, Role in Society and Eclipse* (JSPSup, 30; Sheffield: Sheffield Academic Press, 1998).

Koukouli-Chrysantaki, Chaido, 'Colonia Iulia Augusta Philippensis', in Charalambos Bakirtzis and Helmut Koester (eds), *Philippi at the Time of Paul and after His Death* (Harrisburg: Trinity Press International, 1998), pp. 5–35.

Krentz, Edgar, *The Historical-Critical Method* (Guides to Biblical Scholarship, Old Testament Series; Philadelphia: Fortress Press, 1975).

Kressel, Gideon M., 'An Anthropologist's Response to the Use of Social Science Models in Biblical Studies', *Semeia* 68 (1996), pp. 153–60.

Küster, Erich, *Die Schlange in der griechischen Kunst und Religion* (Religionsgeschichtliche Versuche und Vorarbeiten, Band 13, Heft 2; Giessen: Alfred Töpelmann, 1913).

Ladouceur, David, 'Hellenistic Preconceptions of Shipwreck and Pollution as a Concept for Acts 27–28', *HTR* 73 (1980), pp. 435–49.

Lake, Kirsopp, 'The Ascension', in Kirsopp Lake and Henry J. Cadbury (eds) *Additional Notes to the Commentary*, vol. V in F.J. Foakes-Jackson and Kirsopp Lake (eds), *The Beginnings of Christianity*. I. *The Acts of the Apostles* (London: MacMillan, 1933), pp. 16–22.

—'Localities in and Near Jerusalem Mentioned in Acts', in Kirsopp Lake and Henry J. Cadbury (eds), *Additional Notes to the Commentary*. V, in F.J. Foakes-Jackson and Kirsopp Lake (eds), *The Beginnings of Christianity*. I. *The Acts of the Apostles* (London: MacMillan, 1933), pp. 474–86.

—'Your Own Poets', in Kirsopp Lake and Henry J. Cadbury (eds), *Additional Notes to the Commentary*, vol. 5 of F.J. Foakes-Jackson and Kirsopp Lake (eds), *The Beginnings of Christianity*. I. *The Acts of the Apostles* (London: MacMillan, 1933), pp. 246–51.

Lake, Kirsopp and Henry J. Cadbury, *English Translation and Commentary*, vol. 6 of F.J. Foakes-Jackson and Kirsopp Lake (eds), *The Beginnings of Christianity*. I. *The Acts of the Apostles* (London: MacMillan, 1933).

Lambert, Michael, 'Ancient Greek and Zulu Sacrificial Ritual: A Comparative Analysis', *Numen* 40 (1993), pp. 293–318.

Lämmer, Manfred, 'Griechische Wettkampfe in Jerusalem und ihre politischen Hintergrunde', *Kölner Beiträge zur Sporwissenschaft* 2 (1973), pp. 182–227.

—'Die Kaiserspiele von Caesarea im Dienste der Politik des Königs Herodes', *Kölner Beiträge zur Sporwissenschaft* 3 (1974), pp. 95–164.

—'Grieschische Wettkampfe in Galilea unter der herrschaft des herodes Antipas', *Kölner Beiträge zur Sporwissenschaft* 3 (1976), pp. 36–67.

Lane, Eugene N., 'Sabazius and the Jews in Valerius Maximus', *JRS* 69 (1979), pp. 35–38.

Lane Fox, Robin, 'Hellenistic Culture and Literature', in John Boardman, Jasper Griffin, and Oswyn Murray (eds), *Greece and the Hellenistic World* (OHCW; Oxford: Oxford University Press, 1988), pp. 332–58.

Lardinois, André., 'Greek Myths for Athenian Rituals: Religion and Politics in Aeschylus' Eumenides and Sophocles' Oedipus Colonus', *GRBS* 33 (1992), pp. 313–27.

Latte, Kurt, 'The Coming of the Python', *HTR* 33 (1949), pp. 9–18.

Lauffer, Siegfried, 'Pytho', PW 24 (1963), pp. 569–80.

Leary, T.J., 'The "Aprons" of St. Paul – Acts 19:12', *JTS* 41 (1990), pp. 527–29.

Lehmann, Karl, Review of *Studies in Roman Imperial Art* by Per G. Hamber, *Art Bulletin* 29 (1947), p. 138.

Lerle, Ernst, 'Die Predigt in Lystra (Acta XIV 15–18)', *NTS* 7 (1960–61), pp. 46–55.

Levick, Barbara, *Roman Colonies in Asia Minor* (Oxford: Oxford University Press, 1967).

Levin, Saul, 'The Old Greek Oracles in Decline', *ANRW* II/18, part 2 (1989), pp. 1598–1649.

Levinskaya, Irina, *The Book of Acts in Its Diaspora Setting* V, in Bruce W. Winter (ed.), *The Book of Acts in its First Century Setting* (Grand Rapids: Eerdmanns, 1996).

Lewis, David M., 'Temple Inventories in Ancient Greece', in Michael Vickers (ed.), *Pots & Pans: A Colloquium on Precious Metals and Ceramics in the Muslim, Chinese, and Graeco-Roman Worlds* (Oxford: Board of the Faculty of Oriental Studies, University of Oxford; Oxford University Press, 1986), pp. 71–81; repr. in David M. Lewis, *Selected Papers in Greek and Near Eastern History* (Cambridge: Cambridge University Press, 1997), pp. 40–50.

Lieu, Judith M., *Neither Jew Nor Greek?: Constructing Early Christianity* (Studies of the New Testament in its World; London: T&T Clark Internation, YEAR?).

Linders, Tullia, 'Ritual Display and the Loss of Power', in Pontus Hellström and Brita Alroth (eds), *Religion and Power in the Ancient Greek World: Proceedings of the Uppsala Symposium 1993* (Acta Universitatis Upsaliensis; Boreas, Uppsala Studies in Ancient Mediterranean and Near Eastern Civilizations, 24; Uppsala: Academia Upsaliensis, 1996), pp. 120–24.

Linders, Tullia and Gullög Nordquist (eds), *Gifts to the Gods: Proceedings of the Uppsala Symposium 1985* (Acta Universitatis Upsaliensis; Boreas, Uppsala Studies in Ancient Mediterranean and Near Eastern Civilizations, 15; Uppsala: Academia Upsaliensis, 1987).

Lloyd, Alan B., 'The Egyptian Elite in the Early Ptolemaic Period. Some Hieroglyphic Evidence', in Daniel Ogden (ed.), *The Hellenistic World: New Perspectives* (Swansea, England: The Classical Press of Wales, 2002), pp. 117–36.

Lloyd-Jones, Hugh, *The Justice of Zeus* (Sather Classical Lectures, 41; Berkeley: University of California Press, 1971).

Lohfink, Gerhard, *Die Himmelfahrt Jesu: Untersuchungen zu den Himmelfahrts- und Erhöhungstexten bei Lukas* (SANT, 26; Munich: Kösel, 1971).

Long, Charlote R., *The Twelve Gods of Greece and Rome* (EPRO, 107; Leiden: Brill, 1987).

Lösch, Stephan, *Deitas Jesu und Antike Apotheose: Ein Beitrag zur Exegese und Religionsgeschichte* (Rottenburg, Germany: Bader, 1933).

Louw, Johannes P. and Eugene A. Nida (eds), *Greek-English Lexicon of the New Testament Based on Semantic Domains* (New York: United Bible Societies, 1988).

MacDonald, Dennis Ronald, 'Luke's Eutychus and Homer's Elpenor: Acts 20:7–12 and *Odyssey* 10–12', *Journal of Higher Criticism* 1 (1994), pp. 5–24.

—*Christianizing Homer: the Odyssey, Plato, and the Acts of Andrew* (Oxford: Oxford University Press, 1994).

—*The Homeric Epics and the Gospel of Mark* (New Haven: Yale University Press, 2000).

—*Does the New Testament Imitate Homer: Four Cases from the Acts of the Apostles* (New Haven: Yale University Press: 2003).

Macgregor, G.H.C., 'Principalities and Powers: The Cosmic Background of Paul's Thought', in Harvey K. McArthur (ed.), *New Testament Sidelights: Essays in Honor of Alexander Converse Purdy* (Hartford, CN: The Hartford Seminary Foundation Press, 1960), pp. 88–104.

MacMullen, Ramsay, *Enemies of the Roman Social Order: Treason, Unrest, and Alienation in the Empire* (Cambridge, MA: Harvard University Press, 1966; paperback edn, London: Routledge, 1992).

—*Paganism in the Roman Empire* (New Haven: Yale University Press, 1981).

—*Christianizing the Roman Empire: A.D. 100–400* (New Haven: Yale University Press, 1984).

McVann, Mark, 'Introduction' to *Transformations, Passages, and Processes: Ritual Approaches to Biblical Texts, Semeia* 67 (1994), pp. 7–12.

McRay, John, 'Gerasenes', *ABD* II, pp. 991–92.

Magie, David, *Roman Rule in Asia Minor* (2 vols; Princeton: Princeton University Press, 1950).

Majercik, Ruth, 'Rhetoric and Oratory in the Greco-Roman World', *ABD* V, pp. 710–12.

Malina, Bruce J., *The New Testament World: Insights from Cultural Anthropology* (rev. edn; Louisville, KY: Westminster/John Knox Press, 1993).

Malina, Bruce J. and Jerome H. Neyrey, 'Honor and Shame in Luke-Acts: Pivotal Values of the Mediterranean World', in Neyrey (ed.), *The Social World of Luke-Acts*, pp. 25–66.

Marcus, Joel, 'Jesus' Baptismal Vision (Satan Falling From Heaven)', *NTS* 41 (1995), pp. 512–21.

—'Blanks and Gaps in the Markan Parable of the Sower', *BibInt* 5 (1997), pp. 247–67.

Marinatos, Nanno, 'The Imagery of Sacrifice: Minoan and Greek', in Robin Hägg, Nanno Marinatos and Gullög C. Nordquist (eds), *Early Greek Cult Practice: Proceedings of the Fifth International Symposium at the Swedish Institute at Athens, 26–29 June, 1986* (Skrifter Utgivna av Svenska Institutet i Athen, 4°, 38; Stockholm: Svenska Institutet i Athen, 1988), pp. 9–20.

Marshall, I. Howard and David Peterson (eds), *Witness to the Gospel: The Theology of Acts* (Grand Rapids: Eerdmanns, 1997).

Martin Jr, Hubert M., 'Areopagus', *ABD* I, pp. 370–72.

Martin, Luther H., 'Gods or Ambassadors of God? Barnabas and Paul in Lystra', *NTS* 41 (1995), pp. 152–56.

Martitz, Peter Wülfing von, 'υἱός', *TDNT* VIII (1972), pp. 334–40.

Mastromarco, Giuseppe, *The Public of Herondas* (London Studies in Classical Philology, 11; Amsterdam: J.C. Gieben, 1984).

Mattingly, Harold, *Coins of the Roman Empire in the British Museum* (London: British Museum, 1923–1950).

Mbachu, Hilary, *Survey and Method of Acts Research from 1826–1995* (Deutsche Hochschulschriften, 1051; Egelsbach, Germany: Hänsel-Hohenhausen, 1995).

Meijer, P.A., 'Philosophers, Intellectuals and Religion in Hellas', in H.S. Versnel (ed.), *Faith, Hope, and Worship: Aspects of Religious Mentality in the Ancient World* (Studies in Greek and Roman Religion, 2; Leiden: Brill, 1981), pp. 216–64.

Menoud, Phillipe H., 'The Additions to the Twelve Apostles According to the Book of Acts', in *idem, Jesus Christ and the Faith: A Collection of Studies* (PTMS, 18; Pittsburgh: Pickwick, 1978), pp. 133–48.

Metzger, Bruce M., *A Textual Commentary on the New Testament* (Stuttgart: Deutsche Bibegesellschaft and United Bible Societies, 2nd edn, 1994).

Meyers, Carol L. and Eric M. Meyers, *Zechariah 9–14* (AB, 25C; New York: Doubleday, 1993).

Michaelis, Wilhelm, 'πίπτω', *TDNT* VI (1968), pp. 161–66.

Mikalson, Jon D., *Religion in Hellenistic Athens* (Hellenistic Culture and Society; Berkeley: University of California Press, 1998).

Miles, Gary B. and Garry Trompf, 'Luke and Antiphon: The Theology of Acts 27–28 in the Light of Beliefs about Divine Retribution, Pollution, and Shipwreck', *HTR* 69 (1976), pp. 259–67.

Millar, Fergus, 'The World of *The Golden Ass*', *JRS* 71 (1981), pp. 63–75.

Mitropoulou, Elpis, *Horses' Heads and Snake in Banquet Reliefs and Their Meaning* (Athens: Pyli Editions, 1976).

—*Deities and Heroes in the Form of Snakes* (2nd edn; Athens: Pyli Editions, 1977).

Morkot, Robert, *The Penguin Historical Atlas of Ancient Greece* (London: Penguin, 1996).

Moxnes, Halvor, ' "He saw that the city was full of idols" (Acts 17.16): Visualizing the World of the First Christians', *ST* 49 (1995), pp. 107–31.

Müller, Ulrich B., 'Vision und Botschaft: Erwagungen zur prophetischen Struktur der Verkündigung Jesu', *ZThK* 74 (1977), pp. 416–48.

Mussies, Gerard, 'Identification and Self-Identification of Gods in Classical and Hellenistic Times', in R. van den Broek, T. Baarda and J. Mansfeld (eds), *Knowledge of God in the Graeco-Roman World* (EPRO, 112; Leiden: Brill, 1988), pp. 1–18.

Mylonas, George E., *Eleusis and the Eleusinian Mysteries* (Princeton: Princeton University Press, 1961).

Nappa, Christopher, Review of Stephen Hinds, *Allusion and Intertext. Dynamics of Appropriation in Roman Poetry* (Cambridge: Cambridge University Press, 1998), in *BMCR* (online), http://ccat.sas.upenn.edu/bmcr/1998/1998–09–08.html.

Nestle, Wilhelm, 'Legenden vom Tod der Gottesverächter', *ARW* 33 (1936), pp. 246–69.

—'Anklange an Euripides in der Apostelgeschichte', in *idem*, *Griesche Studien, Untersuchung zur Religion, Dichtung und Philosophie der Griechen* (Stuttgart: Hannsman, 1948), pp. 226–39.

Newell, E.T., *The First Seleucid Coinage of Tyre* (Numismatic Notes and Monographs, 10: New York: American Numismatic Society, 1921).

—*The Seleucid Coinages of Tyre* (Numismatic Notes and Monographs, 36; New York: American Numismatic Society, 1936).

Newton, Derek, *Deity and Diet: The Dilemma of Sacrificial Food at Corinth* (JSNTSup, 169; Sheffield: Sheffield Academic Press, 1998).

Neyrey, Jerome H. (ed.), *The Social World of Luke-Acts: Models for Interpretation* (Peabody, MA: Hendrickson, 1991).

—'Acts 17, Epicureans, and Theodicy', in Balch (ed.), *Greeks, Romans, and Christians*, pp. 118–34.

Nilsson, Martin, 'Die Prozessionstypen im griechischen Kult', in *Opuscula Selecta* (3 vols; Skrifter Utgivna av Svensak Institute I Athen, 8°, ser. 2, no. 2; Lund: Gleerup, 1951), I, pp.166–213.

—'Roman and Greek Domestic Cult', *Opuscula Romana* 18 (1954), pp. 77–85.

Nilsson, Martin P., *Greek Popular Religion* (1940; repr. *Greek Folk Religion*; Torchbook Editions, 78; The Cloister Library; New York: Harper, 1961).

Nock, Arthur Darby, Colin Roberts and Theodore C. Skeat, 'The Guild of Zeus Hypsistos', *HTR* 9 (1936), pp. 9–88; repr., Arthur Darby Nock, *Essays on Religion and the Ancient World* (Zeph Stewart, ed.; Oxford: Clarendon, Oxford University Press, 1986), I, pp. 414–43.

Norden, Eduard, *Agnostos Theos: Untersuchungen zur Formengeschichte Religiöser Rede* (Leipzig: Teubner, 1913; repr., Darmstadt: Wissenschaftliche Buchgesellschaft, 1956).

North, John, 'Sacrifice and Ritual: Rome', in Michael Grant and Rachel Kitzinger (eds), *Civilization of the Ancient Mediterranean* (New York: Scribners, 1988), II, pp. 981–86.

Oberleitner, W., *Funde aus Ephesos und Samothrake* (Kunsthistorisches Museum, Wien, Katalog der Antikensammlung, 2; Vienna: Kunsthistorisches Museum, 1978).

O'Brien, P.T. 'Prayer in Luke-Acts', *TynBul* 23 (1973).

O'Day, Gail R., 'Acts', in Carol A. Newsom and Sharon H. Ringe (eds), *Women's Bible Commentary* (expanded edn; Louisville, KY: Westminster John Knox, 1998) pp. 394–402.

Office, Roberta, *Public Office in Early Rome: Ritual Procedure and Political Practice* (Ann Arbor: University of Michigan Press, 1998).

Ogden, Daniel, *Greek and Roman Necromancy* (Princeton: Princeton University Press, 2001).

Oliver, James H., 'Epaminondas of Acraephia', *GRBS* 12 (1971), pp. 221–237.

Orr, David G., 'Roman Domestic Religion: The Evidence of the Household Shrines', *ANRW* 16/2 (1978), pp. 1557–91.

Osborne, Robin., 'Women and Sacrifice in Classical Greece', *ClQ* 43 (1993), pp. 392–405.

Oster, Richard E. 'The Ephesian Artemis as an Opponent of Early Christianity', *JAC* 19 (1976), pp. 24–44.

—'Numismatic Windows into the Social World of Early Christianity: A Methodological Inquiry', *JBL* 101 (1982), pp. 195–223.

Ott, Willhelm, *Gebet und Heil: Die Bedeutung der Gebetsparänese in der lukanischen Theologie* (SANT, 12; Munich: Kösel, 1965).

Overman, J. Andrew, Jack Olive and Michael Nelson, 'Discovering Herod's Shrine to Augustus: Mystery Temple Found at Omrit', *BARev* 29.2 (March/April; 2003), pp. 40–49, 67–68.

Park, Robert Christopher Townley, 'Dioskuri', *OCD* (rev. 3rd edn, 2003) 484.

Parke, H.W., *Greek Oracles* (Hutchinson University Library, Classical History and Literature; London: Hutchinson, 1967).

—*The Oracles of Zeus: Dodona, Olympia, Ammon* (Oxford: Basil Blackwell, 1967).

—'Three Enquiries from Dodona', *JHS* 87 (1969), pp. 132–33.

—*The Oracles of Apollo in Asia Minor* (London: Croom Helm, 1985).

Parke, H.W., *Sibyls and Sibylline Prophecy in Classical Antiquity* (ed. B.C. McGing; London: Routledge, 1988).

Parke, H.W. and D.E. Wormell, *The Delphic Oracle, Its Responses and Operations, with a Catalogue of Responses* (2 vols; Oxford: Basil Blackwell, 1956).

Parker, Robert, *Miasma: Pollution and Purification in Early Greek Religion* (Oxford: Clarendon Press, 1983).

—'Festivals of the Attic Demes', in Tullia Linders and Gullög Nordquist (eds), *Gifts to the Gods: Proceedings of the Uppsala Symposium 1985* (Acta Universitatis Upsaliensis; Boreas, Uppsala Studies in Ancient Mediterranean and Near Eastern Civilizations, 15; Uppsala: Academia Uppsaliensis, 1987), pp. 137–48.

—*Athenian Religion: A History* (Oxford: Clarendon Press, Oxford University Press, 1996).

Parsons, Mikeal G., *The Departure of Jesus in Luke-Acts: The Ascension Narratives in Context* (JSNTSup, 21; Sheffield: JSOT Press, 1987).

Pearcy, Lee T., *The Shorter Homeric Hymns* (Bryn Mawr, PA: Bryn Mawr Greek Commentaries, 1989).

Pervo, Richard I., *Profit with Delight: The Literary Genre of the Acts of the Apostles* (Philadelphia: Fortress Press, 1987).

Pesch, Rudolf, *Die Apostelgeschichte* (2 vols; EKKNT, 5; Zürich: Benziger; Neukirchen: Neukirchener Verlag, 1986).

Peterson, Erik, 'Εἷς Θεός' (FRLANT, n.s. 24; Göttingen: Vandenhoeck & Ruprecht, 1926).

—'Die Einholung des Kyrios', *ZST* 7 (1929–30), pp. 682–702.

Petersen, Leiva, *Zur Geschichte der Personifikation in griechischer Dichtung und Bildener Kunst* (Würzburg: Konrad Triltsch, 1939).

Picard, Gilbert Charles and Colette Picard, *Carthage: A Survey of Punic History and Culture from its Birth to the Final Tragedy* (Great Civilizations Series; London: Sidgwick & Jackson, 1987).

Pilhofer, Peter, *Philippi*. I. *Die erste christliche Gemeinde Europas* (WUNT, 87; Tübingen: Mohr, 1995).

Piña-Cabrel, Joãode, 'The Mediterranean as a Category of Regional Comparison: A Critical View', *Current Anthropology* 30 (1989), pp. 399–406.

Plümacher, Eckhardt, *Lukas als hellenistischer Schriftsteller* (Göttingen: Vandenhoeck & Ruprecht, 1972).

Plymale, Steven F., 'Luke's Theology of Prayer', *SBLSP* 29 (1990), pp. 529–51.

Portefaix, Lilian, *Sisters Rejoice: Paul's Letter to the Philippians and Luke-Acts as Received by First-Century Philippian Women* (ConBNT, 20; Stockholm: Almqvist & Wiksell, 1988).

—'Ancient Ephesus: Processions as Media of Religious and Secular Propaganda', in Tore Ahlbäck (ed.), *The Problem of Ritual: Based on Papers Read at the Symposium on Religious Rites at Åbo, Finland, on the 13th–16th of August 1991* (Scripta Instituti Donneriani Aboensis, 15 ; Stockholm: Almqvist & Wicksell, 1993), pp. 195–210.

Potter, D.S., *Prophets and Emperors: Human and Divine Authority from Augustus to Theodosius* (Cambridge, MA: Harvard University Press, 1994).

Pottier, E., 'Les représentations allégoriques dans les peintues de vases grecs', *Monuments Grecs* 17–18 (1889–90), pp. 15ff.

Poulsen, Brite, 'The Dioscuri and Ruler Ideology', *SO* 66 (1991), pp. 235–48.

Poulsen, Brite and Jesper Karlsen, 'A Relief from Croceae: Dioscuri in Roman Laconia', *Acta Hyperborea: Danish Studies in Classical Archaeology* 3 (1991), pp. 235–48.

Powell, Mark Allan, *What Are They Saying About Luke?* (New York: Paulist Press, 1989).

Praeder, Susan Marie, 'Acts 27:1–28:16: Sea Voyages in Ancient Literature and the Theology of Luke-Acts', *CBQ* 46 (1984), pp. 683–706.

Prag, A.J.N.W., *The Oresteia: Iconography and Narrative Tradition* (Chicago: Bolchazy-Carducci; Warminster, Great Britain: Aris & Phillips, 1985).

Pred, Allan, *Making Histories and Constructing Human Geographies: The Local Transformation of Practice, Power Relations, and Consciousness* (Boulder, CO: Westview, 1990).

Price, Robert M., *The Widow Traditions in Luke-Acts: A Feminist-Critical Scrutiny* (SBLDS, 155; Atlanta: Scholars Press, 1997).

Price, Simon R.F., 'Between Man and God: Sacrifice in the Roman Imperial Cult', *JRS* 70 (1980), pp. 28–43.

—'Gods and Emperors: The Greek Language of the Roman Imperial Cult', *JHS* 104 (1984), pp. 79–95.

—*Rituals and Power: The Roman Imperial Cult in Asia Minor* (Cambridge: Cambridge University Press, 1984).

—'Delphi and Divination', in P.E. Easterling and J.V. Muir (eds), *Greek Religion and Society* (Cambridge: Cambridge University Press, 1985), pp. 128–54.

—'The History of the Hellenistic Period', in John Boardman, Jasper Griffin and Oswyn Murray (eds), *Greece and the Hellenistic World* (OHCW; Oxford: Oxford University Press, 1988), pp. 309–31.

—'Religion, Roman', *OCD* (rev. 3rd edn, 2003), pp. 1306–7.

Rabinowitz, Peter J., 'Truth in Fiction: A Reexamination of Audiences', *Critical Inquiry* 4 (1977), pp. 121–141.

—*Before Reading: Narrative Conventions and the Politics of Interpretation* (Ithaca, NY: Cornell University Press, 1987).

—'Whirl Without End: Audience Oriented Criticism', in G. Douglas Atkins (ed.), *Contemporary Literary Criticism* (Amherst, MA: University of Massachusetts Press, 1989) pp. 81–100.

Radl, Walter, 'Befreiung aus dem Gefängnis: die Darstellung eines biblischen Grundthemas in Apg 12', *BZ* 27 (1983), pp. 81–96.

Räisänen, Heikki, 'Coexistence and Conflict: Early Christian Attitudes to Adherents of Traditional Cults', *Temenos: Studies in Comparative Religion* 31 (1995), pp. 163–80.

Ramsay, William M., *St. Paul the Traveler and the Roman Citizen* (New York: Putnam's, 1902).

—*The Cities of St. Paul: Their Influence on His Life and Thought* (The Dale Memorial Lectures; New York: George H. Doran; London: Hodder and Stoughton, 1907).

—'Colonia Caesarea (Pisidean Antioch) in the Augustan Age', *JRS* 6 (1916), pp. 83–134.

—'Studies in the Roman Province Galatia VI. Some Inscriptions of Colonia Caesarea Antiochea', *JRS* 14 (1924), pp. 172–205.

—*The Social Basis of Roman Power in Asia Minor* (Aberdeen: Aberdeen University Press, 1941; repr., Amsterdam: Hakkert, 1967).

Ramsey, John T. and A. Lewis Licht, *The Comet of 44 B.C. and Caesar's Funeral Games*; (American Classical Studies, 39; Atlanta: American Philological Association, Scholars Press, 1997).

Ravens, David, *Luke and the Restoration of Israel* (JSNTSup, 119; Sheffield: Sheffield Academic Press, 1995).

Rawson, Elizabeth, 'The Expansion of Rome', in John Boardman, Jasper Griffin, and Oswyn Murray (eds), *The Oxford Illustrated History of the Roman World* (Oxford: Oxford University Press, 1988) pp. 39–59.

Read-Heimerdinger, Jenny, 'Barnabas in Acts: A Study of his Role in the Text of Codex Bezae', *JSNT* 72 (1998), pp. 23–66.

—*The Bezan Text of Acts: A Contribution of Discourse Analysis to Textual Criticism* (SNTSup, 236; Sheffield: Sheffield Academic Press, 2003).

Reeder, Ellen D., 'The Mother of the Gods and a Hellenistic Bronze Matrix', *AJA* 91 (1987), pp. 423–40.

Reicke, Bom, 'πρός', *TDNT* VI (1968), pp. 683–88.

Reid, Barbara E., OP, *The Transfiguration: A Source- and Redaction-Critical Study of Luke 9:28–36* (CahRB, 32; Paris: J. Gabalda, 1993).

Reimer, Ivoni Richter, *Women in the Acts of the Apostles: A Feminist Liberation Perspective* (Minneapolis: Fortress Press, 1995).

Rey-Coquais, Jean-Paul, 'Decapolis', *ABD* II, pp. 116–21.

Rhoads, David, *The Challenge of Diversity: The Witness of Paul and the Gospels* (Minneapolis: Fortress Press, 1996).

Rhodes, P.J., *The Athenian Boule* (corrected edn with additions; Oxford: Clarendon, Oxford University Press, 1985).

Richardson, R.B., 'A Sacrificial Calendar from the Epakia', *AJA* 10 (1895), pp. 209–26.

Robert, J. and L. Robert, *Bulletin Epigraphique* (1976).

—*Bulletin Epigraphique* (1983).

Robbins, Frank Egleston, 'The Lot Oracle at Delphi', *CP* 11 (1916), pp. 278–92.

Robbins, Vernon K., 'The Social Location of the Implied Author of Luke-Acts', in Neyrey (ed.), *The Social World of Luke-Acts*, pp. 305–32.

—*Exploring the Texture of Texts: A Guide to Socio-Rhetorical Interpretation* (Valley Forge, PA: Trinity, 1996).

Robinson, David Moore, 'Greek and Latin Inscriptions from Asia Minor', *TAPA* 57 (1926), pp. 195–237.

Rogers, E., *The Second and Third Seleucid Coinages of Tyre* (Numismatic Notes and Monographs, 34; New York: American Numismatic Society, 1927).

Rogers, Guy MacLean, 'Demetrios of Ephesos: Silversmith and Neopoios', *Belletin Türk tarih Kurumu* 50 (1986), pp. 877–83.
—*The Sacred Identity of Ephesos: Foundation Myths of a Roman City* (New York: Routledge, 1991).
Roloff, Jürgen, *Die Apostelgeschichte* (NTD; Göttingen: Vandenhoeck & Ruprecht, 1981).
Roscher, Wilhelm (ed.), *Ausführliches Lexicon der griechischen und römischen Mythologie* (Leipzig: Teubner, 1884–86; repr., Hildesheim: G. Olms, 1992–93).
Rose, H.J., 'The Religion of the Greek Household', *Euphrosyne* 1 (1957), pp. 95–116.
Rose, Herbert Jennings and B.C. Dietrich, 'Erinyes', *OCD* (rev. 3rd edn; 2003) p. 556.
Rosenstein, Nathan 'Sorting Out the Lot in Republican Rome', *AJP* 116 (1995) pp. 43–75.
Rosivach, Vincent J., *The System of Public Sacrifice in Fourth-Century Athens* (American Classical Studies, 34; Atlanta: American Philological Association, Scholars Press, 1994).
Roth, S. John, *The Lame, The Blind, and the Poor: Character Types in Luke-Acts* (JSNTSup, 144; Sheffield: Sheffield Academic Press, 1997).
Rouse, William Henry Denham, *Greek Votive Offerings* (Cambridge: Cambridge University Press, 1902; repr., Ancient Religion and Mythology; New York: Arno, 1975).
—'Votive offerings', in James Hastings (ed.), *Encyclopedia of Religion and Ethics* (New York: Scribner's, 1922), vol. 12, pp. 641–43.
Rowe, C. Kavin, 'Luke-Acts and the Imperial Cult: A Way Through the Conundrum', *JSNT* 27 (2005) pp. 279–300.
Rudhardt, Jean and Olivier Reverdin (eds), *Le Sacrifice dans L'Antiquité* (Entretiens sur L'Antiquité Classique, 27; Geneva: Fondation Hardt pur L'Étude de L'Antiquité Classique, 1980).
Rupp, E. Gordon, *Principalities and Powers; Studies in the Christian Conflict in History* (New York: Abingdon-Cokesbury Press, 1952).
Russell, Donald Andrew Frank Moore, 'Rhetoric, Greek', *OCD* (rev. 3rd edn, 2003), pp. 1312–14.
Sanders, Jack T., 'The Prophetic Use of the Scriptures in Luke-Acts', in Craig A. Evans and W.F. Stinespring (eds), *Early Jewish and Christian Exegesis: Essays in Honor of W.H. Brownlee* (Homage, 10; Atlanta: Scholars Press, 1987), pp. 191–98.
Sanders, Todd K., 'A New Approach to 1 Corinthians 13:1', *NTS* 36 (1990), pp. 614–18.
Sandys, John Edwin, *A History of Classical Scholarship*. I. *From the Sixth Century B.C. to the End of the Middle Ages* (Cambridge: Cambridge University Press, 1958; repr., New York: Hafner, 1967).
Sarian, Haigamich and Peter Delev, 'Erinyes', *LIMC* (Zurich: Artemis, 1986), III/1, pp. 826–43; III/2, pp. 595–606.
Schauf, Scott, *Theology as History, History as Theology: Paul in Ephesus in Acts 19* (BZNW, 133; Berlin: Walter de Gruyter, 2005).
Scheid, John, 'Religion, Roman, terms relating to', *OCD* (3rd edn, 1996), p. 1307.
Schillig, Robert and Jörg Rüpke, 'Roman Religion: The Early Period', *ER* (2nd edn), vol. 12, pp. 7997–8008,
Schneider, Gerhard, *Die Apostelgeschichte* (2 vols; HTKNT; Freiburg: Herder, 1980–82).
Schowalter, Daniel N., *The Emperor and the Gods: Images From the Time of Trajan* (HDR, 28; Minneapolis: Fortress Press, 1993).
Schreiber, Stefan, *Paulus als Wundertäter: Redaktionsgeschichtliche Untersuchungen zur Apostelgeschichte und den authentischen Paulusbriefen* (BZNW, 79; Berlin: Walter de Gruyter, 1996).
Schröder, Stephan, *Plutarchs Schrift, 'De Pythiae Oraculis': Text, Einleitung und Kommentar* (Beiträge zur Altertumskunde, 8; Stuttgart: Teubner, 1990).
Schürer, Emil, *The History of the Jewish People in the Age of Jesus Christ (175 B.C.– 135 A.D.)* (rev. English edn, Geza Vermes, Fergus Millar, and Matthew Black [eds]; 3 vols; Edinburgh: T&T Clark, 1973).

Schwartz, Daniel R., *Agrippa I: Last King of Judea* (Texte und Studien zum antiken Judentum, 23; Tübingen: Mohr-Siebeck, 1990).

Schweizer, Eduard, 'υἱός', *TDNT* VIII (1972), pp. 363–92.

Scodel, Ruth (ed.), *Theater and Society in the Classical World* (Ann Arbor: The University of Michigan Press, 1993).

Scott, Kenneth, 'Drusus, Nicknamed Castor', *CP* 25 (1930), pp. 155–61.

—'The Dioscuri and the Imperial Cult', *CP* 25 (1930), pp. 379–80.

—*The Imperial Cult Under the Flavians* (Stuttgart: W. Kohlhammer, 1936; repr., Ancient Religion and Mythology; New York: Arno, 1975).

Segal, J.B., *The Hebrew Passover From the Earliest Times to A.D 70* (London Oriental Series, 12; London: Oxford University Press, 1963).

Seltman, Charles, 'The Wardrobe of Artemis', *Numismatic Chronicle*, Series 6, 12 (1952), pp. 33–51.

—*The Twelve Olympians and Their Guests* (rev. and enlarged edn; London: Max Parrish, 1956).

Selvidge, Marla J., 'Acts of the Apostles. A Violent Aetiological Legend', *SBLSP* 25 (1986), pp. 330–40; repr., in *idem, Women, Violence, and the Bible* (Studies in Women and Religion, 37; Lewiston, NY: Edwin Mellen, 1996), pp. 95–109.

Shapiro, Harvey Alan, 'Personification of Abstract Concepts in Greek Art and Literature to the End of the Fifth Century B.C.' (PhD dissertation, Princeton University, 1977).

—'Dike', *LIMC* (Zurich and Munich: Artemis, 1986), III/1, pp. 388–91; III/2 pp. 280–81, pls. 3–16.

—*Personifications in Greek Art: The Representation of Abstract Concepts 600–400 B.C.* (Crescens, 1; Zurich: Akanthus 1993).

Shilbrak, Kevin, 'Religion, Models of, and Reality: Are We Through with Geertz?', *JAAR* 73 (2005) pp. 429–52.

Silberman, Lou H., 'Paul's Viper: Acts 28:3–6', *Forum* 8 (1992), pp. 247–253.

Smallwood, E. Mary, *The Jews Under Roman Rule From Pompey to Diocletian: A Study in Political Relations* (corrected edn; SJLA, 20; Leiden: Brill, 1981).

Smythe, Herbert Weir, *Greek Grammar* (rev. edn; Cambridge, MA: Harvard University Press, 1984).

Soards, Marion, *The Speeches of Acts: Their Content, Context, and Concerns* (Louisville, KY: Westminster/John Knox Press, 1994).

Soffe, Graham, 'Christians, Jews and Pagans in the Acts of the Apostles', in Martin Henig and Anthony King (eds), *Pagan Gods and Shrines of the Roman Empire* (Oxford University Committee for Archaeology Monograph, 8; Oxford: Oxford University Committee for Archaeology, 1986), pp. 239–56.

Solkolowski, F., 'Sur un passage de la convention Delphes-Skiathos', *RArch* 31/32 (1939), pp. 981–84.

Sommerstein, Alan H., 'Aeschylus', *OCD* (rev. 3rd. edn, 2003), pp. 26–29.

Soren, David, Aicha ben Abed ben Khader and Hedi Slim, *Carthage: Uncovering the Mysteries and Splendors of Ancient Tunisia* (New York: Simon & Schuster, 1990).

Sorensen, Eric, *Possession and Exorcism in the New Testament and Early Christianity* (WUNT, 2/157; Tübingen: Mohr-Siebeck, 2002).

Spencer, F. Scott, *Journeying Through Acts: A Literary-Cultural Reading* (Peabody, MA: Hendrickson, 2004).

—'Paul's Odyssey in Acts: Status Struggles and Island Adventures', *BTB* 28 (1998), pp. 150–50.

—'Out of Mind, Out of Voice: Slave-girls and Prophetic Daughters in Luke-Acts', *BibInt* 7 (1999), pp. 133–55.

Spitta, Friedrich, 'Der Satan als Blitz', *ZNW* 9 (1908), pp. 160–63.

Squires, John T., *The Plan of God in Luke-Acts* (SNTSMS, 76; New York: Cambridge University Press, 1993).

St. Denis, E.D., 'Mare clausum (Act. 28.11)', *Revue de étude latine* 25 (1947), pp. 196–214.

Stafford, Emma, *Worshipping Virtues: Personification and the Divine in Ancient Greece* (London: Duckworth, 2004).

Stambaugh, John E. and David L. Balch, *The New Testament in Its Social Environment* (LEC, 2; Philadelphia: Westminster Press, 1986).

Stern, Jacob, 'Herodas Mimiamb 6', *GRBS* 20 (1979), pp. 247–53.

Sternberg, Meir, *The Poetics of Biblical Narrative: Ideological Literature and the Drama of Reading* (Indiana Studies in Biblical Literature; Bloomington, IN: Indiana University Press, 1985).

Stockmeier, Peter, 'Christlicher Glaube und antike Religiosität', *ANRW* II/23, part 2 (1980), pp. 871–909.

Stoops, Ronald, 'Riot and Assembly: The Context of Acts 19:23–41', *JBL* 108 (1989), pp. 73–91.

Stowers, Stanley K. 'Greeks Who Sacrifice and Those Who Do Not', in L. Michael White and O. Larry Yarbrough (eds), *The Social World of the First Christians: Essays in Honor of Wayne A. Meeks* (Minneapolis: Fortress Press, 1995), pp. 293–333.

Strack, Hermann L. and Paul Billerbeck, *Kommentar zum Neuen Testament aus Talmud und Midrash* (5 vols; Munich: Beck, 7th edn, 1978).

Straten, Folkert T. van, 'Gifts for the Gods', in H.S. Versnel (ed.), *Faith, Hope, and Worship: Aspects of Religious Mentality in the Ancient World* (SGRR, 2; Leiden: Brill, 1981), pp. 65–151.

—'The God's Portion in Greek Sacrificial Representations: Is the Tail Doing Nicely?', in Robin Hägg, Nanno Marinatos, and Gullög C. Nordquist (ed.), *Early Greek Cult Practice: Proceedings of the Fifth International Symposium at the Swedish Institute at Athens, 26–29 June, 1986* (Skrifter Utgivna av Svenska Institutet i Athen, 4°, 38; Stockholm: Svenska Institutet i Athen, 1988), pp. 51–68.

—'Greek Sacrificial Representations: Livestock Prices and Religious Mentality', in Tullia Linders and Gullög Nordquist (eds), *Gifts to the Gods: Proceedings of the Uppsala Symposium 1985* (Acta Universitatis Upsaliensis; Boreas, Uppsala Studies in Ancient Mediterranean and Near Eastern Civilizations, 15; Uppsala: Academia Upsaliensis, 1987), pp. 159–70.

—'Votives and Votaries in Greek Sanctuaries', in Albert Schachter (ed.), *Le Sanctuaire Grec* (Fondation Hardt pour L'Étude de l'Antiquité Classique, Entretiens sur l'Antiquité Classique, 37; Geneva: Fondation Hardt, 1992), pp. 247–90.

—*Hierà Kalá: Images of Animal Sacrifice in Archaic and Classical Greece* (RGRW, 127; Leiden: Brill, 1995).

Strelan, Rick, *Paul, Artemis, and the Jews in Ephesus* (BZNW, 80; Berlin: Walter de Gruyter, 1996).

Strom, Mark R., 'An Old Testament Background to Acts 12.20-23', *NTS* 32 (1986), pp. 289–92.

Sullivan, Richard D., 'Priesthoods of the Eastern Dynastic Aristocracy', in Sencer Sahin, Elmar Schwertheim, and Jörg Wagner (eds), *Studien zur Religion und Kultur Kleinasiens: Festschrift für Friedrich Karl Dörner zum 65. Geburstag am 28. Februar 1976* (2 vols; EPRO, 66; Leiden: Brill, 1966), II, pp. 914–39.

—'The Dynasty of Judaea in the First Century', *ANRW* II/8 (1978), pp. 296–354.

Tabory, Joseph, 'Towards a History of the Passover Meal', in Paul F. Bradshaw and Lawrence Hoffman (eds), *Passover and Easter: Origin and History to New Testament Times* (Two Liturgical Traditions, 5; Notre Dame, IN: University of Notre Dame Press, 1999).

Taeger, Fritz, *Charisma. Studien zur Geschichte des antiken Herrscherkultes* (2 vols; Stuttgart: W. Kohlhammer, 1957).

Talbert, Charles H., *Reading Corinthians: A Literary and Theological Commentary on 1 and 2 Corinthians* (New York: Crossroad, 1987).

—*Reading Acts: A Literary and Theological Commentary on The Acts of the Apostles* (Reading the New Testament Series; New York: Crossroad, 1997).

—*Reading Luke-Acts in Its Mediterranean Milieu* (NovTSup, 107; Leiden: Brill, 2003).

Talbert, Charles H. (ed.), *Perspectives on Luke-Acts* (PRSt, Special Studies Series, 5; Danville, VA: Association of Baptist Professors of Religion, 1978).

—*Luke-Acts: New Perspectives from the Society of Biblical Literature Seminar* (New York: Crossroad, 1984).

Talbert, C.H. and J.H. Hayes, 'A Theology of Sea Storms in Luke-Acts', *SBLSP* 34 (1995), pp. 321–36.

Tannehill, Robert, *The Narrative Unity of Luke-Acts: A Literary Interpretation*. II. *The Acts of the Apostles* (Minneapolis: Fortress Press, 1990).

Tatscheva-Hitova, Margareta, 'Dem Hypsistos geweihte Denkmäler in Thrakien. Untersuchungen zur Geschichte der antiken Religionen, III', *Thracia* 4 (1977), pp. 274–90.

—*Eastern Cults in Moesia Inferior and Thracia (5th Century BC–4th Century AD)* (EPRO, 95; Leiden: Brill, 1983).

Taylor, Lily Ross, *The Divinity of the Roman Emperor* (American Philological Association Philological Monographs, 1; Middletown, CT: American Philological Association, 1931).

Thiersch, Hermann, *Artemis Ephesia eine archäologische Untersuchung: I, Katalog der erhaltener Denkmäler. Abhandlungen der Gesellschaft der Wissenschaften zu Göttingen, Philologische-Historische Klasse* (3rd Folge; Berlin: Weidmannsche Buchhandlung, 1935).

Thiessen, Gerd, *The Miracle Stories of the Early Christian Tradition* (Philadelphia: Fortress Press, 1983).

Thompson, Homer A. and R.E. Wycherly, *The Athenian Agora*, vol. XIV in *The Agora of Athens: The History, Stages, and Uses of an Ancient City Center* (Princeton: The American School of Classical Studies at Athens, 1972).

Thornton, L.S., 'The Choice of Matthias', *JTS* 46 (1945), pp. 51–59.

Thurston, Bonnie, Review of Robert M. Price, *The Wisdom Traditions in Luke-Acts* in *Reviews in Biblical Literature* (on-line), www.bookreviews.org/pdf/2182_1297.pdf.

Tiede, David L., *Prophecy and History in Luke-Acts* (Philadelphia: Fortress Press, 1980).

Toorn, K. van der, 'The Nature of the Biblical Teraphim in the Light of the Cuneiform Evidence', *CBQ* 52 (1990), pp. 203–22.

Trebilco, Paul. 'Asia', in David W.J. Gill and Conrad Gempf (eds), *The Book of Acts in Its Graeco-Roman Setting*, vol. 2 of Bruce W. Winter (ed.), *The Book of Acts in Its First Century Setting* (Grand Rapids: Eerdmanns, 1994) pp. 316–57.

—'Paul and Silas—"Servants of the Most High God" Acts 16.16–18', *JSNT* 36 (1989), pp. 51–73.

Tremel, Bernard, 'Voie du salut et religion populaire. Paul et Luc face au resque de paganisation', *Lumière et Vie* 30 (1981), pp. 87–108.

Trites, Allison A., 'The Prayer Motif in Luke-Acts', in Charles H. Talbert (ed.), *Perspectives on Luke-Acts* (Perspectives in Religious Studies Special Series, 5; Danville, VA: Association of Baptist Professors of Religion, 1978).

Trompf, G.W., 'On Why Luke Declined to Recount the Death of Paul: Acts 27–28 and Beyond', in Charles H. Talbert (ed.), *Luke-Acts: New Perspectives from the Society of Biblical Literature Seminar* (New York: Crossroad, 1984), pp. 225–39.

Turner, Victor, *From Ritual to Theatre: The Human Seriousness of Play* (New York: Performing Arts Journal Publications, 1982).

Twelftree, Graham H., *Jesus the Exorcist: A Contribution to the Study of the Historical Jesus* (WUNT, 54; Tübingen: Mohr-Siebeck, 1993; repr., Peabody, MA: Hendrikson, 1994).

Tyson, Joseph B., *Images of Judaism in Luke-Acts* (Columbia: University of South Carolina Press, 1992).

Tyson, Joseph B. (ed.), *Luke-Acts and the Jewish People: Eight Critical Perspectives* (Minneapolis: Augsburg, 1988).

Ustinova, Yulia, *The Supreme Gods of the Bosporan Kingdom: Celestial Aphrodite and the Most High God* (RGRW, 135; Leiden: Brill, 1999).

Van Henton, J.W., 'Python', *DDD* (2nd edn), pp. 669–671.

Van Unnik, W.C., 'Die Anklage gegen die Apostel in Philippi, Apostelgeschichte xvi 20f', in Alfred Stuiber and Alfred Hermann (eds), *Mullus: Für Theodor Klauser* (2 vols; Jahrbuch für Antike und Christentum Ergänzungsband, 1; Münster: Aschendorff, 1964); repr., *Sparsa Collecta: The Collected Essays of W.C. Van Unnik* (NovTSup, 29; Leiden: Brill, 1973), I, pp. 374–86.

Vernant, Jean Pierre, 'A General Theory of Sacrifice and the Slaying of the Victim in the Greek *Thusia*', in Froma I. Zeitlin (ed.), *Mortals and Immortals: Collected Essays, Jean-Pierre Vernant* (Princeton: Princeton University Press, 1991), pp. 290–302.

Versnel, H.S., 'Religious Mentality in Ancient Prayer', in H.S. Versnel (ed.), *Faith, Hope, and Worship: Aspects of Religious Mentality in the Ancient World* (SGRR, 2; Leiden: Brill, 1981), pp. 1–64.

Veyne, Paul, *Did the Greeks Believe Their Myths? A Study in the Constitutive Imagination* (Chicago: University of Chicago Press, 1988).

Vollenweider, Samuel, 'Ich sah den Satan wie einen Blitz vom Himmel fallen (Lk 10:18)', *ZNW* 79 (1988), pp. 187–203.

Wachtel, Klaus review of Jenny Read-Heimerdinger, *The Bezan Text of Acts: A Contribution of Discourse Analysis to Textual Criticism* (SNTSup, 236; Sheffield: Sheffield Academic Press, 2003), *RBL* (online), http://www.bookreviews.org/pdf/3197_3576.pdf (2004).

Walasky, Paul, *'And so we came to Rome': The Political Perspective of St. Luke* (SNTSMS, 49; Cambridge: Cambridge University Press, 1983).

Wallace, R.W., *The Areopagus Council, to 307 BC* (Baltimore: The Johns Hopkins University Press, 1985).

Walters, H.B., *History of Ancient Pottery* (2 vols; New York: Scribners, 1905.)

—*Catalogue of the Greek and Roman Lamps in the British Museum* (London: The British Museum, 1914).

Wallace, Richard and Wynne Williams, *The Acts of the Apostles: A Companion* (Classical Studies Series; London: Bristol Classical Press, 1993).

Wanger-Lux, Ute, K.J.H. Vriezen and Svend Holm Nielsen, 'Gadara', *ABD* II, pp. 866–68.

Waser, Otto, 'Dike', PW, V (1903), pp. 574–78.

Webster, T.B.L., 'Language and Thought in Early Greece', *Memoirs and Proceedings of the Manchester Literary and Philosophical Society* 94 (1952–53) pp. 17–38.

—'Personification as a Greek Mode of Thought', *Journal of the Wartburg and Courtauld Institute* 17 (1954), pp. 10–21.

Wehnert, Jürgen, 'Zu einem neuen These zur den Shiffbruch der Apostels Paulus auf dem Wege nach Rom (Apg. 27–28)', *ZThK* 87 (1990), pp. 67–99.

Weiser, Alfons, *Die Apostelgeschichte* (2 vols; Ökumenischer Taschenbuchkommentar zum Neuen Testament, 5; Gütersloh: Gerd Mohn, 1981–85).

White, L. Michael, 'Visualizing the 'Real' World of Acts 16: Toward Construction of a Social Index', in White and Yarbrough (eds), *Social World of the First Christians*, pp. 234–61.

White, L. Michael and O. Larry Yarbrough (eds), *The Social World of the First Christians: Essays in Honor of Wayne A. Meeks* (Minneapolis: Fortress Press, 1995).

Whittaker, C.R., (ed.), *Pastoral Economics in Classical Antiquity* (Proceedings of the Cambridge Philological Society, 15; Cambridge: Cambridge Philological Society, 1988).

Wiest, Stephen R., 'A Propaedeutic from the *Bacchae* of Euripides for Interpreting Luke's Stephen-Section (Acts 6:1–8:4)'. Paper presented at the annual meeting of the Midwest Region of the SBL, Chicago, Feb. 14, 2000.

—'Stephen and the Angel: A Typological Reading of the Story of Stephen in the Acts of the Apostles' (Ph.D dissertation, Marquette University, Milwaukee, 2001).

Wilamowitz-Moellendorf, Ulrich von and Fr. Zucker, 'Zwei Edickte des Germanicus auf einem Papyrus des Berliner Museums', *Sitzungsbericht der preussischen Akademie der Wissenschaften* (Berlin) 33 (1911), pp. 794–821.

Wildhaber, Bruno, *Paganisme populaire et prédication apostolique, d'après l'exégèse de quelques séquences des Actes* (Le Monde de la Bible; Geneva: Labor et Fides, 1987).

Winter, Bruce W., 'In Public and in Private: Early Christian Interactions with Religious Pluralism', in Andrew D. Clarke and Bruce W. Winter (eds), *One God One Lord in a World of Religious Pluralism* (Cambridge: Tyndale House, 1991), pp. 112–34.

—'Acts and Roman Religion, B. The Imperial Cult', in David W.J. Gill and Conrad Gempf (eds), *The Book of Acts in Its Graeco-Roman Setting*, vol. 2 of Bruce W. Winter (ed.),*The Book of Acts in Its First Century Setting* (Grand Rapids: Eerdmanns, 1994, 1994) pp. 93–104.

—'On Introducing Gods to Athens: An Alternative Reading of Acts 17:18–20', *TynBul* 47 (1996), pp. 71–90.

—'Acts and Food Shortages', in Gill and Gempf (eds), *The Book of Acts in Its Graeco-Roman Setting*, pp. 59–78.

Winterbottom, Michael, 'Rhetoric, Latin', *OCD* (rev. 3rd. edn, 2003), pp. 1314–1316.

Wirgin, Wolf, *Herod Agrippa I: King of the Jews* (Leeds University Oriental Society Monograph Series, 10; 2 vols; Leeds: Leeds University Oriental Society, 1968).

Witherington III, Ben, *The Acts of the Apostles: A Socio-Rhetorical Commentary* (Grand Rapids: Eerdmans, 1997).

Wordelmann, Amy Lorine, 'The Gods Have Come Down: Images of Historical Lycaonia and the Literary Construction of Acts 14' (PhD dissertation, Princeton University, 1994).

Wüst, Ernst, 'Erinyes' (PWSup, 8; 1956), pp. 82–166.

Wycherly, W.E., 'Two Notes on Athenian Topography', *JHS* 75 (1953), pp. 117–21.

—*The Athenian Agora*, vol. 3, *Literary and Epigraphical Testimonia* (Princeton: American School of Classical Studies at Athens, 1957).

Wycherly, R.E., 'St. Paul in Athens', *JTS* 19 (1968), pp. 619–21.

Yerkes, Royden Keith, *Sacrifice in Greek and Roman Religions and Early Judaism* (The Hale Lectures. New York: Scribner's, 1952).

York, John O., *The Last Shall Be First: The Rhetoric of Reversal in Luke* (JSNTSup, 46; Sheffield: JSOT Press, 1991).

Zaidman, Louise Bruit and Pauline Schmitt Pantel, *Religion in the Ancient Greek City* (Cambridge: Cambridge University Press, 1992).

Zeitlin, Froma I. (ed.), *Mortals and Immortals: Collected Essays of Jean-Pierre Vernant* (Princeton: Princeton University Press, 1991).

Zweck, Dean William, 'The Function of Natural Theology in the Areopagus Speech' (ThD dissertation, Lutheran School of Theology at Chicago, 1985).

Zwiep, Arie W., *Judas and the Choice of Matthias: A Study on Context and Concern of Acts 1:15–26* (WUNT, 2/187; Tübingen: Mohr-Siebeck, 2004).

INDEXES

INDEX OF REFERENCES

BIBLE

OTHER ANCIENT SOURCES

Xenophon of Ephesus
Ephesiaka
1.2	76
3.3	77
5.15.2	77

Papyri and Inscriptions
CIG
14.60	114

CIL
3.6837	72
3.14400	72

I.Eph.
7.2.3801	46
22212.a.6–7	95

IG
II² 1358	74
II² 4326	95

IGR
1.467	100
3.977	114
4.1608C	46
4.353	50

ILS
3.6832	72
5081	72
9052–53	72

MAMA
8.12	72

SEG
10.321	97